Communications in Computer and Information Science 3079

Rationale

The CCIS series is devoted to the publication of proceedings of computer science conferences. Its aim is to efficiently disseminate original research results in informatics in printed and electronic form. While the focus is on publication of peer-reviewed full papers presenting mature work, inclusion of reviewed short papers reporting on work in progress is welcome, too. Besides globally relevant meetings with internationally representative program committees guaranteeing a strict peer-reviewing and paper selection process, conferences run by societies or of high regional or national relevance are also considered for publication.

Topics

The topical scope of CCIS spans the entire spectrum of informatics ranging from foundational topics in the theory of computing to information and communications science and technology and a broad variety of interdisciplinary application fields.

Information for Volume Editors and Authors

Publication in CCIS is free of charge. No royalties are paid, however, we offer registered conference participants temporary free access to the online version of the conference proceedings on SpringerLink (http://link.springer.com) by means of an http referrer from the conference website and/or a number of complimentary printed copies, as specified in the official acceptance email of the event.

CCIS proceedings can be published in time for distribution at conferences or as post-proceedings, and delivered in the form of printed books and/or electronically as USBs and/or e-content licenses for accessing proceedings at SpringerLink. Furthermore, CCIS proceedings are included in the CCIS electronic book series hosted in the SpringerLink digital library at http://link.springer.com/bookseries/7899. Conferences publishing in CCIS are allowed to use our online conference service (Meteor) for managing the whole proceedings lifecycle (from submission and reviewing to preparing for publication) free of charge.

Publication process

The language of publication is exclusively English. Authors publishing in CCIS have to sign the Springer CCIS copyright transfer form, however, they are free to use their material published in CCIS for substantially changed, more elaborate subsequent publications elsewhere. For the preparation of the camera-ready papers/files, authors have to strictly adhere to the Springer CCIS Authors' Instructions and are strongly encouraged to use the CCIS LaTeX style files or templates.

Abstracting/Indexing

CCIS is abstracted/indexed in DBLP, Google Scholar, EI-Compendex, Mathematical Reviews, SCImago, Scopus. CCIS volumes are also submitted for the inclusion in ISI Proceedings.

How to start

To start the evaluation of your proposal for inclusion in the CCIS series, please send an e-mail to ccis@springer.com

Mohammed Saqr · Kamila Misiejuk ·
Sonsoles López-Pernas
Editors

Innovations in Analytics of Learning Dynamics

First International Workshop, TNA 2026
Bergen, Norway, April 27, 2026
Proceedings

Springer

Editors
Mohammed Saqr
University of Eastern Finland
Joensuu, Finland

Kamila Misiejuk
FernUniversität in Hagen
Hagen, Germany

Sonsoles López-Pernas
University of Eastern Finland
Joensuu, Finland

ISSN 1865-0929 ISSN 1865-0937 (electronic)
Communications in Computer and Information Science
ISBN 978-3-032-34156-3 ISBN 978-3-032-34157-0 (eBook)
https://doi.org/10.1007/978-3-032-34157-0

This Springer imprint is published by the registered company Springer Nature Switzerland AG
The registered company address is: Gewerbestrasse 11, 6330 Cham, Switzerland

Preface

This volume contains the proceedings of the 1st Transition Network Analysis (TNA) Workshop: *A Hands-on Tutorial with a Focus on Modeling Human-AI Interaction*, co-located with the 16th International Conference on Learning Analytics and Knowledge 2026 in Bergen, Norway. Learning analytics has developed powerful tools for measuring what learners know and how they perform, but the temporal dimension of learning, how behavior unfolds, shifts, and stabilizes over time, has proved harder to capture. TNA addresses this directly: it maps transitions between states, tests whether these transitions are statistically meaningful, and surfaces the sequential structure of learning processes that aggregate measures leave invisible. As AI becomes an active participant in learning rather than a mere delivery mechanism, this capacity becomes even more important. Understanding whether a student is engaging productively with an AI tutor or drifting into shallow interaction loops requires methods that can examine processes, not just outcomes.

A total of 16 submissions were received for the workshop proceedings. Each submission underwent a double-blind peer review process and was evaluated by two independent reviewers. Based on the reviewers' recommendations and the overall quality and relevance of the contributions, 14 papers were accepted for publication in this volume. The 14 peer-reviewed contributions gathered here reflect this breadth and are organized into three themes.

The **methodological contributions** introduce new variants of TNA, examine how core analytical decisions shape the networks that emerge, and connect TNA to broader theoretical and computational frameworks. The Dynalytics framework provides a comprehensive methodological ecosystem for the analysis and validation of dynamical systems. Heterogeneous TNA introduces different node classes within the same network, making it possible to model human-AI collaboration in a way that distinguishes human prompts from the AI response. Change point detection combined with idiographic TNA allows longitudinal analysis to respect the natural phases of an individual process rather than averaging over them. Topological data analysis replaces arbitrary time boundaries with data-driven segmentation that locates genuine intervention windows. Network Transformative Learning connects TNA to transformative learning theory, making the temporal unfolding of meaning-making observable through transition patterns. Further contributions examine how the choice of co-occurrence window shapes network structure and interpretation, and how TNA metrics such as entropy and recurrence can characterize stability in learning systems.

The contributions focused on modeling **learning trajectories** span clickstream data from primary school students, process data from the PISA international assessment, experience sampling data from PhD students using generative AI, and eye-tracking data from clinical teams in VR simulations. They also include a direct comparison of sequence analysis and TNA applied to the same dataset, exploring how the two methods complement each other and what each reveals that the other cannot, and a demonstration of how change point detection combined with TNA can reveal the shifting phases of an individual's writing process over the course of a master's thesis.

Finally, empirical papers focusing on **collaboration dynamics** examine both human-human and human-AI interactions, and show in each case how TNA reveals things about learning quality that frequency counts and outcome measures would leave invisible: how collaborative discourse can be dominated by social coordination at the expense of cognitive engagement, how learner proficiency shapes the behavioral loops that emerge in interaction with an AI writing tutor, and how students who differ in prompting style, sentiment, and depth of engagement with generative AI show correspondingly distinct sequential interaction patterns when examined through TNA.

This volume is intended for researchers and practitioners in learning analytics, educational technology, and the learning sciences who are interested in process-oriented approaches to studying learning. Whether you are new to TNA or looking to extend an existing familiarity with network-based methods, we hope the contributions here offer both practical guidance and theoretical provocation. The field needs methods that can keep pace with the complexity of learning as it actually happens. We believe TNA is one of them, and we hope this workshop becomes a recurring forum for the community developing it.

May 2026

Kamila Misiejuk
Sonsoles López-Pernas
Mohammed Saqr

Organization

General Chair

Mohammed Saqr	University of Eastern Finland, Finland

Program Committee Chairs

Sonsoles López-Pernas	University of Eastern Finland, Finland
Kamila Misiejuk	FernUniversität in Hagen, Germany

Program Committee

Hesham Ahmed	University of Eastern Finland, Finland
Awais Ilyas Baig	National University of Sciences and Technology, Pakistan
Fitsum Deriba	University of Eastern Finland, Finland
Ramy Elmoazen	University of Eastern Finland, Finland
Haoting Gao	University of Michigan, USA
Hitoshi Inoue	Nakamura Gakuen University, Japan
Hibiki Ito	Kyoto University, Japan
Daniel Jerez	University of Alberta, Canada
Eduardo Oliveira	University of Melbourne, Australia
Yaroslav Opanasenko	University of Tartu, Estonia
Godwin Sani	Federal University Lokoja, Nigeria
Tomi Suovuo	University of Eastern Finland, Finland
Steve Woollaston	Kyoto University, Japan
Volkan Yücepur	FernUniversität in Hagen, Germany

Contents

Methodological Contributions

Dynalytics: The Birth of a Framework for Rigorous Analytics of Dynamical Systems

Mohammed Saqr[1(✉)], Sonsoles López-Pernas[1], and Kamila Misiejuk[2]

[1] University of Eastern Finland, Joensuu, Finland
{mohammed.saqr,sonsoles.lopez}@uef.fi
[2] FernUniversität in Hagen, Hagen, Germany
kamila.misiejuk@fernuni-hagen.de

Abstract. In this paper, we introduce *Dynalytics*, an overarching framework and methodological ecosystem designed for the analysis and rigorous validation of dynamics of and dynamical systems. The framework encompasses a diverse family of models, including transition networks, co-occurrence networks, psychological networks, and higher-order networks. Central to *Dynalytics* is the application of a multi-level confirmatory testing battery to validate the supported models and support any analytical claim: split-half reliability for internal consistency, bootstrapping for edge-level stability, case dropping for centrality stability, and permutation-based group comparisons. The framework is supported by an open-source software ecosystem including R, Python, and Javascript libraries, as well as web and desktop applications. More importantly, *Dynalytics* is grounded in a "scientific contract" in which every analytical claim must be matched by evidence appropriate to the structure, scope, and complexity of the inference being made.

Keywords: Dynalytics · Network Analysis · Process Analysis · Complex Dynamic Systems · Transition Network Analysis

1 Introduction: From Transition Network Analysis to *Dynalytics*

Research on learning processes has a long and methodologically rich history of contributions from multiple disciplines and evolving analytical traditions. Scholars have drawn on a wide spectrum of methods to understand how the learning process progresses over time, ranging from in-depth qualitative methods—such as ethnography, discourse analysis, and case studies—to computational and data-driven methods like network analysis, process mining, and sequence analysis [1]. Each of these approaches offers a distinct lens that allows the modeling of patterns, structures, and temporal dynamics across diverse contexts and learning scenarios. Over time, this interdisciplinary exchange has generated a substantial body of knowledge, with methods often adapted and appropriated from other fields to address the complexity of learning processes [1]. However, while the appropriation of methods from other disciplines has been productive, it has often been accompanied by limitations in scope, contextual alignment, and theoretical grounding. In many cases, methods developed for different phenomena are hard to align

M. Saqr et al. (Eds.): TNA 2026, CCIS 3079, pp. 3–17, 2026.
https://doi.org/10.1007/978-3-032-34157-0_1

with the nature of learning, resulting in analyses that are methodologically sophisticated but insufficiently attuned to the theoretical foundations of learning processes and the learning sciences.

Take, for instance, process mining, which aims at discovering, describing, and optimizing processes based on event logs [2]. While useful for identifying workflows and deviations from expected paths, it is primarily oriented toward conformance to predefined models and efficiency of execution of business processes. As such, it often lacks a strong inferential framework and may impose normative process structures on learning interactions that are inherently agentic, emergent, and context-sensitive [3]. Other methods, such as Social Network Analysis (SNA), have been extensively used to model relationships and interactions among learners, teachers, and peers [4, 5]. Yet, SNA's theories and methods were designed to capture who connects with whom and how those connections shape behaviour—a fundamentally different question from how a learning process unfolds [4]. While researchers have successfully adapted SNA, its statistical validation methods were hard to apply to the learning processes—where the actors are not learners, e.g., steps or actions of a process—that are essentially temporal, interdependent, and follow a non-social structure.

In the grand scheme of things, our research landscape, theoretical or empirical claims about the processes are frequently based on observations, with limited assurance that these patterns would withstand rigorous statistical validation or replicate across contexts. Such a foundation is not conducive to either robust research or reliable practice. For findings to inform practice, policymakers and educators need confidence that identified patterns are stable, generalizable, and not artifacts of specific samples, coding decisions, or analytical choices.

Transition Network Analysis (TNA) [6] was introduced to fill this gap by providing a principled, multi-level confirmatory framework—spanning several methodologies that validate the process as a whole and its structure, the individual transitions that make up the fabrics of the learning process, the patterns, the comparisons between them, as well as the important events that shape the process. The framework embeds extensive confirmatory testing procedures that ensure analytical findings reflect genuine system behaviour rather than noise or chance. Entire network models can be assessed through null-model testing [7], split-half reliability [8], and bootstrap analysis [9]. Individual edges can be examined using bootstrap procedures, and centrality measures can be evaluated through case-dropping techniques [9]. Comparative analyses benefit from resampling strategies, permutation approaches, and graph-theoretic significance assessments, all designed to substantiate the validity of observed patterns. In this way, TNA functions not only as a conceptual guide to dynamic systems analysis but also as a rigorously validated methodological ecosystem dedicated to producing reliable, interpretable, and scientifically robust insights.

Whereas some of these statistical tests have been used before either in other fields (e.g., psychology) or traditional psychometrics, the contribution of TNA lies in adapting and validating these tests using vast datasets and robust simulation studies. More importantly, TNA has set the foundation and the methodological formalism of these tests, defining their scope, underlying assumptions, statistical procedures, and appropriate application boundaries.

To achieve these goals, TNA development followed several stages. First, we conducted a comprehensive review of validation approaches in education and in adjacent fields that have recently advanced network modeling, particularly psychological networks and network science. Second, each verification method was rigorously examined against its underlying assumptions, with particular attention to their suitability for sequential and process-oriented data. This was followed by systematic validation of each test using established methods such as the use of simulated data with known properties to assess whether TNA procedures could accurately recover expected patterns. In addition, both empirical checks and formal mathematical scrutiny were applied to audit the behavior, boundaries, and reliability of the proposed methods. As such, each statistical method or test in TNA has been carefully calibrated, rigorously validated, and subjected to an extensive battery of simulation-based evaluations, empirical checks, and formal analytical scrutiny to ensure its reliability, robustness, and appropriate fit of application.

Nevertheless, the conceptual groundwork of TNA testing battery and confirmatory framework applies broadly to networks derived from event data or estimated from empirical observations—in other words, to networks constructed from observed interactions, sequences, or co-occurrence processes where structure emerges from underlying data-generating mechanisms rather than being assumed a priori or observed [6]. Whether applied to social, behavioral, or social systems, the testing framework offers a unified lens through which inferences can be examined—capturing how patterns form, stabilize, transform, or characterize different groups, to mention a few. This expansive scope underscores TNA's dual contribution. Its value transcends the narrow focus on the analysis of transitions, extending instead to providing a unified theoretical and methodological framework for describing change and stability in any dynamic system.

Dynalytics is the name that we use to refer to this overarching framework, which encompasses TNA and the diverse family of models and statistical methods that use the same unified philosophy of scientific rigor and a consistent confirmatory testing battery.

2 Dynalytics Promise and Philosophy

Dynalytics is built and grounded in the "scientific contract" principle in which every analytical claim must be matched by evidence appropriate to the structure, scope, and complexity of the inference being made. The framework (outlined in Fig. 1) assumes that methodological validity is established through the alignment between the substantive claim, the underlying data-generating process, the representational model, and the confirmatory procedures used to evaluate it. As such, inference is treated as conditional on evidence based on strong and appropriate statistical foundations.

In *Dynalytics*, different forms of interpretation require appropriate forms of validation. Claims concerning the reliability or structure of an entire network require evidence of structural reproducibility and stability [10]. Claims about specific transitions require uncertainty estimation at the edge level. Claims regarding influential states require demonstrations that centrality structures remain stable under perturbation and resampling. Comparative claims between groups, conditions, or temporal phases require permutation-based inference and structural comparison procedures capable of distinguishing genuine reorganisation from stochastic variation.

The same logic extends to temporal, heterogeneous, and higher-order phenomena. More importantly, these standards extend to other forms of analysis supported by the framework that are not essentially network models. For instance, claims about sequential dependency require evidence that the assumed memory structure is supported by the data-generating process. Claims regarding latent subgroups or process typologies require clustering or mixture-based evidence. Claims involving polyadic, multilayer, or higher-order interaction structures require representational frameworks capable of preserving those dependencies rather than reducing them to pairwise approximations. Mechanistic claims about behavioural or cognitive processes require pathway and pattern evidence that reconnects network structure to the trajectories from which it emerged.

The framework adopts a proportional and progressive view of scientific evidence: the complexity of the evidential standard must match the complexity of the claim. Simple descriptive observations require descriptive support, whereas mechanistic, comparative, or structural interpretations require stronger forms of confirmatory evidence. *Dynalytics* therefore treats estimation, validation, robustness assessment, and interpretation as inseparable components of a single inferential system designed to ensure that conclusions remain faithful to the empirical process that generated the data. All the more so, conclusions must be supported by evidence proportionate to the scope, explanatory depth, and inferential demands of the claims being advanced.

3 Estimation Methods

Analysis, estimation, and the production of evidence represent the cornerstone of the method's operationalization and the primary mechanism through which empirical observations are transformed into structured, interpretable, and scientifically defensible conclusions. For instance, network estimation defines the empirical object under study and encompasses a wide array of approaches suited to different analytical questions. The research question, the assumed data-generating mechanism, and the theoretical orientation jointly determine which estimation strategy is appropriate, and this choice carries substantive implications for both the resulting structure and the conclusions drawn from it. A transition network captures how events unfold through directed temporal dependencies, whereas a co-occurrence network reflects associative proximity without implying sequence or temporal ordering [6]. An attention network, in turn, models multi-step influence and the propagation of activity or focus across interconnected elements [11]. Although these networks may appear structurally similar at the level of graph representation, they rest on different assumptions regarding what constitutes a relation, how dependency is operationalized, and which processes the network is intended to represent. A wide array of analytical methods exist across several types of data and empirical questions that go beyond networks contributing to a rich toolset of analytical methods.

Estimation or analysis are the entry point to inference, and the choice of method constrains every downstream interpretation. The framework is organised around a common registry of named models, so a method is added or replaced without altering the surrounding inferential machinery. A study that progresses from TNA to a Higher-Order Network, or from a co-occurrence network to a simplicial complex, inherits the confirmatory approach e.g., bootstrap, permutation, reliability, and stability tools, and the

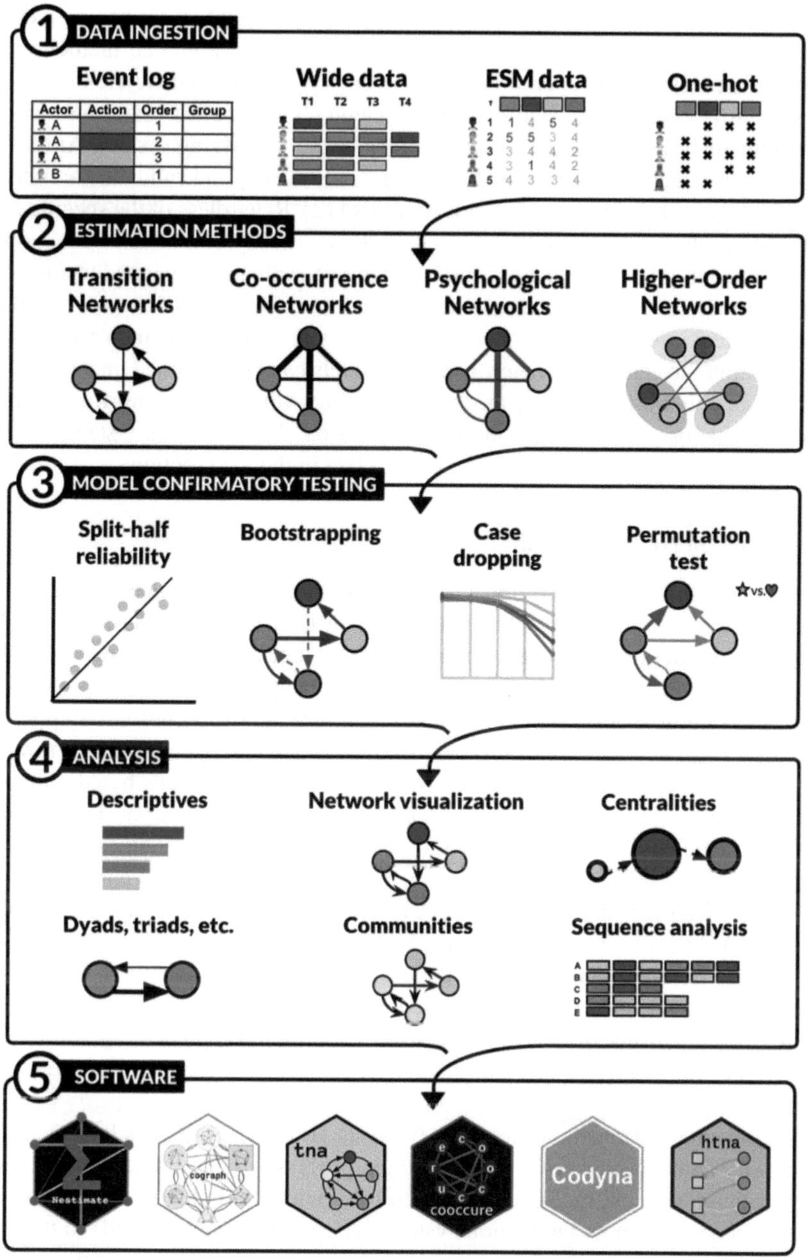

Fig. 1. Overview of Dynalitics' layers

named-model discipline keeps the analyst, the reader, and the software in agreement about which object is under examination at each stage.

Within the *Dynalytics* framework, each approach is therefore treated as a distinct model in which the estimator and the resulting output form a unified methodological entity. Different estimators operationalize different forms of dependency, temporal structure, stochastic assumptions, and relational meaning, allowing the same empirical data to generate analytically distinct representations of the underlying system. At the same time, these approaches benefit from the broader confirmatory and validation architecture established through Transition Network Analysis [12]. Regardless of the specific model employed, results can be examined through a rigorous ecosystem of estimation, robustness assessment, inferential testing, and comparative evaluation designed to ensure that observed structures reflect genuine system behaviour rather than stochastic variation or methodological artefacts. Consequently, *Dynalytics* provides a common methodological foundation through which heterogeneous models can be examined under consistent standards of reliability, validity, and interpretability while preserving the theoretical and analytical specificity of each modeling approach. As we currently stand, the main methods supported by the framework are described in the next section

3.1 Transition Network Family

TNA models estimate directed transition probabilities from sequence data. Each edge expresses the conditional probability of a target state given a source state, and the network is a Markov model of order one over the observed states [6]. TNA answers questions about sequential dynamics: which actions or states tend to follow which prior actions, which behavioural states lead to later states, and how a process unfolds step by step. Relatedly, Frequency Transition Network Analysis (FTNA) [13] preserves the raw count of observed transitions rather than their row-normalised proportions based on Markov models like TNA. The resulting network captures empirical frequencies. The distinction from TNA matters for interpretation. A transition can have a high conditional probability under TNA because its source state is rare, and a different transition can have a lower probability while accounting for a much larger share of the observed process under FTNA. TNA describes relative tendency; FTNA describes observed frequencies. Both are estimated from the same sequence data, and the choice between them is a choice of a substantive question [13]. Attention-based Transition Network Analysis (ATNA) [11] captures the influence across the timeline using a multi-step approach that addresses the limitations of limited memory models, such as TNA. Earlier events continue to shape later ones.

Heterogeneous Transition Network Analysis (HTNA) [14] models sequences in which two or more actor types share a single process—for example, human and AI agents within a session, multiple participant roles within a dialogue, or different categories of nodes within an interaction system. Heterogeneity also extends to the nature of the edges themselves. In this sense, HTNA can be viewed as a generalization of bipartite network structures, in which multiple node classes coexist within the same graph, but differs by allowing edges to form both within and across node types, thereby supporting transition structures that capture sequential dynamics among heterogeneous actors. Meta-path analysis identifies actor-level pathways such as human → AI → human sequences. Relatedly, Multicluster Multilayer Networks (MCML) preserve layered organisation when the data are stratified by group, cluster, time slice, or actor.

MCML stores within-layer transition structure together with the between-layer aggregate, which keeps comparisons across strata available without collapsing the data into a single matrix.

3.2 Co-Occurrence Networks

Co-occurrence Network Analysis (CNA) represents associations (instances where the state or action co-occur, happen, or are associated with each other) within an observational unit—a session, a window, a person, a document [15]. The relation is associative rather than sequential. Window-based Transition Network Analysis (WTNA) makes use of binary data (data coded as 0 s and 1 s) and computes transitions and co-occurrences inside local temporal neighbourhoods of fixed size. Furthermore, WTNA makes use of both the fact that events co-occur together in the same window and also that each window follows the other. WTNA are thus mixed network models with both types of interactions in the same network, which is a novel and innovative approach to taking the full advantage of the data.

3.3 Beyond Traditional Networks

For relations that cannot be reduced to dyads, the *Dynalytics* framework offers further analysis types. In other words, *Dynalytics* is not constrained, restricted or dogmatically attached to networks, or a certain type of models. Therefore, *Dynalytics* include novel models that go beyond its foundational approaches. Hypergraph networks represent polyadic relations directly through hyperedges that connect more than two nodes, with hypergraph centralities and hypergraph structural measures that respect the polyadic geometry. Simplicial complex networks represent nested relations among sets of nodes. Namely, *Dynalytics* includes rich functions for Higher-Order Networks (HON, HONEM, HYPA, MOGen) [16], which encode explicit temporal memory and account for multiple dependencies, structural complexities, and cases where interaction patterns cannot be reduced to simple pairwise steps (e.g., simplicial complexes [17]). Put another way, they are designed for situations in learning where what a learner does next depends on the sequence of prior actions rather than only the most recent one. We expect that HON will have extensive applications in the analysis of complex processes, structures, and human-AI interactions and therefore, they make an important part of the Nestimate R package [18].

3.4 Psychological Networks

The *Dynalytics* framework extends to association methods for association, ecological, and panel data, again named in correspondence with the network each method produces. Correlation networks describe pairwise linear association. Partial correlation networks condition each pairwise association on the remaining variables and recover the direct-dependence structure after controlling for shared variance [19]. Gaussian graphical models estimated by graphical lasso (EBICglasso) add L1 regularisation under the extended Bayesian information criterion, producing sparse partial-correlation networks suited to high-dimensional data [20]. Ising networks fit the same logic to binary data through L1-penalised nodewise logistic regression. Mixed graphical model networks (MGM) extend nodewise regression to data that combine continuous and categorical variables, with EBIC lambda selection and Lin–Wei thresholding. Multilevel vector-autoregression networks (mlVAR) estimated from intensive longitudinal data return three named networks at distinct time scales—a temporal network of fixed-effect lagged coefficients, a contemporaneous network of within-person residual partial correlations, and a between-person network of partial correlations among person means. GIMME networks apply group-iterative multiple-model estimation to subject-specific connectivity in fMRI and ESM data [21]. All of such models are offered through the network estimation main network approach Nestimate [18].

4 Confirmatory Testing

The *Dynalytics* framework relies on a rigorous and strict approach to validation. The estimated models must be examined for internal reproducibility, sampling uncertainty, robustness to information loss, comparability across groups, and adequacy of their temporal assumptions. The confirmatory layer of the framework operationalises each of these requirements through a specific statistical procedure rooted in an established scientific principle according to the methods used.

4.1 Model Suitability

Dynalytics incorporates a suite of diagnostic tools to determine model suitability, beginning with an evaluation of the memoryless assumption. Markov-order adequacy testing provides the empirical basis for this assessment and examines whether a first-order transition structure sufficiently represents the system or if the underlying process necessitates modeling longer temporal dependencies [22]. On the one hand, a first-order model is deemed appropriate; TNA would be appropriate. On the other hand, if higher-order dependencies emerge, another type of model is then necessary that attends to and preserves the structural fidelity to the data generation process e.g., ATNA, FTNA or HON. Following the determination of model order, path-dependence diagnostics pinpoint the specific loci where temporal memory influences the system.

4.2 Model Reliability

To validate model reliability, we rely on split-half reliability, which draws its logic from classical test theory [23]. A reliable instrument should yield similar scores when the items are partitioned into two equivalent halves. Translated to network estimation, the instrument is the estimator, and the score is the matrix of edge weights. Cases are randomly partitioned, two networks are estimated independently, and the matrices are compared through edge-wise correlation and absolute deviation. Repeated splits provide a distribution of agreement values. The test answers whether the estimated network is internally reproducible within the available data. Low reliability indicates that the network is too sample-dependent to support strong interpretation. Split-half reliability does not address external generalisation; it addresses internal consistency.

4.3 Edge-Level Stability

Bootstrap analysis evaluates edge uncertainty through resampling procedures designed to ensure that estimated parameters genuinely reflect the underlying data-generating process [9]. Resampling preserves the inherent temporal dependencies and structural fidelity of the system to ensure that uncertainty estimates capture authentic variability rather than methodological artefacts. This confirmatory approach allows researchers to verify that individual edges are statistically consistent rather than spurious reflections of noise. Consequently, bootstrap procedures provide the empirical substantiation necessary for validating theoretical assumptions and constructing robust models that could remain reproducible across diverse datasets.

Other methods of examining edge stability include edge-weight case-dropping stability, which evaluates robustness to information loss [9]. The procedure repeatedly removes increasing proportions of cases, re-estimates the network, and compares the reduced-sample edge vector with the full-sample vector through rank correlation. High edge stability supports interpretation of the network as a stable map of relations; low edge stability indicates that the structure is fragile and should be reported as sample-specific. Usually, both methods agree on the strong, stable edges, which provide evidence of these stable, consistent structures across different stability methods.

In the same way, centrality stability utilize case-dropping procedures to verify the structural significance of key states or events. Generally, researchers use centrality to advance theoretical assertions—characterizing a state as either a bridge, an influential hub, or a peripheral event. These inferences demand empirical proof that structural rankings persist even when information loss is introduced. Therefore, in *Dynalytics*, centrality analysis entails a dual process: estimation of the centrality measure and stability analysis confirms whether that position reflects a genuine system property capable of supporting substantive interpretation.

4.4 Model Comparison

Network analysis is often used to compare groups, sessions, or subpopulations such as high and low achievers, yet many of these comparisons remain descriptive, visual, or subjective in nature [24]. *Dynalytics* addresses this limitation by providing a structured inferential framework for network comparison that is grounded in formal statistical testing rather than visual inspection alone. Network comparison testing extends permutation to structural hypotheses through a set of complementary statistics. *Dynalytics* provides a multi-level network comparison framework for contrasting transition networks across groups, conditions, or time points. At the edge level, the focus is on identifying which specific transitions differ between networks. At the summary level, overall similarity is assessed using correlation, dissimilarity, and deviation-based measures. At the centrality level, comparisons examine whether structural roles of nodes are preserved or redistributed across networks. At the network level, global properties such as density, centralization, and reciprocity are contrasted to assess broader structural organization. Each level is accompanied by permutation-based inference to ensure that observed differences can be distinguished from variation expected under chance, and thereby grounding comparative claims in a coherent statistical framework.

Permutation testing provides inference under exchangeability [25]. Under the null hypothesis of no group difference, group labels are arbitrary. If cases are exchangeable across groups, shuffling the labels generates a valid null distribution for any function of the two networks—global strength, edge-wise differences, centrality differences, pattern frequencies. The observed difference is then located within this empirical null and assigned a p-value.

Permutation testing is also distribution-free in the same sense as the bootstrap: it dispenses with a parametric distribution for the test statistic, but it requires that the permuted units are genuinely exchangeable under the null. Designs with paired or clustered structure must preserve that structure during shuffling. The permutation test is the natural device for group comparison in the framework, because two networks estimated separately almost always look different when plotted side by side, and the relevant question is whether the observed difference exceeds what arises by chance under exchangeability.

4.5 Other Confirmatory Methods

The *Dynalytics* framework includes several other analytical methods and tools that, for instance, estimate the transition entropy and quantify the dispersion of outgoing transitions from a state and help establish the type of model needed. Markov stability evaluates whether the modular structure persists across scales of a transition process. Passage-time analysis estimates the expected number of steps required to reach one state from another through the transition process. It extends interpretation beyond direct edges to eventual reachability. A state can be dynamically close to an outcome through a chain of intermediate steps even when the direct edge between them is weak. Passage-time analysis supports claims about accessibility, gateway states, and temporal distance that the immediate adjacency matrix cannot articulate.

5 The Analysis Layer

The models in *Dynalytics* benefit from a unified analysis layer that operates consistently across estimation types. The analysis layer sits between model estimation and interpretation, and it applies through a shared system in which all estimators return a common structure. Several families of operations define the *Dynalytics* analysis layer: descriptives, centrality, community detection, visualisation, and pattern analytics, among others. These functions apply widely and can be implemented across TNA, FTNA, CNA, ATNA, WTNA, HTNA, and higher-order networks when appropriate.

Descriptive analysis characterises the empirical foundation of the model. State frequencies, base rates, initial and terminal distributions, and transition structure provide the contextual grounding for interpreting edges, centrality, and group differences. Descriptive measures define the distributional landscape on which all subsequent inference depends. In other words, these descriptive measures offer the base backgrounds upon which interpretation relies and widen the picture to different perspectives of the data.

Centrality analysis captures structural roles within the network. Measures such as in-strength, out-strength, betweenness, closeness, and eigenvector-based influence define and measure the importance of events or states according to the network model and operationalisation of the data [5]. Community detection identifies modular structures within the network [26]. Communities can be interpreted as functional or thematic groupings depending on the domain, and are used for cross-scale and cross-group comparisons.

Visualisation and network comparison, together with bootstrap plots, help communicate structure and provide a summary view of the data in an intuitive form. Because plotting is decoupled from estimation, similar plots can be rendered across multiple visual modalities without altering their inferential content.

Sequence-pattern analytics recover and mine patterns that are not easily visible through inspection. *Dynalytics* offers a wide array of pattern mining methods [27], e.g., n-gram and gapped-pattern mining, motif detection, association rules, sequence patterns, and pattern–outcome models, reconnecting network structure to the underlying trajectories that generated it. This layer moves analysis from dyadic associations to temporally extended mechanisms, linking local transitions to higher-order behavioural or cognitive sequences.

Dynalytics integrates clustering methods that group individuals based on similarity in their data [28], identifying distinct behavioural profiles or process typologies within a population. Pattern mining operates within and across clusters to characterise the sequential signatures that distinguish each group, revealing not only that individuals differ but also how their temporal dynamics differ in terms of specific transitions and sequential patterns. *Dynalytics* supports the integration of external covariates with cluster assignments, enabling researchers to examine how individual characteristics—such as achievement, demographics, prior knowledge, or motivational profiles—relate to membership in behaviourally defined clusters. This bridges the gap between person-level variables and process-level typologies, allowing researchers to test whether theoretically meaningful covariates predict distinct patterns of temporal behaviour.

5.1 Validation of *Dynalytics* Analysis Routines

Dynalytics follows a multistructure strict equivalence and validation policy to ensure that every statistical procedure is both theoretically correct and empirically faithful to the data-generating process. Each *Dynalytics* method is required to implement the exact statistical question it is intended to answer, including correct resampling units in bootstrap procedures, correct exchangeability assumptions in permutation tests, correct conditional-independence structures in Markov-order tests, and correct re-estimation logic in stability and higher-order analyses. This alignment is enforced through a strict numerical equivalence framework.

Validation is carried out through four complementary strategies that together follow current software-engineering best practice: numerical agreement, generative calibration, input/data validation, and behavioural testing of happy and unhappy paths. First, each implementation is benchmarked against established R and Python packages to ensure that outputs match reference results within extremely tight numerical tolerances. Second, and more fundamentally, Dynalytics tests are assessed on simulated data where the true data-generating process is known, allowing direct evaluation of whether each test recovers the correct structures, parameters, and model choices under controlled conditions; transition-network estimators, for instance, have been assessed on millions of datasets spanning diverse configurations, sample sizes, sequence lengths, and missing-data regimes, and bootstrap stability procedures have demonstrated near-perfect sensitivity and very high specificity in identifying true and false transitions with predictable performance across a wide array of variations. Third, every public function performs explicit data validation at entry—checking types, shapes, admissible ranges, identifier consistency, and temporal ordering—so that malformed inputs fail fast with informative errors rather than producing silently incorrect results. Fourth, the test suite covers both happy paths (well-formed inputs under canonical assumptions) and unhappy paths (missing data, ties, empty sequences, singleton trajectories, degenerate transition matrices, non-stationary inputs, and adversarial edge cases), ensuring that estimators degrade gracefully and that error states are themselves part of the verified contract. Continuous integration runs the full suite on every change, so each release inherits the same guarantees rather than relying on ad-hoc verification.

Across all other tests, including permutation-based comparison tests, centrality stability measures, Markov-order selection, mixed graphical models, and higher-order estimators, followed the same dual validation mechanisms to reproduce known reference implementations and correctly recover known ground-truth structures in simulated data. Only after passing both criteria—numerical equivalence and generative recovery—are procedures considered valid for use. This makes validation an integral part of the methodological framework rather than a post hoc check, ensuring that every implemented test is both computationally correct and substantively meaningful.

6 Software Implementations

Dynalytics is implemented as a layered ecosystem of open-source software packages designed to separate estimation, analysis, and visualisation while maintaining a unified analytical workflow. The R ecosystem serves as the reference implementation, complemented by an ecosystem for browser-based and desktop applications. Across both ecosystems, packages share common data structures and interoperable object schemas, allowing methods to operate consistently across estimation types and analytical contexts. More importantly, a rigorous validation process ensures that these apps deliver consistent results across different environments.

The original TNA implementation is provided through *tna* [29], which offers transition-network estimation, centrality analysis, bootstrapping, permutation testing, case-dropping procedures, and the visual conventions used in published TNA research. Complex-network analysis and rendering are handled through *cograph* [30], which provides community detection, multilayer and heterogeneous network visualisation, centrality analysis, and a broad suite of plotting methods including transition, comparison, bootstrap, heatmap, trajectory, and alluvial plots. Cograph functions as the dedicated rendering layer and operates independently from the estimation engine through object-based dispatch.

At the core of the framework is *Nestimate* [18], the main estimation and inference engine. Nestimate implements the major computational components of the framework, including transition-network estimation, bootstrap and permutation inference, split-half reliability, case-dropping procedures, centrality stability, network comparison testing,

Markov-order analysis, path-dependence diagnostics, mixed Markov models, multilevel VAR, mixed graphical models, higher-order networks, hypergraphs, and simplicial analyses. Its architecture is based on a registry and dispatch system in which estimators are accessed through a unified interface and custom methods can be integrated alongside built-in estimators. Documentation is available online.

Specialised extensions support additional methodological families. The *htna* package provides Heterogeneous Transition Network Analysis (HTNA) for modelling sequences involving multiple interacting actor groups such as humans and AI systems. The *coo ccure* package implements Co-occurrence Network Analysis with multiple similarity normalisations and flexible data input structures for bipartite, binary, sequence, and delimited formats [31].

A defining feature of the software architecture is the strict separation between computation, inference, and rendering. Estimation packages generate shared netobject structures and specialised subclasses, while downstream analytical and visualisation functions dispatch behaviour based on object class rather than direct package dependencies. This modular architecture allows methods, interfaces, and rendering systems to evolve independently while preserving a coherent analytical framework across the entire *Dynalytics* ecosystem.

The aforementioned packages have been originally developed in the R programming language. However, alternatives in other common languages exist as well as graphical interfaces for non-technical users. For instance, *tna* is also offered for the Python language (*tnapy*) [32]. TNA is also available as a web app based on R Shiny [33] as well as for desktop as part of the Jamovi app [34]. A newer, more comprehensive web application that combines the complete *Dynalytics* framework is also available online. Dynalytics has also been implemented from scratch in JavaScript (*dynajs*) and can be used to implement real-time dashboards.

References

1. López-Pernas, S., Misiejuk, K., Kaliisa, R., Conde-González, M.Á., Saqr, M.: Capturing the wealth and diversity of learning processes with learning analytics methods. In: Learning Analytics Methods and Tutorials, pp. 1–14. Springer Nature Switzerland, Cham (2024)
2. van der Aalst, W.M.P.: Process mining: a 360 degree overview. In: Lecture Notes in Business Information Processing, pp. 3–34. Springer International Publishing, Cham (2022)
3. López-Pernas, S., Saqr, M.: The why, the how and the when of educational process mining in R. In: Learning Analytics Methods and Tutorials, pp. 467–488. Springer Nature Switzerland, Cham (2024)
4. Saqr, M., Poquet, O., Lopez-Pernas, S.: Networks in education: a travelogue through five decades. IEEE Access **10**, 32361–32380 (2022). https://doi.org/10.1109/access.2022.3159674
5. Saqr, M., López-Pernas, S., Conde-González, M.Á., Hernández-García, Á.: Social network analysis: a primer, a guide and a tutorial in R. In: Learning Analytics Methods and Tutorials, pp. 491–518. Springer Nature Switzerland, Cham (2024)
6. Saqr, M., López-Pernas, S., Törmänen, T., Kaliisa, R., Misiejuk, K., Tikka, S.: Transition network analysis: a novel framework for modeling, visualizing, and identifying the temporal patterns of learners and learning processes. In: Proceedings of Learning Analytics & Knowledge (LAK'25). ACM, New York, NY, USA (2025) p in–press

7. Váša, F., Mišić, B.: Null models in network neuroscience. Nat. Rev. Neurosci. **23**, 493–504 (2022). https://doi.org/10.1038/s41583-022-00601-9
8. Cronbach, L.J.: A case study of the split-half reliability coefficient. J. Educ. Psychol. **37**, 473–480 (1946). https://doi.org/10.1037/h0054328
9. Epskamp, S., Borsboom, D., Fried, E.I.: Estimating psychological networks and their accuracy: a tutorial paper. Behav. Res. Methods. **50**, 195–212 (2018). https://doi.org/10.3758/s13428-017-0862-1
10. Andreotti, J., Jann, K., Melie-Garcia, L., Giezendanner, S., Dierks, T., Federspiel, A.: Repeatability analysis of global and local metrics of brain structural networks. Brain Connect **4**, 203–220 (2014). https://doi.org/10.1089/brain.2013.0202
11. López Pernas, S., Tikka, S., Misiejuk, K., Oliveira, E., Saqr, M.: Modeling the dynamics and impact of human-AI interactions with attention transition network analysis. Soc. Sci. Res. Netw. (2026)
12. Saqr, M., López-Pernas, S., Tikka, S.: Mapping relational dynamics with transition network analysis: a primer and tutorial. In: Advanced Learning Analytics Methods, pp. 371–411. Springer Nature Switzerland, Cham (2026)
13. Saqr, M., Misiejuk, K., Törmänen, T., Kaliisa, R., Tikka, S., López-Pernas, S.: Frequency transition network analysis (FTNA). In: Proceedings of the International Conference on Computer-Supported for Collaborative Learning. International Society of the Learning Sciences, pp. 276–280 (2025)
14. López-Pernas, S., Misiejuk, K., Tikka, S., Saqr, M.: Role dynamics in student–AI collaboration: a heterogeneous transition network analysis approach. In: Innovations in Analytics of Learning Dynamics: Proceedings of the 1st Workshop on Transition Network Analysis (TNA). Springer (2026)
15. Misiejuk, K., Oliveira, E., Song, Y., López-Pernas, S., Saqr, M.: Modeling observation lens in co-occurrence network analysis: four window approaches and implementations. In: Innovations in Analytics of Learning Dynamics: Proceedings of the 1st Workshop on Transition Network Analysis (TNA). Springer (2026)
16. Bianconi, G.: Higher-Order Networks: an Introduction to Simplicial Complexes. Cambridge University Press, Cambridge, England (2021)
17. Shi, D., Chen, G.: Simplicial networks: a powerful tool for characterizing higher-order interactions. Natl. Sci. Rev. **9**, nwac038 (2022). https://doi.org/10.1093/nsr/nwac038
18. Saqr, M., López-Pernas, S.: Nestimate: Network Estimation, Bootstrap, and Higher-Order Analysis. Contributed Packages, CRAN (2026)
19. Epskamp, S., Fried, E.I.: A tutorial on regularized partial correlation networks. Psychol. Methods. **23**, 617–634 (2018). https://doi.org/10.1037/met0000167
20. Epskamp, S., Waldorp, L.J., Mõttus, R., Borsboom, D.: The Gaussian graphical model in cross-sectional and time-series data. Multivar. Behav Res. **53**, 453–480 (2018). https://doi.org/10.1080/00273171.2018.1454823
21. Beltz, A.M., Gates, K.M.: Network mapping with GIMME. Multivar. Behav Res. **52**, 789–804 (2017). https://doi.org/10.1080/00273171.2017.1373014
22. Besag, J., Mondal, D.: Exact goodness-of-fit tests for Markov chains. Biometrics **69**, 488–496 (2013). https://doi.org/10.1111/biom.12009
23. Savage, M.: Reliability, Split-Half. The SAGE Encyclopedia of Communication Research Methods (2017)
24. Elmoazen, R., Saqr, M., Tedre, M., Hirsto, L.: A systematic literature review of empirical research on epistemic network analysis in education. IEEE Access **10**, 17330–17348 (2022). https://doi.org/10.1109/access.2022.3149812
25. van Borkulo, C.D., et al.: Comparing network structures on three aspects: a permutation test. Psychol. Methods **28**, 1273–1285 (2023). https://doi.org/10.1037/met0000476

26. Hernández-García, Á., Cuenca-Enrique, C., Traxler, A., López-Pernas, S., Conde-González, M.Á., Saqr, M.: Community detection in learning networks using R. In: Learning Analytics Methods and Tutorials, pp. 519–540. Springer Nature Switzerland, Cham (2024)
27. Mooney, C.H., Roddick, J.F.: Sequential pattern mining — approaches and algorithms. ACM Comput. Surv. **45**, 1–39 (2013). https://doi.org/10.1145/2431211.2431218
28. Murphy, K., López-Pernas, S., Saqr, M.: Dissimilarity-based cluster analysis of educational data: a comparative tutorial using R. In: Saqr, M., López-Pernas, S. (eds.) Learning Analytics Methods and Tutorials, pp. 231–283. Springer Nature Switzerland, Cham (2024)
29. Tikka, S., López-Pernas, S., Saqr, M.: Tna: an R package for transition network analysis. Appl. Psychol. Meas. (2025). https://doi.org/10.1177/01466216251348840
30. Saqr, M., López-Pernas, S.: cograph: Analysis and Visualization of Complex Networks. CRAN: Contributed Packages (2026)
31. Saqr M, López-Pernas S, Misiejuk K.: cooccure: Co-Occurrence Network Construction and Manipulation. CRAN: Contributed Packages (2026)
32. Saqr, M., Tikka, S., López-Pernas, S.: TNA: Transition Network Analysis for Python (2026)
33. López-Pernas, S., Tikka, S., Misiejuk, K., Saqr, M.: Tna-web: advanced analytics just a few clicks away. In: Proceedings TEEM 2025: Thirteennth International Conference on Technological Ecosystems for Enhancing Multiculturality. TEEM 2025 Lecture Notes in Computer Science. Springer, Berlin, Germany (2026)
34. López-Pernas, S., Girault, D., Tikka, S., Saqr, M.: JTNA: a desktop software for transition network analysis. In: Proceedings of ICSLE 2025. The Changing Landscape of Smart Learning Environments: Pedagogy, Collaborative Intelligence, and Ethics. Springer, LNET (2026)

Role Dynamics in Student–AI Collaboration: A Heterogeneous Transition Network Analysis Approach

Sonsoles López-Pernas[1](✉), Kamila Misiejuk[2], Santtu Tikka[3], and Mohammed Saqr[1]

[1] University of Eastern Finland, Joensuu 80100, Finland
sonsoles.lopez@uef.fi
[2] FernUniversität in Hagen, Hagen 58097, Germany
[3] University of Jyväskylä, Jyväskylä 40100, Finland

Abstract. In this study, we introduce Heterogeneous Transition Network Analysis (HTNA), a variant of Transition Network Analysis (TNA) that acknowledges different node classes within the same network. We propose this method as an analytical solution to model human-AI collaboration where humans take different intents and AI enacts appropriate roles in response. We exemplify the method in a case study examining the collaborative problem-solving process between students and AI through their dialogic exchanges. Our dataset includes 1,915 student-AI interactions from 95 unique students collected in a programming course which were annotated to capture the students' intents as well as the role assumed by AI in its response. We used HTNA to model the iterative flow of these exchanges and identify recurring typed patterns that characterise how students and the AI respond to one another across multiple steps. The approach captures these higher-order structures while preserving core TNA features such as bootstrapping, and it can be extended with additional measures, including centrality measures, communities and cliques, to further examine the dynamics of human–AI collaboration.

Keywords: student-AI interactions · transition network analysis · heterogeneous networks · human-AI collaboration · learning analytics · collaborative roles · computer science education

1 Introduction

A large body of research on generative artificial intelligence (AI) focuses on examining the range of tasks these systems can handle, their performance, and the outcomes they can produce. Much of this assessment relies on benchmarking studies that compare AI performance with that of humans to evaluate how closely AI systems approach—or even surpass—human capabilities. In the specific case of education, many studies evaluate Generative AI's performance in

M. Saqr et al. (Eds.): TNA 2026, CCIS 3079, pp. 18–33, 2026.
https://doi.org/10.1007/978-3-032-34157-0_2

tasks such as multiple-choice question generation [18], feedback provision [20] or generation of learning materials [12]. Others focus on studying the impact of Generative AI on students, teachers and education outcomes at large. For example, a recent meta-analysis [7] investigated the impact of AI-generated feedback (including Generative AI) on students' performance and learning dispositions and found no statistically significant differences between AI-generated feedback and human-provided feedback on all the tested outcomes.

Recent calls emphasize the need to move beyond outcome-based evaluations and instead focus on the process—that is, how students interact with generative AI, learn, progress, regress, or advance their understanding [12]. Most studies adopting this process-oriented perspective have compared interaction patterns between high- and low-performing students. These studies generally report that higher-performing students tend to engage more with AI [27,31], and that self-regulated learning [8,17], critical thinking [3,9,15,33], and higher-order cognition [28] are associated with higher performance. In contrast, relying on AI primarily as an information source, failing to evaluate AI outputs, and engaging in lower-order cognitive processes have been associated with lower performance.

Other research has focused on identifying distinct patterns or profiles of student–AI interactions—for example, students who engage deeply with AI versus those who are more efficiency-oriented [2,16,29]; structured versus exploratory interaction patterns [4]; or profiles distinguished by different levels of behavioral, emotional, and cognitive engagement [32].

This strand of research mirrors a long tradition of learning analytics literature aimed at capturing students' learning strategies as well as engagement and regulation patterns from their trace log data when interacting with different learning tools, such as Learning Management Systems (LMSs) [21,22]. In such studies, technology is a relatively passive medium that supports students' learning. However, when it comes to students' interactions with AI, this passive role is not entirely fitting, since AI contributes ideas, proposes directions, and responds in ways shaped by previous interactions [35]. Therefore, it stands to reason that AI should be modeled as an active participant in the learning process. In the present study, we concur with this view (AI as a partner) where AI is not a mere tool but rather a collaborator that influences students' learning, emotions and regulation [6].

Transition Network Analysis (TNA) has proven to be a suitable method for mapping student–AI interactions. It has been used to examine students' prompting processes when generating synthetic network data [12,24], to study students' self-regulation in problem-solving [13], and to compare the writing process across various AI-supported writing tasks [10]. However, despite these contributions, a notable gap remains: prior TNA studies have treated AI primarily as a background tool or response mechanism rather than as an active, analyzable agent within the interaction network. As a result, the full dynamics of student–AI collaboration—particularly how learners and AI systems co-construct problem-solving processes—remain underexplored.

This gap motivates the present study. We advance TNA by explicitly modeling the AI as an active participant within multi-type interaction sequences, thereby enabling a richer account of how learners and AI systems influence one another over time. Using Heterogeneous Transition Network Analysis (HTNA), a variant of TNA that acknowledges different node classes within the same network, we uncover cross-type collaboration patterns and examine how specific forms of learner–AI interaction relate to students' self-regulation, engagement, and learning. In doing so, we aim to address the following research question: *What are the role dynamics in the student-AI collaboration process?*.

2 Heterogeneous Transition Network Analysis (HTNA)

Heterogeneous Transition Network Analysis (HTNA) [23] can help map the collaborative process between students and AI, taking into account the different nature and dynamics of both students' and AI's dialogic exchanges. A heterogeneous network, also referred to as a multitype or typed network (depending on the context), is a network that contains two or more distinct types of nodes, with edges representing interactions either across or within node types [26]. In the context of student–AI collaboration, the two node types correspond to learners and AI agents (see Fig. 1). Specifically, HTNA is a method that models and visualizes sequences of interactions in a network composed of distinct node types (learners and AI roles in our case) connected by edges representing dialogic or behavioral interactions. In this two-typed network, learners and AI roles are treated as separate node classes, allowing us to examine not only patterns of student-to-student or AI-to-AI interactions (if relevant) but, more importantly, the cross-type interactions that occur between learners and AI. HTNA captures the dynamic interplay of contributions from human and artificial agents, revealing how students' learning behaviors, self-regulation, and cognitive engagement evolve in response to AI inputs. Understanding the transitions in this two-typed network helps identify collaboration patterns, such as reciprocal exchanges, AI-initiated scaffolding, or learner-driven regulation, and how these patterns relate to learning outcomes and engagement.

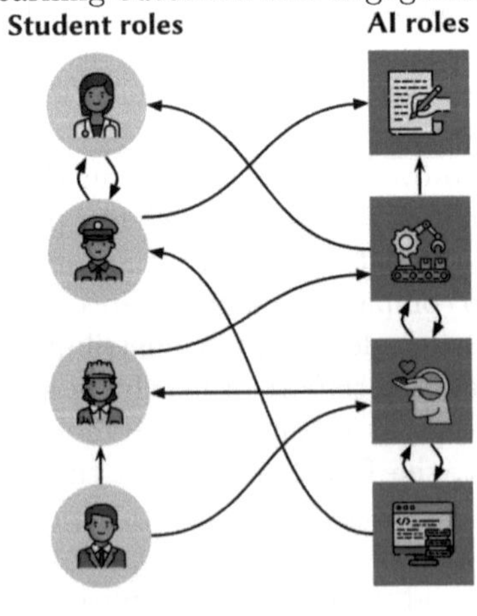

Fig. 1. Heterogeneous network where nodes represent either student or AI roles

A fundamental construct in heterogeneous networks (Fig. 1) is the *meta-path*, which refers to a sequence of node types and edge types (relationships) specified at the network schema level [26]. Meta-paths define composite relationships across different node classes and allow analysts to trace meaningful semantic and cross-type interaction patterns. In our student–AI heterogeneous network, a temporal meta-path such as *Learner-Instruct* → *AI-Tutor* or *Learner-Seek.Help* → *AI-Supporter* represents an interpretable chain of dialogic actions, capturing how a learner's behavioral move is followed by—and potentially shaped by—a specific AI role. The edges in the network in Fig. 1 illustrate strong cross-type transitions where learner actions like *Instruct*, *Seek.Help*, or *Debug* frequently lead to AI responses such as *Tutor*, *Supporter*, or *Coder*. Such meta-paths highlight not just direct interactions but also the functional relationship between sequential behaviors and emergent AI role enactment. Another important analytical capability in heterogeneous networks is *link prediction*, which quantifies the probability that a particular type of relationship will form between two nodes based on observed structural patterns [26]. In the context of our student–AI network, link prediction can be used to anticipate whether a learner action (e.g., *Inquire*) is likely to elicit a specific AI role (e.g., *Coder*), or whether recurrent instances of *Seek Help* predict subsequent AI scaffolding as a *Supporter*. For instance, if learners who frequently *Debug* tend to receive *Tutor*-type responses (as the strong *Debug* → *Tutor* edge in the visualization suggests), link prediction could quantify the likelihood that future debugging attempts will systematically trigger an AI tutoring response. Incorporating meta-paths and link prediction into HTNA expands its analytical power, enabling richer inferences about how interaction patterns emerge, stabilize, and contribute to cognitively productive student–AI collaboration.

Weighted, multi-type networks are particularly valuable in student–AI interactions where edge weights capture meaningful pedagogical information: a heavily weighted *Debug* → *Tutor* transition suggests consistent, reliable scaffolding, while a light-weighted transition may indicate sporadic or context-dependent support. Because these weights encode pedagogically meaningful variation, they provide essential signals that advanced link prediction algorithms can leverage to forecast both the presence and magnitude of future links. Advanced link prediction methods can incorporate multiple network features simultaneously—including node centrality, neighborhood overlap, meta-path patterns, and historical edge weights—to forecast not just future connections but their expected strength. Weighted link prediction enables more nuanced anticipation of collaboration dynamics by predicting both the existence and intensity of future interactions. In doing so, it helps identify which learner behaviors are likely to generate robust AI support versus tentative engagement, and inform adaptive system design that strengthens productive interaction patterns while addressing underutilized or weak pedagogical pathways.

HTNA builds on the solid methodological foundations of traditional TNA while extending its analytical reach to systems composed of multiple interacting entity types, behaviors, or modalities. HTNA allows transitions to span categories—such as learner actions, AI responses, and contextual states— and thus provides a richer and more ecologically valid representation of complex learning environments. This extension is paired with a robust confirmatory framework that ensures observed patterns reflect genuine system behavior rather than artifacts of sampling error, noise, or model bias. Entire network structures can be evaluated through rigorous null-model testing, split-half reliability checks, and perturbation analyses that assess stability under controlled distortions. At the micro level, individual transitions and edge weights can be verified using bootstrap-based confidence estimation, while node-level indicators such as centrality or influence can be validated through case-dropping and resampling procedures. For comparative analyses, HTNA incorporates permutation techniques, cross-group resampling, and graph-theoretic significance assessments to determine whether differences between networks exceed what would be expected by chance. Together, these confirmatory tools help HTNA to yield reliable, interpretable, and scientifically trustworthy insights into dynamic, multi-type interaction processes.

3 A Case Study

3.1 Context

The context of our study is an introductory Web Programming university course. As part of the course, students were given an assignment in which they had to create a web version of the familiar Nokia-style snake game. Throughout the development process, students could turn to ChatGPT whenever they wished: to sketch out their design, write code, resolve errors, or clarify ideas about any of the required technologies. Their use of ChatGPT was left entirely open, making it possible to observe how they spontaneously interacted with Generative AI to complete the task. Once they finished the assignment, they provided the publicly shared links to their ChatGPT conversations. The content of the conversations was then collected through the R package `chatGPTscrapeR` [11], resulting in a dataset of 1,915 exchanges between 95 students and the AI, split evenly between student messages and ChatGPT replies.

3.2 Qualitative Data Coding

We annotated the collected conversations through qualitative coding supported by an AI-based workflow. The process began with an inductive phase in which two members of the research team reviewed a subset of the interactions and collaboratively constructed a data-driven codebook:

Student intent

- **Instruct**: Student asks the AI for new code, a new feature in the existing code, a fix, or a similar task
- **Seek.Help**: Student asks the AI for direction on how to proceed
- **Inquire**: Student asks the AI a question about the problem or domain
- **Debug**: Student asks the AI to identify problems in the code or help when facing difficulties (e.g., solving an error)
- **Socialize**: Student engages in social interactions or conversation management with the AI

AI roles

- **Tutor**: The AI explains concepts, ideas, or solutions often in response to a question

- **Analyzer**: The AI analyzes how to solve a task step by step or suggests next steps
- **Coder**: The AI supplies code or related artifacts often accompanied by structure and explanations
- **Supporter**: The AI provides feedback on the code provided by the student
- **Sycophant**: The AI pleases the user or agrees with what he says

After finalizing the codebook, we used the `ellmer` R package [30] to annotate every student prompt and every ChatGPT reply. For this stage, we prepared separate system prompts tailored to each interaction type and refined them through several rounds of testing. During coding, the model received only a single utterance at a time as the user message, but could return more than one code (a comma-separated list). In total 2,009 codes were generated at the coding stage.

3.3 Data Analysis

We analyzed the student-AI collaboration process using the `htna` R package [14]. For the HTNA model, we specified the conversation as the *actor*, the code generated through the qualitative coding process as the *action*, and the position of each code within the conversation as the *order*, allowing for the possibility that a single interaction contained multiple codes.

HTNA captures how actions unfold over time by estimating the probability that one coded event follows another while preserving the hierarchical structure of the coded data. The model treats observed pairs of consecutive codes as transitions and uses them to compute transition probabilities under a first-order Markov assumption. We visualized the resulting model using a customized layout and visualization settings, such as color and shape, to distinguish codes corresponding to student intents from those corresponding to AI roles.

To examine the stability of the estimated transitions, we carried out bootstrapping, also through the `htna` package. Bootstrapping re-estimates the HTNA model repeatedly from samples drawn with replacement to evaluate how consistently each transition appears across resampled datasets. This process yields confidence intervals and significance assessments for every transition, which helps determine which transitions in the model are recurring and therefore constitute the backbone of the underlying interaction process. Through this procedure, we identified transitions that can be interpreted as stable elements of how students and the AI interacted with one another while collaboratively working on the assignment.

Capitalizing on the heterogeneous networks framework, we applied meta-path detection to capture higher-order structures that emerge when transitions follow a specific pattern of node types. We focused on the schema *Student* → *AI* → *Student*, which reflects the alternation between a student intent, an AI response, and the subsequent student intent. To complement the meta-path analysis, we also examined recurring local patterns in the interaction sequences by extracting n-grams of length four to six. The n-grams capture contiguous sequences of interactions that occur in exactly the same order, independent of the underlying schema used for meta-paths.

3.4 Results

Table 1 presents the descriptive statistics of the coded interactions in our dataset, separated into student actions and AI roles. On the student's side, the most frequent behavior is *Instruct* with 429 coded instances, appearing in 83 conversations and averaging 5.17 occurrences per student. *Debug* is the next most common, with 266 instances across 61 conversations (mean = 4.36). *Inquire* and *Seek.Help* appear more moderately, with just below 100 occurrences each and lower mean values, although *Seek.Help* occurs in 66 conversations. *Socialize* is relatively rare, with only 37 instances across 22 conversations, and its mean frequency is the lowest in the student set.

On the AI's side, the dominant role is *Supporter*, with 593 occurrences across 75 conversations and the highest mean (7.91 per conversation, though with a wide SD). *Tutor* also appears prominently, with 256 instances across 38 conversations, and so does *Coder*, with 185 instances. *Analyzer* roles occur less frequently (38 times), while *Sycophant* is rare, with only 13 coded instances across 7 conversations.

Table 1. Descriptive statistics of the qualitatively coded data. *Total* = Number of occurrences of the code. *Nc* = Number of unique conversations in which the code appears. *M* = Mean number of occurrences per conversation. *SD* = Standard deviation of the number of occurrences per conversation

	Code	Total	Nc	M	SD
Student	Instruct	429	83	5.17	5.46
	Seek.Help	94	66	1.42	0.93
	Inquire	98	37	2.65	4.17
	Debug	266	61	4.36	5.60
	Socialize	37	22	1.68	1.09
AI	Analyzer	38	13	2.92	2.33
	Coder	185	69	2.68	3.87
	Supporter	593	75	7.91	9.47
	Tutor	256	38	6.74	9.05
	Sycophant	13	7	1.86	1.46

Figure 2 shows the heterogeneous transition network of student-AI collaboration, where the left-hand nodes represent student intents and the right-hand nodes represent AI roles enacted in the responses. Significant transitions identified through bootstrapping are highlighted in blue. From the donut chart around the nodes, we can see that students tend to initiate their conversations through

Seek.Help or *Instruct* intents, which indicates that most learners turn to AI with a specific need or a directive prompt rather than in an exploratory way. From *Instruct*, there are two statistically significant transitions. The strongest transition leads to *Supporter*, indicating that directive prompts position the AI as an assistant that offers feedback or scaffolding. For *Socialize*, *Debug* and *Inquire*, the only significant transition is also to *Supporter*. Both *Instruct* and *Seek.Help* transition to *Coder*, indicating that the AI only adopts this role when asked for help or when instructed specifically. Regarding the transitions in the opposite direction, only two intents are likely to emerge from AI's responses —*Instruct* and *Debug*— which occur in response to *Supporter*, *Tutor*, or *Coder*. *Sycophant* appeared isolated in the bootstrapped network with no significant transitions. *Analyzer* only significantly led to *Coder*, which indicates that the LLM first analyzed the problem at hand and then provided the code to solve the problem within the same response. Other transitions between nodes of the same type were infrequent and not statistically significant.

The link between *Supporter* and *Debug* forms a reciprocal feedback loop. Students often respond to AI's feedback by implementing changes in their code and, therefore, encounter new errors. As such, the AI tends to return to the *Supporter* role when students bring new *Debug* attempts or follow-up errors. This pattern seems to be a central mechanism of student-AI collaboration: the AI helps students interpret issues or revise their code, which leads students to test or repair, and this cycle repeats until the problem is resolved.

The meta-path analysis revealed a set of recurring heterogeneous transition structures that describe how students' intentions and the AI agent's roles intertwine during problem-solving episodes. Table 2 shows the top 20 meta-paths in our dataset. The meta-paths show a consistency in how student intent and AI roles interact, with *Instruct* → *Supporter* → *Instruct* dominating both support (0.3789) and lift (459.83). This pattern, along with its longer variants—such as the four-step sequence with nearly identical support (0.3684) and high lift (447.09)—highlights a strong reinforcing loop in which instruction-seeking prompts supportive responses that, in turn, encourage students to continue refining or extending their inquiries. Debug-related chains like *Debug* → *Supporter* → *Instruct* (*support* 0.2526; *lift* 306.55) *and Debug* → *Supporter* → *Debug* variants (lift around 281) reveal that moments of troubleshooting often broaden into conceptual clarification or oscillate between identifying issues and seeking explanation, showing that debugging is not isolated but embedded within students' broader knowledge-building efforts. Although less frequent, paths involving *Tutor* or *Coder* roles—such as *Instruct* → *Tutor* → *InstructorInstruct* → *Coder* → *Tutor* → *Instruct* —reflect deeper cognitive engagement where students require more structured guidance, yet their lower supports (mostly around 0.05–0.08) suggest these episodes are more situational than foundational. At the same time, some short and low-lift patterns, like *Debug* → *Debug* → *Supporter* or *Supporter* → *Supporter* → *Debug*, appear to represent more surface-level exchanges that lack the iterative depth seen in the major chains. Overall, the dominant meta-paths reveal a highly stable interaction dynamic where the AI's

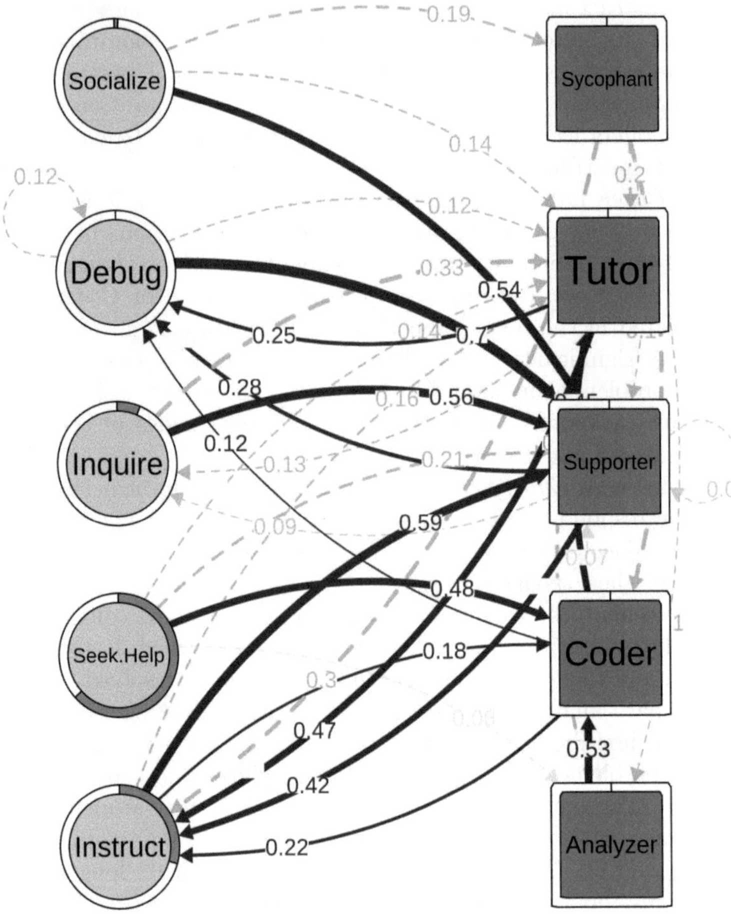

Fig. 2. Heterogeneous transition network of student–AI interactions. Nodes represent qualitative codes assigned to each conversational turn, with yellow circles representing student codes and purple squares representing AI codes. Directed edges denote transitions between codes across the full dataset, with edge thickness reflecting transition probability. Blue edges are found statistically significant after bootstrapping. (Color figure online)

Supporter role acts as the central connective mechanism, enabling sustained learning-oriented dialogue, while the smaller, shallower paths indicate occasional, less cognitively demanding detours within the broader structure of student–AI interaction.

The sequential patterns (Table 3) reinforce the same structure seen in the meta-paths but with even stronger evidence of how persistent and cyclic the dominant sequences are. The most frequent patterns—*Instruct* → *Supporter* → *Instruct* → *Supporter* (support 0.3684, lift 3684) and its five-step extension with

Table 2. Top 20 meta-paths

Pattern	Lgth	N	N_s	Support	Prop.	Lift
Instruct → Supporter → Instruct	3	136	36	0.3789	0.0262	459.83
Instruct → Supporter → Instruct → Supporter	4	130	35	0.3684	0.0251	447.09
Instruct → Supporter → Instruct → Supporter → Instruct	5	76	22	0.2316	0.0147	281.07
Debug → Supporter → Instruct	3	53	24	0.2526	0.0102	306.55
Debug → Supporter → Instruct → Supporter	4	49	22	0.2316	0.0095	281.07
Instruct → Coder → Tutor	3	46	13	0.1368	0.0089	166.02
Debug → Supporter → Debug	3	44	22	0.2316	0.0085	281.07
Instruct → Supporter → Debug	3	44	23	0.2421	0.0085	293.81
Instruct → Supporter → Debug → Supporter	4	43	23	0.2421	0.0083	293.81
Debug → Supporter → Debug → Supporter	4	40	22	0.2316	0.0077	281.07
Debug → Supporter → Supporter	3	31	3	0.0316	0.0060	38.35
Instruct → Tutor → Instruct	3	31	6	0.0632	0.0060	76.70
Debug → Debug → Supporter	3	30	2	0.0211	0.0058	25.61
Debug → Debug → Supporter → Supporter	4	30	2	0.0211	0.0058	25.61
Instruct → Coder → Tutor → Instruct	4	29	8	0.0842	0.0056	102.18
Instruct → Tutor → Instruct → Tutor	4	26	5	0.0526	0.0050	63.83
Instruct → Supporter → Debug → Supporter → Instruct	5	25	13	0.1368	0.0048	166.02
Debug → Supporter → Instruct → Supporter → Instruct	5	24	15	0.1579	0.0046	191.63
Instruct → Coder → Tutor → Instruct → Coder	5	23	8	0.0842	0.0044	102.18
Debug → Supporter → Supporter → Debug	4	22	2	0.0211	0.0042	25.61

nearly identical support (0.2842) and very high lift—show that once students initiate an instructional query, they tend to remain in this mode through repeated rounds of supportive AI responses. The recurrence of these high-lift chains (many exceeding 20,000 and some reaching 168,000) signals exceptionally stable behavioral loops: an *Instruct* intent leads almost deterministically to a *Supporter* reply, which then elicits another *Instruct* follow-up. This structure suggests that the AI's consistent scaffolding not only sustains but amplifies students' inclination to refine or deepen their questions.

The data also show that *Debug* pathways, while less dominant, integrate into these sequences rather than forming isolated islands. For example, *Instruct → Supporter → Instruct → Supporter → Debug → Supporter* (support 0.1684; lift 168,400) reveals that troubleshooting moments often emerge midstream in a longer instructional chain, suggesting that problem-solving is folded into broader conceptual exploration. Similarly, repeated patterns such as *Supporter → Debug → Supporter → Instruct → Supporter* (support around 0.20) indicate that students use debugging not just to fix errors but as a gateway back into clarification and deeper inquiry. In sum, these n-grams present a coherent picture: the *Supporter* role is the structural backbone of the interaction network, repeatedly attracting both instructional and debugging intents into long, stable, and often cognitively rich sequences.

Table 3. Top 20 n-grams

Pattern	Lgth	N	N_s	Support	Prop.	Lift
Instruct → Supporter → Instruct → Supporter	4	130	35	0.3684	0.0264	3684
Supporter → Instruct → Supporter → Instruct → Supporter	5	112	27	0.2842	0.0227	28420
Instruct → Supporter → Instruct → Supporter → Instruct → Supporter	6	74	22	0.2316	0.0150	231600
Supporter → Instruct → Supporter → Instruct → Supporter → Instruct	6	69	21	0.2211	0.0140	221100
Instruct → Supporter → Instruct → Supporter → Instruct	5	76	22	0.2316	0.0154	23160
Supporter → Instruct → Supporter → Debug → Supporter	5	40	22	0.2316	0.0081	23160
Supporter → Instruct → Supporter → Instruct	4	117	28	0.2947	0.0238	2947
Instruct → Supporter → Instruct → Supporter → Debug → Supporter	6	20	16	0.1684	0.0041	168400
Supporter → Debug → Supporter → Instruct → Supporter	5	42	19	0.2000	0.0085	20000
Debug → Supporter → Instruct → Supporter → Instruct → Supporter	6	23	15	0.1579	0.0047	157900
Supporter → Debug → Supporter → Debug → Supporter	5	35	18	0.1895	0.0071	18950
Instruct → Supporter → Debug → Supporter	4	43	23	0.2421	0.0087	2421
Supporter → Debug → Supporter → Instruct → Supporter → Instruct	6	21	14	0.1474	0.0043	147400
Debug → Supporter → Instruct → Supporter	4	49	22	0.2316	0.0099	2316
Debug → Supporter → Debug → Supporter	4	40	22	0.2316	0.0081	2316
Supporter → Instruct → Supporter → Debug	4	40	22	0.2316	0.0081	2316
Supporter → Debug → Supporter → Instruct	4	46	21	0.2211	0.0093	2211
Supporter → Instruct → Supporter → Debug → Supporter → Instruct	6	24	13	0.1368	0.0049	136800
Instruct → Supporter → Debug → Supporter → Instruct → Supporter	6	24	13	0.1368	0.0049	136800
Supporter → Instruct → Supporter → Instruct → Supporter → Debug	6	17	13	0.1368	0.0035	136800

4 Discussion

4.1 About the Method

Modeling two types of nodes is commonly performed with two-mode bipartite networks [1], which allow connections only between the two sets but not within each set. While useful for simple interactions, this approach often requires projecting the network into a one-mode form, which can lose important relational information. Heterogeneous information networks (HINs), in contrast, support multiple node and edge types, including both cross-type and within-type connections, preserving the full structure of the data [25]. This flexibility allows HINs to capture complex, higher-order relationships and enables more detailed analysis of interactions through mechanisms such as meta-paths. In this study, we have implemented the principle behind HINs in a transition network, resulting in a heterogeneous transition network.

Modelling the interaction data as a heterogeneous transition network provides a representation that retains both the temporal nature of the exchanges and the semantic distinctions between student intents and AI roles. HTNA allows us to move beyond isolated transitions toward patterns that emerge only when sequences are examined holistically. Meta-paths play a central role here because they describe recurring typed transitions that reflect how one class of actions is typically followed by responses from another class. In our study, meta-paths have revealed structures that repeatedly appear when students and the AI system interact, such as cycles of instructive actions paired with supportive responses.

In addition to the analytical advantages introduced by heterogeneity, the framework retains the methodological strengths of TNA more broadly. The model still supports validation techniques such as bootstrapping, which provides a way to evaluate the stability of observed patterns. There are other features of TNA that could be integrated into future work using HTNA, including centrality measures capable of quantifying the prominence of specific events or roles within the larger interaction system. As such, the heterogeneous transition network developed in the present study forms a foundation that can be expanded with the full range of the TNA toolkit while retaining the ability to model distinct node types and complex relational structures.

4.2 About the Results

The results show that student AI interactions often begin with students asking for help and the AI responding with generated code. Another strong pattern is that students request new code or features and then receive feedback or explanations on what the code does. There is also a notable link between the AI analyzing a task and then producing code, as well as between code generation and follow-up explanation. A central finding is that the AI's feedback role is activated by many different student moves, including domain questions, social conversation, and debugging attempts. When the AI takes on a tutoring role, students frequently respond by asking for help with coding, requesting fixes for errors, or asking for new code entirely. Interestingly, the *Coder* role of AI, where AI provides students with code, appears only once among the top patterns, specifically in the sequence *Instruct* → *Coder* → *Tutor*. This suggests that direct code generation is not a dominant standalone behavior. Instead, when the AI does produce code, it often shifts immediately into a tutoring mode, explaining the solution rather than leaving the code without interpretation. Although the data cannot reveal whether students actually internalized the AI's feedback, tutoring, and explanations or were simply prompting repeatedly until they obtained a working solution, the interaction patterns show that they were at least consistently exposed to tutoring and feedback from the AI side.

Similar patterns were found in Pan et al. [19], who reported that students mainly received step-by-step guidance or strategic advice from the AI, while their own queries were largely solution-focused. This aligns with our finding that students approach the AI with concrete goals and that the AI responds by structuring the path toward a solution. To better understand these interaction patterns, it is also important to consider individual differences. Hao et al. [5] showed that students with different levels of prior knowledge engage with AI in distinct ways: concept-focused questions triggered knowledge-building sequences supported by AI scaffolding, while more advanced learners were able to co-regulate the learning process with the AI. Students with less background knowledge, in contrast, tended to rely more on direct cognitive support. Zheng et al. [34] further demonstrated that the main challenge is not excessive dependence on AI but difficulty applying AI guidance effectively. Many students struggled to translate advice into correct solutions, sometimes disengaging after an unproductive first attempt or becoming stuck in repeated cycles of unsuccessful application. Their results highlight that productive human–AI collaboration requires not only access to AI guidance but also the skills to evaluate and implement it. As such, future research on student–AI collaboration should account for both individual differences and how students actually apply AI scaffolding, in order to develop a more comprehensive understanding of this complex phenomenon.

5 Limitations

Our study is of a methodological nature and aimed at illustrating HTNA as an extension of TNA. We do so through an empirical case study in student-AI interactions in programming education. However, since our study is not focused on the empirical results, the case study has several limitations. First, it is situated within a single introductory Web Programming course at a single university, which limits the extent to which the findings can be transferred to other courses, disciplines, or institutional settings. The sample size, although sufficient for analysis, remains moderate and reflects the practices of a specific cohort working on a particular programming assignment. Such contextual features may influence both the nature of student–AI interactions and the roles that the AI and the students adopt. Also, the study focused on one type of AI (ChatGPT): other AI models or subsequent versions of ChatGPT may yield different results. Another constraint concerns the qualitative annotation process. Although we developed a data-driven codebook and applied careful prompt engineering, the coding was performed by a large language model. This introduces the possibility of misclassifications that may differ from human judgment. Several methodological constraints are also relevant. (H)TNA relies on Markovian assumptions that treat each code as conditionally dependent only on the preceding one, which may oversimplify longer conversational dependencies. The model captures observable sequences but does not include latent factors such as prior coding experience, students' confidence, or their familiarity with AI tools, all of which may have shaped how students interacted with ChatGPT.

Acknowledgments. This article has been co-funded by the European Commission through the ISILA (2023-1-FI01-KA220-HED-000159757) project and the Research Council of Finland through the project CRETIC (360746).

References

1. Borgatti, S.P., Everett, M.G.: Network analysis of 2-mode data. Soc. Netw. **19**, 243–269 (1997)
2. Cai, Y., Tian, S.: Investigating student translators' human–GENAI interaction patterns: an exploratory study using cluster analysis and epistemic network analysis. Interpret. Transl. Trainer, 1–19 (2025). https://doi.org/10.1080/1750399x.2025.2543209
3. Chu, X., et al.: Enhancing the flipped classroom model with generative AI and metaverse technologies: insights from lag sequential and epistemic network analysis. Educat. Technol. Res. Develop.: ETR & D **73**(3), 1539–1567 (2025). https://doi.org/10.1007/s11423-025-10457-2

4. Dang, B., Huynh, L., Gul, F., Rosé, C., Järvelä, S., Nguyen, A.: Human- AI collaborative learning in mixed reality: examining the cognitive and socio-emotional interactions. Br. J. Edu. Technol. **56**(5), 2078–2101 (2025). https://doi.org/10.1111/bjet.13607
5. Hao, Z., Cao, J., Li, R., Yu, J., Liu, Z., Zhang, Y.: Mapping student-AI interaction dynamics in multi-agent learning environments: supporting personalised learning and reducing performance gaps. arXiv preprint arXiv:2506.02993 (2025)
6. Järvelä, S., Nguyen, A., Hadwin, A.: Human and artificial intelligence collaboration for socially shared regulation in learning. Br. J. Educ. Technol. **54**(5), 1057–1076 (2023). https://doi.org/10.1111/bjet.13325
7. Kaliisa, R., Misiejuk, K., López-Pernas, S., Saqr, M.: How does artificial intelligence compare to human feedback? A meta-analysis of performance, feedback perception, and learning dispositions. Educ. Psychol. (Lond.), 1–32 (2025). https://doi.org/10.1080/01443410.2025.2553639
8. Lai, J.W., et al.: Leveraging process-action epistemic network analysis to illuminate student self-regulated learning with a socratic chatbot. J. Learn. Analy. **12**(1), 32–49 (2025). https://doi.org/10.18608/jla.2025.8549
9. Liu, J., Li, S., Dong, Q.: Collaboration with generative artificial intelligence: an exploratory study based on learning analytics. J. Educat. Comput. Res **62**(5), 1234–1266 (2024). https://doi.org/10.1177/07356331241242441
10. López-Pernas, S., Misiejuk, K., Inga Bulanova, G., Emara, M., Siddika, A.N.M., Saqr, M.: The changing landscape of Smart learning environments: pedagogy, collaborative intelligence, and ethics. In: Proceedings of ICSLE 2025, LNET. Springer (2026). A process-oriented view of human-AI interactions: Comparing argumentative vs. creative writing
11. López-Pernas, S., Misiejuk, K., Jovanović, J., Raspopović Milić, M., Conde, M.A., Saqr, M.: ChatGPTScraper: a tool for retrieving student-ai interactions. In: Proceedings of the 2025 International Conference on Advanced Learning Technologies (ICALT), pp. 134–136. IEEE, Piscataway, NJ, USA (2025). https://doi.org/10.1109/ICALT64023.2025.00044
12. López-Pernas, S., Misiejuk, K., Kaliisa, R., Saqr, M.: Capturing the process of students' AI interactions when creating and learning complex network structures. IEEE Trans. Learn. Technol. **18**, 556–568 (2025). https://doi.org/10.1109/tlt.2025.3568599
13. López-Pernas, S., Misiejuk, K., Oliveira, E., Saqr, M.: The dynamics of the self-regulation process in student-AI interactions: the case of problem-solving in programming education. In: Proceedings of the 25th Koli Calling International Conference on Computing Education Research, pp. 1–12. ACM, New York, NY, USA (2025). https://doi.org/10.1145/3769994.3770043
14. López-Pernas, S., Misiejuk, K., Saqr, M.: Heterogeneous Transition Network Analysis [R package htna version 0.3.1] (2026). CRAN. https://doi.org/10.32614/CRAN.package.htna
15. Misiejuk, K., López-Pernas, S., Kaliisa, R., Saqr, M.: Learning together: modeling the process of student-ai interactions when generating learning resources. In: Molina Carmona, R.E.A. (ed.) Proceedings of TEEM 2024. Lecture Notes in Educational Technology, pp. 448–458. Lecture Notes in Educational Technology, Springer Nature Singapore, Singapore (2025)
16. Nguyen, A., Ilesanmi, F., Dang, B., Vuorenmaa, E., Järvelä, S.: Hybrid intelligence in academic writing: examining self-regulated learning patterns in an AI-assisted writing task. In: HHAI 2024: Hybrid Human AI Systems for the Social Good.

Frontiers in artificial intelligence and applications, IOS Press (2024). https://doi.org/10.3233/faia240198
17. Nguyen, H., Nguyen, A.: Reflective practices and self-regulated learning in designing with generative artificial intelligence: an ordered network analysis. J. Sci. Educ. Technol. (2024). https://doi.org/10.1007/s10956-024-10175-z
18. Olney, A.: Generating multiple choice questions from a textbook: LLMs match human performance on most metrics. In: Workshop on Empowering Education with LLMs - the Next-Gen Interface and Content Generation at the AIED'23 Conference. CEUR (2023). https://ceur-ws.org/Vol-3487/paper7.pdf
19. Pan, Z., Ba, S., Jiang, Z., Li, C.: Patterns of inquiry, scaffolding, and interaction profiles in learner-AI collaborative math problem-solving. In: Proceedings of the Artificial Intelligence in Measurement and Education Conference, pp. 297–305., AIME-Con (2025) Full Papers
20. Rüdian, S., Podelo, J., Kužílek, J., Pinkwart, N.: Feedback on feedback: student's perceptions for feedback from teachers and few-shot LLMs. In: Proceedings of the 15th International Learning Analytics and Knowledge Conference, pp. 82–92. ACM, New York, NY, USA (2025). https://doi.org/10.1145/3706468.3706479
21. Saint, J., Gašević, D., Matcha, W., Uzir, N.A., Pardo, A.: Combining analytic methods to unlock sequential and temporal patterns of self-regulated learning. In: Proceedings of the Tenth International Conference on Learning Analytics & Knowledge, pp. 402–411. LAK '20, Association for Computing Machinery, New York, NY, USA (2020). https://doi.org/10.1145/3375462.3375487
22. Saqr, M., López-Pernas, S., Jovanović, J., Gašević, D.: Intense, turbulent, or wallowing in the mire: a longitudinal study of cross-course online tactics, strategies, and trajectories. internet high **57**, 100902 (2023). https://doi.org/10.1016/j.iheduc.2022.100902, https://www.sciencedirect.com/science/article/pii/S1096751622000586
23. Saqr, M., López-Pernas, S., Törmänen, T., Kaliisa, R., Misiejuk, K., Tikka, S.: Transition network analysis: a novel framework for modeling, visualizing, and identifying the temporal patterns of learners and learning processes. In: Proceedings of Learning Analytics & Knowledge (LAK '25), pp. in–press. ACM, New York, NY, USA (2025)
24. Saqr, M., Misiejuk, K., López-Pernas, S.: Human-AI collaboration or obedient and often clueless AI in instruct, serve, repeat dynamics? arXiv [cs.HC] (2025). https://doi.org/10.48550/arXiv.2508.10919, http://arxiv.org/abs/2508.10919
25. Shi, C., Philip, S.Y.: Heterogeneous Information Network Analysis and Applications. Springer (2017)
26. Sun, Y., Han, J.: Mining heterogeneous information networks: a structural analysis approach. SIGKDD Explor. **14**(2), 20–28 (2013). https://doi.org/10.1145/2481244.2481248
27. Urban, M., et al.: Prompting for creative problem-solving: a process-mining study. Learn. Instr. **99**, 102156 (2025). https://doi.org/10.1016/j.learninstruc.2025.102156
28. Wang, F., Tang, X., Yu, S.: Cognitive outsourcing based on generative artificial intelligence: an analysis of interactive behavioral patterns and cognitive structural features. Xin li xue bao.Acta psychologica Sinica **57**(6), 967 (2025). https://doi.org/10.3724/sp.j.1041.2025.0967
29. Wang, X., et al.: What matters in AI-supported learning: a study of human-ai interactions in language learning using cluster analysis and epistemic network analysis. Comput. Educat. **194**(104703), 104703 (2023). https://doi.org/10.1016/j.compedu.2022.104703

30. Wickham, H., Cheng, J., Jacobs, A., Aden-Buie, G., Schloerke, B.: ELLMER: chat with large Language Models (2025). https://CRAN.R-project.org/package=ellmer, r package version 0.4.0
31. Woollaston, S., Flanagan, B., Ocheja, P., Toyokawa, Y., Ogata, H.: Archie: exploring language learner behaviors in LLM chatbot-supported active reading log data with epistemic network analysis. In: Proceedings of the 15th International Learning Analytics and Knowledge Conference, pp. 642–654. ACM, New York, NY, USA (2025). https://doi.org/10.1145/3706468.3706556
32. Yin, X., Ye, J., Yu, S., Li, H., Liu, Q., Zhao, G.: The association between groups' interactions with the visual-GENAI learning analytics feedback and student engagement in cscl. Comput. Educat. **239**(105434), 105434 (2025). https://doi.org/10.1016/j.compedu.2025.105434
33. Zhao, Y., Xu, Y., Long, T.: Understanding pre-service science teachers' collaborative discourse patterns in a GENAI integrated collective reflection: A network analytic approach. J. Sci. Educ. Technol. (2025). https://doi.org/10.1007/s10956-025-10241-0
34. Zheng, J., et al.: Do students rely on AI? analysis of student-ChatGPT conversations from a field study. In: Proceedings of the AAAI/ACM Conference on AI, Ethics, and Society, vol. 8, pp. 2796–2807 (2025)
35. Ziegler, J., Donkers, T.: From explanations to human-AI co-evolution: charting trajectories towards future user-centric AI. I-Com **23**(2), 263–272 (2024). https://doi.org/10.1515/icom-2024-0020

Modeling Observation Lens in Co-Occurrence Network Analysis: Four Window Approaches and Implementations

Kamila Misiejuk[1(✉)], Eduardo Araujo Oliveira[2], Yige Song[2], Sonsoles López-Pernas[3], and Mohammed Saqr[3]

[1] CATALPA, FernUniversität in Hagen, Hagen, Germany
kamila.misiejuk@fernuni-hagen.de
[2] Melbourne University, Melbourne, Australia
eduardo.oliveira@unimelb.edu.au, yige.song@unimelb.edu.au
[3] University of Eastern Finland, Kuopio, Finland
sonsoles.lopez@uef.fi, mohammed.saqr@uef.fi

Abstract. Modeling how collaboration unfolds in digital learning environments requires analytical approaches that account for both temporal structure and the local organization of learner actions. Co-occurrence Network Analysis (CNA) offers a flexible framework for representing these relationships; however, the choice of co-occurrence window remains an under-examined methodological decision with substantial interpretive consequences. We present a systematic comparison of four window implementations: single-message, multi-message, fixed-duration, and duration-gap. Using two simulated datasets that represent synchronous (dense) and asynchronous (sparse) collaboration patterns, we examine how each window approach shapes the resulting network structures, including co-occurrence patterns, self-connections, cross-actor links, and their sensitivity to different temporal dynamics. Our findings underscore that defining the co-occurrence window is not a neutral pre-processing step but a central modeling decision that directly shapes the interpretation and conceptualization of collaborative processes.

Keywords: Co-Occurrence Network Analysis · Stanza Window · Adaptive Window · Learning Analytics

1 Introduction

Understanding how learning processes unfold over time requires analytical approaches that capture both the temporal and relational structure of learners' actions [8,15] as well as their *dialogic trajectories* [5]. Network-based models have become popular in education [4,13], as they allow researchers to represent the complexity of events and concepts as interconnected structures and

M. Saqr et al. (Eds.): TNA 2026, CCIS 3079, pp. 34–50, 2026.
https://doi.org/10.1007/978-3-032-34157-0_3

can model interaction temporality. Co-occurrence models, in particular, are central for examining how actions, concepts, or discourse elements connect within meaningful units by capturing contributions that appear together within a local interaction segment, such as a short exchange, discussion turn, or moment of joint problem-solving. Network-based co-occurrence methods are widely used in studies of collaborative problem solving, group regulation, and knowledge building, where contributions within the same episode are assumed to share functional or cognitive relationships (e.g., [3,11,18]). A key design choice in these models is the definition of a *window*, the breadth or range of interaction chain included in each window (for example, a single message, a short sequence of messages, or a fixed time interval) within which events are treated as related [6]. Here, contributions refer to the coded actions or utterances, such as asking a question, giving an explanation, or expressing agreement. The window in this context defines which coded actions may be combined together, and the boundaries establish the segmentation mechanism.

Although the need for temporal analysis and the appropriate granularity of such analysis have long been discussed in learning analytics [2,4,6,12,17], methodological guidance on how different window definitions shape resulting network structures remains limited. [14] compared two window approaches in Epistemic Network Analysis (ENA): the moving window, which generates overlapping windows of set length across a conversation, and the whole-conversation window, which treats all utterances within an activity as mutually co-occurring. They found that the whole-conversation window captured team-level patterns but failed to identify individual contributions, whereas the moving window captured both activity-level connections and the contributions of individual students. [19] extended this work by comparing three ENA window types: the moving window of set length, the infinite-stanza window that relates all utterances regardless of position, and the whole-conversation window. The analysis showed that each window type embeds different assumptions about the importance of temporal proximity, conversational boundaries, or cumulative co-occurrence across an activity, which in turn produces different network structures and interpretations. Finally, [7] compared timestamp-based moving windows with analyses that used only ordered data in Socio-semantic Network Analysis. Using timestamp windows revealed meaningful temporal fluctuations in idea development, including periods of intense idea revision and periods of idea maintenance, which were not visible when utterances were treated as evenly spaced.

In this paper, we examine four window implementations within a Co-Occurrence Network Analysis (CNA) framework from the Transition Network Analysis toolkit [9], ranging from temporally agnostic approaches that group messages by count to time-sensitive approaches that respond to actual gaps in activity. To ground our comparison in realistic collaborative contexts, we apply these implementations to both synchronous and asynchronous interaction settings. Our contributions are threefold: (1) we provide R implementations for four co-occurrence window approaches (single-message, multi-message, fixed-duration, and duration-gap), (2) we use simulated synchronous and asynchronous datasets to show how methodological differences are amplified under different temporal conditions, and (3) we discuss the implications of each implementation for network construction, interpretation, and alignment with different types of research questions. Together, these contributions aim to help researchers make informed analytical choices when applying CNA to complex educational datasets.

2 Methods

2.1 Datasets

We created two simulated datasets that represent typical synchronous and asynchronous collaboration scenarios, in which students' messages are coded using a predefined coding scheme. These codes serve as placeholders for common collaborative or cognitive behaviors, such as questioning, explaining, or monitoring. The datasets were generated using reproducible R scripts that produced random student identifiers for four students and fictitious binary coding for each message (the message content itself was not generated, as our focus lies solely on the coding patterns). Each dataset contains 500 messages authored by the four students, with every message coded for the presence or absence of five analytic codes. Dataset 1 (or synchronous dataset) uses small and consistent inter-message gaps to emulate continuous communication, while Dataset 2 (or asynchronous dataset) introduces irregular pauses and extended periods of inactivity. Both datasets share the same distribution of messages per student and the same frequencies of coded occurrences (see Table 1). The sole distinction lies in the temporal distribution of messages (see Fig. 1). Dataset 1 spans nearly four hours, while Dataset 2 covers almost two days, thereby modeling synchronous and asynchronous collaboration settings, respectively. As the binary coding of messages is identical across both datasets and only the temporal spacing differs, this design allows us to isolate the effect of temporal structure on co-occurrence windows while keeping all other properties constant. Full R code for generating the datasets is provided in Appendix A.1.

Table 1. Frequency of messages and codes per student and overall totals.

Student ID	Messages	code1	code2	code3	code4	code5	Total # of codes
student1	109	41	65	39	48	45	**238**
student2	116	32	68	44	50	38	**232**
student3	136	54	84	45	64	44	**291**
student4	139	55	84	48	50	46	**283**
Total # of codes	**500**	**182**	**301**	**176**	**212**	**173**	**1044**

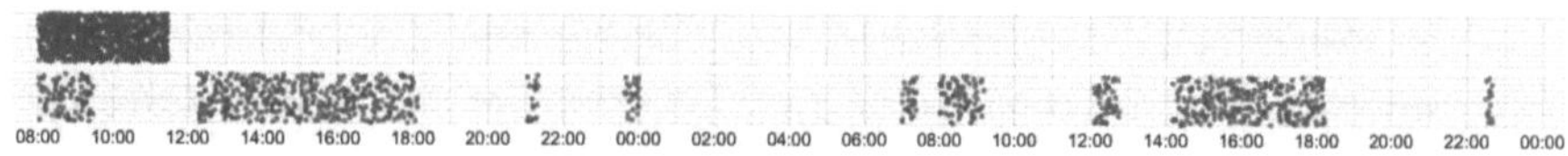

Fig. 1. Time series of the messages distribution for Dataset 1 (top) and Dataset 2 (bottom). Message points are jittered for better readability.

2.2 Analysis

In this paper, we present four possible implementations of a co-occurrence window in CNA: (1) single-message (window = 1 message), (2) multi-message (window = 3 messages), (3) fixed-duration (window = 5-minutes), and (4) duration-gap (window = 5-minutes-gap) (see Fig. 2). The specific parameter values were selected for illustrative purposes to demonstrate the methodological differences between window implementations clearly. Rather than optimizing for a specific dataset or research context, these values were chosen to produce interpretable and comparable networks that highlight the conceptual distinctions between approaches. Researchers applying these implementations to authentic datasets should select parameters based on the temporal structure of their data and the specific research questions being addressed.

CNA is a network method that models the co-occurrence of states or codes within a sequence. The co-occurrence is computed based on the selected *actor* parameter, which defines the unit of analysis within which connections are counted (e.g., an utterance, chat, or lesson). A CNA graph includes nodes that represent the states or codes being modeled, while the strength of the edges represents the cumulative number of connections between the nodes. Unlike standard TNA, which assumes large datasets to meet the statistical requirements of Markov modeling, CNA can be effectively applied to smaller datasets. Moreover, CNA does not account for the directionality of connections, unlike both standard TNA and Frequency-based TNA (FTNA) [10]—the latter also focuses on connection frequencies but captures their directional nature.

We used the `tna` R package [16] to construct CNA networks from the coded data. For each window implementation, we developed two models: one representing synchronous interactions (using Dataset 1) and one representing asynchronous interactions (using Dataset 2). Connections in each model were scaled using min-max normalization to scale values into a 0–1 range while preserving the overall distribution. We also generated subtraction CNA networks to highlight differences between synchronous and asynchronous interactions. Finally, we generated comparison networks across windowing approaches and evaluated them in terms of edge weights, code centralities, network weight densities, and Pearson correlations.

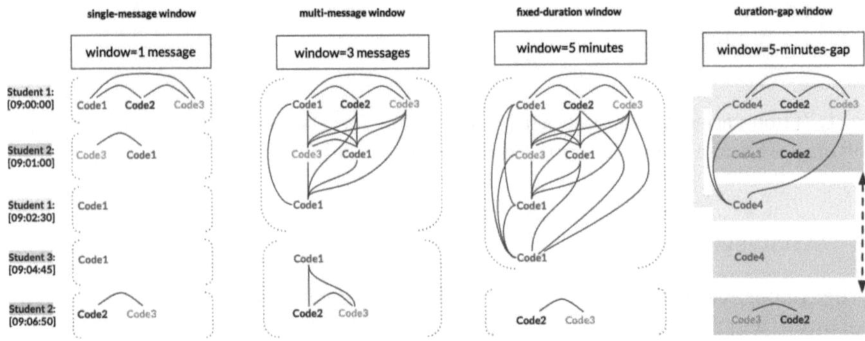

Fig. 2. Overview of window implementations in CNA.

3 Results

3.1 Single-message Window

The single-message window approach utilizes a window of only 1 message. To achieve that we set "message_id" as the *actor* to constrain the algorithm to count co-occurrences only within a single row, not across rows, meaning the algorithm examines each row to determine which codes are present (see Fig. 3a). This means that if a row contains a 1 for *code1* and a 1 for *code2*, the corresponding entry in the co-occurrence matrix for *code1–code2* will be incremented by one. Each co-occurrence contributes one count per code, and since each code can only be annotated as present/absent once per message, there are no self-connections (e.g., *code1–code1*). This results in a symmetric co-occurrence matrix. As such, this implementation does not require any additional data pre-processing, and *time* or *order* parameters can be omitted entirely.

As the *window = 1 message* approach does not consider the time or the order of messages, it produced identical results for Dataset 1 and Dataset 2 (see Fig. 3b). Across all sessions, the total number of windows is 477, indicating that 23 messages either had no codes or only a single code. Since each message can be coded with a maximum of five codes (this was the total number of codes in our simulated code scheme), this also represents the maximum number of connections that can be recorded per window.

(a)

```
# Prepare data using message_id as actor
cna_df = prepare_data(dataset, actor=("message_id", action = "code")
# Create CNA object and scale edge weights
cna = cna(cna_df, scaling = "minmax")
# Plot the CNA network
plot(cna)
```

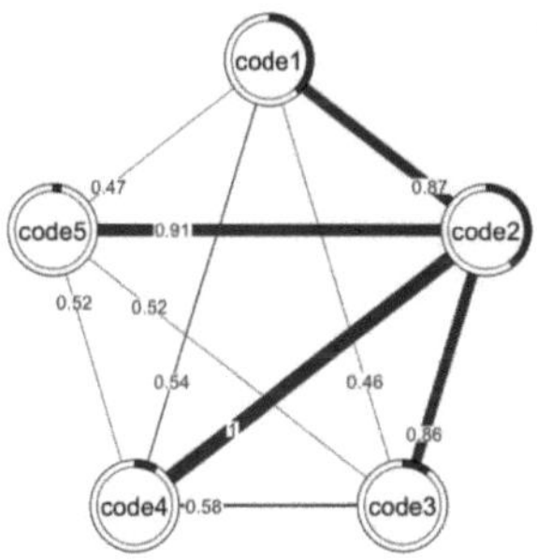

(b)

Fig. 3. *Window = 1 message* approach: (a) CNA parameters and (b) CNA network with scaled edges.

3.2 Multi-message Window

The second implementation counts code co-occurrences across multiple consecutive messages, which requires manipulating the message IDs so that groups of consecutive messages are merged and treated as a single window (see Fig. 4a). We set the window size (*actor*) to an ID representing three consecutive messages (see Fig. 4b). Because the *window = 3 messages* approach counts all co-occurrences within these three-message groups, code self-occurrences are additionally generated. In this approach, the *time* and *order* parameters can be omitted entirely.

As the *window = 3 messages* approach does not consider collaboration settings or the temporal and ordinal aspects of co-occurrences, it produces identical results for Dataset 1 and Dataset 2 (see Fig. 4c). This is because the window is defined purely by message count, meaning that three consecutive messages are always grouped together regardless of when they were sent or how much time elapsed between them. As a result, the same groupings are produced whether messages were exchanged in rapid succession or separated by hours of inactivity. Across all sessions, there are 167 windows in total with a maximum of 11 codes per window.

(a)

```
#Sort by Time
dataset = dataset %>% arrange(Time)
#Create new message_id that repeats each original ID 3 times
dataset$three_messages_id = rep(dataset$message_id, each = 3)[1:nrow(dataset)]
```

(b)

```
#Prepare data and use three_messages_id as actor
cna_df = prepare_data(dataset, actor = "three_messages_id", action = "code")
#Create a CNA object and scale the edge weights
cna = cna(cna_df, scaling = "minmax")
#Create a CNA network
plot(cna)
```

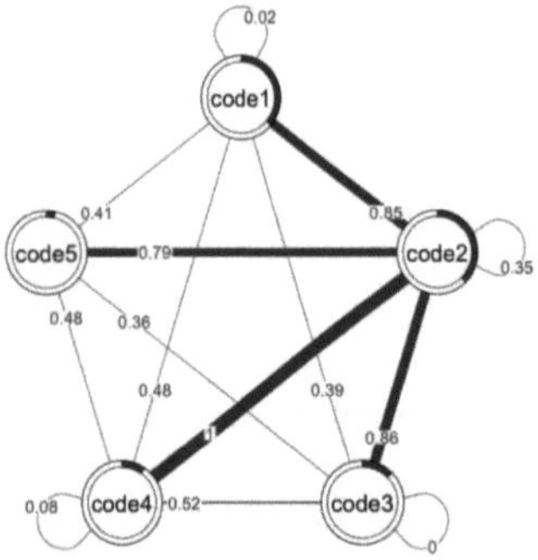

(c)

Fig. 4. *Window = 3 messages* approach: (a) 3-message ID generation, (b) CNA parameters, and (c) CNA network with scaled edges.

3.3 Fixed-Duration Window

Another approach involves developing a fixed-duration window, where each window starts with the first message that follows the end of the previous one. This design makes the windows dynamic rather than fixed to the initial timestamp. To ensure that the analysis is strictly limited to five-minute intervals, we specified only the *actor* parameter and omitted the *order* and *time* parameters (see Fig. 5a).

Using the *window = 5-minutes* approach produces distinct networks for synchronous and asynchronous collaboration settings, as co-occurrence counting depends on whether message timestamps fall within or exceed the defined five-minute intervals (see Fig. 5b and Fig. 5c). Dataset 1 (synchronous collaboration) resulted in 40 sessions, with up to 35 codes recorded per window, whereas Dataset 2 (asynchronous collaboration) produced 146 sessions, with a maximum of 13 codes per window. The difference in the number and size of sessions reflects how the five-minute window interacts with the temporal structure of collaboration. In the synchronous collaboration, denser message exchanges

(a)

```
#Sort dataset by timestamp
dataset = dataset %>% arrange(Time)
#Initialize SessionID column and counters
dataset$SessionID = NA
session_id = 1
i = 1
n = nrow(dataset)
#Assign 5-minute session IDs
while (i <= n) {
  start_time = dataset$Time[i]
  end_time = start_time + minutes(5)
  dataset$SessionID[i:n] = ifelse(dataset$Time[i:n] <= end_time, session_id,
  ↪  dataset$SessionID[i:n])
  i = which(dataset$Time > end_time)[1]
  if (is.na(i)) break
  session_id = session_id + 1
}
```

(b)

```
#Prepare data and use SessionID as actor
cna1_df = prepare_data(dataset1, actor = "session_id", action = "code")
cna1 = cna(cna1_df, scaling = "minmax")
cna2_df = prepare_data(dataset2, actor = "session_id", action = "code")
cna2 = cna(cna2_df, scaling = "minmax")
#Plot CNA networks
plot(cna1)
plot(cna2)
#Compare networks to highlight differences
plot_compare(cna1, cna2)
```

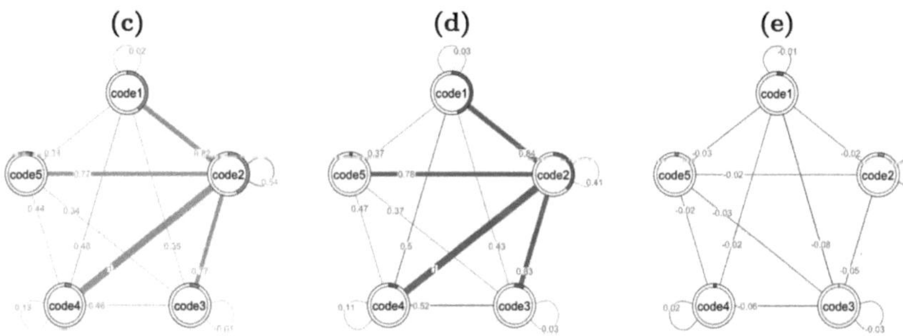

Fig. 5. *Window = 5-minutes* approach: (a) session ID generation, (b) CNA parameters, (c) synchronous CNA network, (d) asynchronous CNA network, and (e) comparison network with scaled edges (green: stronger edges for asynchronous collaboration; orange: stronger edges for synchronous collaboration). (Color figure online)

result in fewer but more code-rich windows, whereas the asynchronous collaboration shows more numerous, smaller windows with fewer co-occurrences per interval. Although overall scaled edge weight differences were small, structural variations were observed. The largest difference occurred in the *code2–code2* self-connection, which was higher in the synchronous condition (0.13), followed by *code3-code1* connection (0.08) and *code3-code4* being stronger for the asynchronous model. Overall, both self-connections and cross-code connections were generally stronger in the asynchronous model than in the synchronous model.

3.4 Duration-Gap Window

In the duration-gap window approach, we utilize the in-built functions: the *time_threshold* and *time* parameters. *Time_threshold* was set to five minutes (300 s). The *actor* was defined as *student_id*, and timestamps were used to represent the *time* variable (see Fig. 6a). This parameter defines a dynamic session window, where a new session begins whenever the gap between consecutive actions of the same *actor* exceeds five minutes. In our case, this means that a new session is initiated whenever the time between two consecutive messages from the same student is greater than five minutes (recall Fig. 2). Another feature of this approach is that co-occurrences of codes are counted only within messages of each individual *actor* (student) for the specified threshold, and not across messages from other actors.

Using the *window* = *5-minutes-gap* approach, the total number of windows differed between synchronous and asynchronous data: 24 windows for syn-

(a)

```
# Prepare data and set parameters
cna1_df = prepare_data(dataset1, actor = "student_id", action = "code",
time_threshold = 300, time = "Time")
cna1 = cna(cna1_df, scaling = "minmax")
cna2_df = prepare_data(dataset2, actor = "student_id", action = "code",
time_threshold = 300, time = "Time")
cna2 = cna(cna2_df, scaling = "minmax")
# Plot CNA networks
plot(cna1)
plot(cna2)
# Compare networks to highlight differences
plot_compare(cna1, cna2)
```

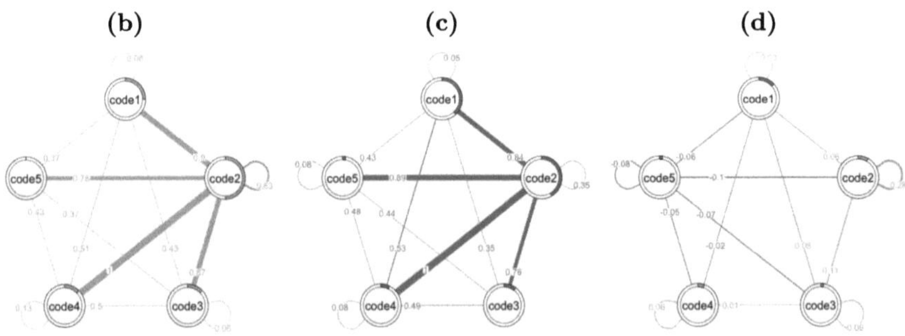

Fig. 6. *Window* = *5-minutes-gap* approach: (a) CNA parameters, (b) synchronous CNA network, (c) asynchronous CNA network, and (d) comparison network with scaled edges (green: stronger edges for asynchronous collaboration; orange: stronger edges for synchronous collaboration). (Color figure online)

chronous communication with a maximum of 121 codes per window, compared to 261 windows for asynchronous communication with a maximum of 20 codes per window. The largest difference in edge weights was observed for the *code2–code2* self-connection (0.28) and *code2–code3* (0.11), which were stronger in synchronous interactions, followed by *code5–code2* (0.1) stronger in asynchronous interaction (see Fig. 6e). Self-connections were generally stronger in the synchronous network (4 out of 5). The cross-code connections were more evenly distributed (5 out of 9 stronger in asynchronous collaboration, 4 out of 9 stronger in synchronous collaboration).

3.5 Comparison of Window Implementations

Conceptually, different temporal windows reflect variations in granularity, temporal sensitivity (for example, the ability to adapt to different collaboration settings), and collaboration dynamics (see Table 2). Using the *single-message window*, networks captured highly granular interactions, but temporality, periods of inactivity, and cross-student connections were ignored. The *multi-message window* revealed links between concepts over multiple messages; however, temporal gaps were not considered, so some connections spanned periods of inactivity. The *time-fixed window* produced networks that were sensitive to both temporality and cross-student connections. Finally, the *duration-gap window* defined sessions based on actual activity gaps rather than fixed intervals. Compared to the *time-fixed window*, the *duration-gap window* highlighted temporal patterns more clearly, although collaboration was primarily represented as individual activity accumulation rather than direct cross-student connections.

Table 2. Comparison of window implementations for co-occurrence modeling

	single-message	multi-message	fixed-duration	duration-gap
Connections in a single message	✓			
Connections across messages		✓	✓	✓
Cross-actor connections		✓	✓	
Code self-connections		✓	✓	✓
Temporal sensitivity			✓	✓

Although the conceptual differences between windowing approaches are substantial, models using different window-modeling strategies produced relatively similar results in both synchronous and asynchronous collaboration settings. A comparison of centralities across all models showed that while the overall patterns remain consistent, the magnitudes of the differences vary depending on the window modeling approaches, with largest discrepancies in diffusion centrality (see Appendix A.2 for a full comparison of the networks generated using the four windowing approaches across both collaboration settings).

The comparison of weight density across different window approaches within synchronous and asynchronous networks shows which models are most similar to each other (see Fig. 8). Within asynchronous networks, the most similar are the *multi-message window* vs. the *fixed-duration window (syn.)*, with a Pearson correlation of $r = 0.997$, followed by the *multi-message window* vs the *duration-gap window (asyn.)* at $r = 0.986$, and the *fixed-duration window (asyn.)* vs the *duration-gap window (asyn.)* at $r = 0.982$. The least similar are the *single-message window* vs the *fixed-duration window (syn.)* ($r = .946$), the *single-message window* vs the *multi-message window* ($r = 0.957$), and the *single-message window* vs the *duration-gap window (asyn.)* ($r = 0.963$).

Within synchronous networks, larger differences are observed across window implementations. The highest similarities occur between the *fixed-duration window (syn.)* and the *duration-gap window (syn.)* ($r = 0.993$), and between the *multi-message window* and the *fixed-duration window (syn.)* ($r = 0.984$). Conversely, the greatest dissimilarities are seen for the *single-message window* compared to the *duration-gap window (syn.)* ($r = 0.887$), the *single-message window* compared to the *fixed-duration window (syn.)* ($r = 0.904$), and the *multi-message window* compared to the *duration-gap window (syn.)* ($r = 0.977$).

Overall, while all window approaches capture general trends in centrality and weight density, the magnitude of differences depends strongly on the specific window modeling method. Asynchronous networks tend to be more similar across different window definitions, whereas synchronous networks show larger variability, particularly for extreme comparisons involving the *single-message window* versus longer or gap-based windows. This indicates that the choice of window can meaningfully impact network measures, especially in synchronous settings (Fig. 7).

4 Lessons Learned

The four window implementations collectively highlight the need to reflect more broadly on how window definitions influence what CNA captures and how collaboration is ultimately interpreted. We synthesise insights from our exploratory methodology into some broader lessons:

1. **On granularity:** As shown in the results, fine-grained windows such as single-message or short multi-message spans capture only the concepts that appear together within very small units of activity. This logic extends to implementations with very short fixed-duration windows: such granular windows are effective for analyzing conceptual co-expression, for example identifying which cognitive or collaborative codes tend to co-occur within a single contribution. However, they overlook how interaction unfolds across messages or over time, making them unsuitable for studying turn taking, responsiveness, or cross-actor coordination. In practice, researchers should use granular windows when the focus is on within-message structure, and adopt less granular windows when the emphasis is on uncovering macro-level patterns of interaction. In other words, if the emphasis is on the structure of connections in individual messages, then a single-message window may be the most

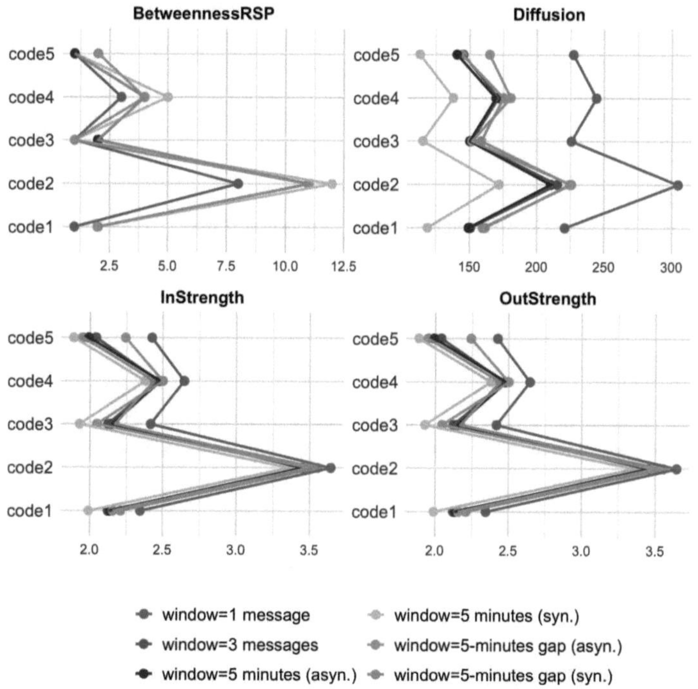

Fig. 7. Centralities of codes by window implementations.

appropriate. However, if the emphasis is on the structure and relationships in the conversation, larger windows that combine multiple messages may be the optimal choice.

2. **On window definition:** We presented two types of window definitions: windows can be based on messages (e.g., multi-message implementation) or on duration (e.g., fixed-duration implementation), and they can be continuous (e.g., fixed-duration implementation) or actor-specific (e.g., duration-gap implementation). Different window definitions implicitly determine how co-occurrences are interpreted. The choice between message-based and duration-based windows is governed by researchers' understanding of collaboration: can it be segmented by exchanges of certain number of messages, or by the temporal span of these interactions? Similar logic applies to the choice between continuous windows and actor-specific windows - whether collaboration should be studied across participants or only within each individual's activity stream. The former treats collaboration as shared participation within a local episode, whereas the latter shifts the analysis toward individual behavioral sequences rather than collective interaction. This means that window choice encodes an assumption about how collaboration is characterized, and researchers should ensure that their window definition aligns with how they conceptualize collaboration in their study.

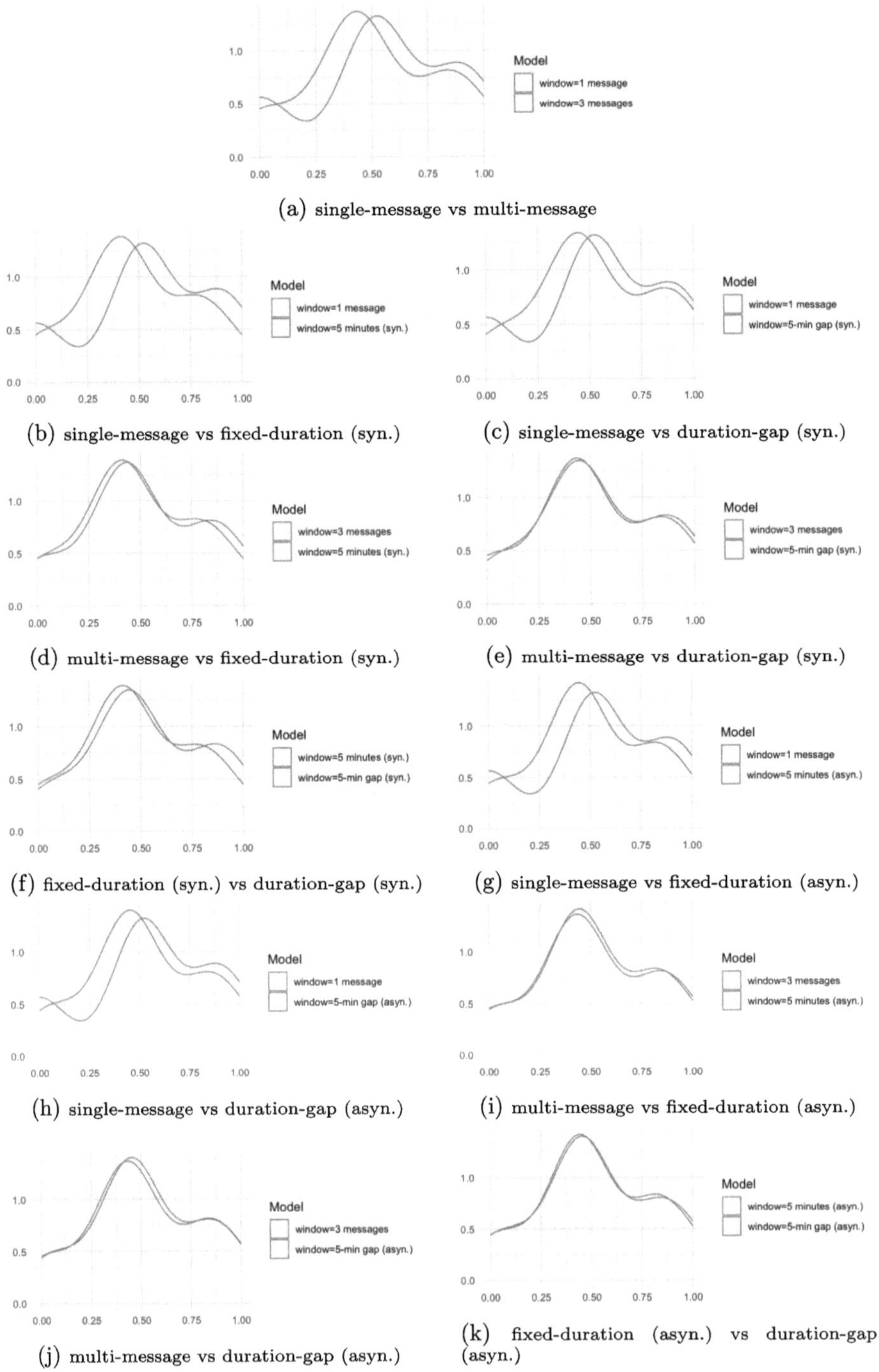

(a) single-message vs multi-message

(b) single-message vs fixed-duration (syn.)

(c) single-message vs duration-gap (syn.)

(d) multi-message vs fixed-duration (syn.)

(e) multi-message vs duration-gap (syn.)

(f) fixed-duration (syn.) vs duration-gap (syn.)

(g) single-message vs fixed-duration (asyn.)

(h) single-message vs duration-gap (asyn.)

(i) multi-message vs fixed-duration (asyn.)

(j) multi-message vs duration-gap (asyn.)

(k) fixed-duration (asyn.) vs duration-gap (asyn.)

Fig. 8. Weight density comparisons using different window approaches for synchronous and asynchronous CNA networks. Each panel compares the weight density distributions of two window models represented by a red line and a green line. Higher overlap between the two lines indicates greater similarity between the models. (Color figure online)

3. **On different dynamics across synchronous and asynchronous contexts:** Self-connections highlight how often the same code recurs within a window, and these patterns differ markedly between synchronous and asynchronous interactions. In fast, synchronous exchanges, rapid back-to-back contributions produce stronger self loops, reflecting concentrated bursts of repeated behaviors. In asynchronous settings, longer pauses and more varied contributions dilute these repetitions, leading to more distributed cross code links instead. These contrasts show that self-connections are not merely technical artifacts but indicators of underlying interaction rhythm. Researchers should interpret self loops as evidence of behavioral pacing rather than treating them as noise.
4. **Window selection must be driven by purpose, not convenience:** There is no single window that performs well across all learning contexts or research aims. Each definition foregrounds some aspects of interaction while obscuring others, which means researchers must first identify whether they aim to capture rapid turn taking, episode level coordination, individual behavior sequences or temporal irregularities. The window should then be chosen to align with that analytic goal, rather than defaulting to common practices such as fixed message counts or standard time intervals [6]. Purpose driven selection helps avoid misleading interpretations and ensures that network structures reflect the phenomena of interest. Clear justification of window choice therefore strengthens both methodological transparency and the validity of resulting claims.

Together, these lessons highlight that co-occurrence windows are not merely technical parameters but active modeling decisions. Careful reflection on interaction patterns, temporal structure and analytic goals is necessary when applying CNA to collaborative learning data.

5 Conclusions

This study was set out to demonstrate and compare different window choices that ranged from limited breadth (a single message), to several message (three) or a group of messages within a temporal window (five minutes) and finally an adaptive window separated by periods of inactivity which capture bouts of conversation of different length.

While the window definitions varied, the difference in networks tended to be small but with some exceptions where some notable differences are visible. These findings partially contrast with prior work, which employed different methods and window choices. In ENA, [14] found that moving windows capture both activity-level connections and individual contributions, whereas whole-conversation windows primarily reveal team-level patterns. [19] showed that moving, infinite-stanza, and whole-conversation windows impose different assumptions about how connections are formed, producing distinct ENA networks. In Socio-semantic Network Analysis, [7] demonstrated that timestamp-based moving windows reveal temporal fluctuations that are not visible when utterances are treated as evenly spaced. In contrast, our models were largely similar across window definitions, suggesting that the specific window conceptualizations tested in CNA may be relatively insensitive to window choice in certain contexts. However, the similarity of the resulting CNA networks may reflect the controlled nature of the simulated datasets. Further research with authentic datasets is needed to determine whether these patterns generalize, as factors such as message density, temporal distribution, and coding schemes could amplify differences between window definitions.

This brings the central question: does window definition matter? Whereas the differences in weights were mostly small, it is important to emphasize that different window definitions reflect different operationalizations and should not be considered interchangeable. A network of individual messages shows the structure of how the concepts co-occur within these message while a network of several messages reflects the broader co-occurrence patterns and the underlying structure of conversations. The choice of the window definition should be driven by the specific research questions being addressed [1,6]. For example, when modeling interactions in instant messaging conversations, where messages are typically exchanged in rapid succession, shorter windows (such brief time intervals) may be more appropriate for capturing the dynamics of immediate interaction in which older messages have no influence. If the researcher goal is to capture bouts of conversations, then a gap window is the most appropriate to capture the full conversation episode.

To summarize, a window reflects the modeled conversation segment and shapes both the resulting network and the insights that can be drawn from it. Therefore, selecting an appropriate window should be directly tied to the research questions, the phenomena the analysis aims to capture and the insights the researchers aim to understand.

Declaration on Generative AI. During the preparation of this work, the authors used ChatGPT to improve on the readability and check language mistakes. After using this tool, the authors reviewed and edited the content as needed and took full responsibility for the content of the publication.

Acknowledgments. K.M. was partially funded by the *Development of the Ecosystem for Novel Learning Resources and Network Data Techniques* project (Postdoktorandinnenförderung: Eigenes Sachkostenbudget funding, FernUniversität in Hagen) and conducted this research in cooperation with the LEAD:FUH project funded by the Stiftung Innovation in der Hochschullehre (1001-3223).

References

1. Hmelo-Silver, C.E., Jeong, H.: An overview of CSCL methods. In: Cress, U., Rosé, C., Wise, A.F., Oshima, J. (eds.) International Handbook of Computer-Supported Collaborative Learning. CCLS, vol. 19, pp. 65–83. Springer, Cham (2021). https://doi.org/10.1007/978-3-030-65291-3_4
2. Knight, S., Wise, A.F., Chen, B.: Time for change: why learning analytics needs temporal analysis. J. Learn. Anal. **4**(3), 7–17 (2017). https://doi.org/10.18608/jla.2017.43.2
3. Lee, S.B., Espino, D.P., Hamilton, E.: Ordered network analysis of prompted student discourse in a collaborative learning context. In: Advances in Quantitative Ethnography, ICQE 2024. CCIS, vol. 2279, pp. 95–103. Springer (2024). https://doi.org/10.1007/978-3-031-76332-8_8
4. López-Pernas, S., Misiejuk, K., Oliveira, E., Saqr, M.: The dynamics of the self-regulation process in student-AI interactions: the case of problem-solving in programming education. In: Proceedings of the 25th Koli Calling International Conference on Computing Education Research, pp. 1–12 (2025). https://doi.org/10.1145/3769994.3770043
5. Mercer, N.: The seeds of time: why classroom dialogue needs a temporal analysis. J. Learn. Sci. **17**(1), 33–59 (2008). https://doi.org/10.1080/10508400701793182
6. Molenaar, I., Wise, A.F.: Temporal aspects of learning analytics-grounding analyses in concepts of time. In: The Handbook of Learning Analytics, pp. 66–76. SoLAR (2022). https://doi.org/10.18608/hla22.007
7. Ohsaki, A., Oshima, J.: Socio-semantic network analysis of knowledge-creation discourse on a real-time scale. In: Ruis, A.R., Lee, S.B. (eds.) ICQE 2021. CCIS, vol. 1312, pp. 170–184. Springer, Cham (2021). https://doi.org/10.1007/978-3-030-67788-6_12
8. Reimann, P.: Time is precious: variable-and event-centred approaches to process analysis in CSCL research. Int. J. Comput.-Support. Collab. Learn. **4**(3), 239–257 (2009). https://doi.org/10.1007/s11412-009-9070-z
9. Saqr, M., López-Pernas, S., Törmänen, T., Kaliisa, R., Misiejuk, K., Tikka, S.: Transition network analysis: a novel framework for modeling, visualizing, and identifying the temporal patterns of learners and learning processes. In: Proceedings of the 15th International Learning Analytics and Knowledge Conference, pp. 351–361 (2025). https://doi.org/10.1145/3706468.3706513
10. Saqr, M., Misiejuk, K., Törmänen, T., Kaliisa, R., Tikka, S., López-Pernas, S.: Frequency transition network analysis (FTNA). In: Computer-Supported Collaborative Learning (2025). https://doi.org/10.22318/cscl2025.901997
11. Saqr, M., Nouri, J.: High resolution temporal network analysis to understand and improve collaborative learning. In: Proceedings of the 10th International Conference on Learning Analytics & Knowledge, pp. 314–319 (2020). https://doi.org/10.1145/3706468.3706513
12. Saqr, M., Peeters, W., Viberg, O.: The relational, co-temporal, contemporaneous, and longitudinal dynamics of self-regulation for academic writing. Res. Pract. Technol. Enhanc. Learn. **16**(1), 1–22 (2021). https://doi.org/10.1186/s41039-021-00175-7
13. Saqr, M., Poquet, O., López-Pernas, S.: Networks in education: a travelogue through five decades. IEEE Access **10**, 32361–32380 (2022). https://doi.org/10.1109/ACCESS.2022.3159674

14. Siebert-Evenstone, A.L., Irgens, G.A., Collier, W., Swiecki, Z., Ruis, A.R., Shaffer, D.W.: In search of conversational grain size: Modeling semantic structure using moving stanza windows. J. Learn. Anal. **4**(3), 123–139 (2017). https://doi.org/10.18608/jla.2017.43.7
15. Song, Y., Oliveira, E., Kirley, M., Thompson, P.: A case study on university student online learning patterns across multidisciplinary subjects. In: Proceedings of the 14th Learning Analytics and Knowledge Conference, pp. 936–942 (2024). https://doi.org/10.1145/3636555.3636939
16. Tikka, S., López-Pernas, S., Saqr, M.: TNA: An r package for transition network analysis. Appl. Psychol. Meas. (2025)
17. Yang, S., Du, X., Tang, H., Hung, J.L., Tang, Y.: Temporal group interaction density in collaborative problem solving: exploring group interactions with different time granularities. Educ. Inf. Technol. **29**(11), 13271–13298 (2024). https://doi.org/10.1007/s10639-023-12373-5
18. Zhang, S., et al.: Understanding student teachers collaborative problem solving: insights from an epistemic network analysis (ENA). Comput. Educ. **183**, 104485 (2022). https://doi.org/10.1016/j.compedu.2022.104485
19. Zörgő, S.: Segmentation and code co-occurrence accumulation: operationalizing relational context with stanza windows. In: Advances in Quantitative Ethnography. ICQE 2022. CCIS, vol. 1785, pp. 146–162. Springer, Cham (2022). https://doi.org/10.1007/978-3-031-31726-2_11

Modeling Stability and Change from a Complex Systems Perspective

Mohammed Saqr[1(✉)], Sonsoles López-Pernas[1], and Santtu Tikka[2]

[1] University of Eastern Finland, Joensuu, Finland
mohammed.saqr@uef.fi
[2] University of Jyväskylä, Jyväskylä, Finland

Abstract. Transition Network Analysis (TNA) provides a solid framework for studying the learning process and the dynamic changes across time in learning systems. TNA maps interactions among system states—including their occurrence or absence, sequential ordering, and the trajectories that unfold over time. Most importantly, TNA incorporates statistical significance testing for transitions and metrics. This study demonstrates how TNA can be used to study stability from a complex systems perspective. We demonstrate how stability can be studied via transition patterns (or the lack thereof), rates of transitions, durations, recurrence, and through state sequences (ordered transitions) via metrics such as entropy, complexity, and feedback loops. These capabilities are demonstrated via a case study where the stability of the engagement states of students across 15 sequential courses is studied.

Keywords: Transition Network Analysis · Complex Systems · Stability · Learning analytics · Engagement

1 Introduction

Transition Network Analysis (TNA) is a novel method that models how states change over time, capturing the changes, as well as the relations between them. In doing so, TNA maps the relational dynamics of change, a unique perspective that is not offered by other methods [8]. What sets TNA apart is the capability to offer detailed analysis coupled with rigor. The rigor of TNA is also evident in its reliance on graph theory and advanced statistical methods, which help ensure that the observed transitions are not merely coincidental, which means that researchers using TNA can confidently claim that the patterns identified in the network represent genuine relationships in the data, and are not artifacts of sampling error or noise [7]. Despite being introduced recently, TNA has been widely adopted across various domains, such as modeling students' interactions with learning environments and understanding how students regulate their interactions in project-based learning.

Nevertheless, most of the existing literature has used TNA to understand changes and dynamics and how they occur over time. Still, the question of stability—or the lack thereof—has not been as widely explored with TNA, although TNA has a rich repertoire

M. Saqr et al. (Eds.): TNA 2026, CCIS 3079, pp. 51–61, 2026.
https://doi.org/10.1007/978-3-032-34157-0_4

of tools and features that can tackle such an important topic. This paper aims to fill this gap and study the stability and resilience from a complex systems' perspective by exploring the options and potentials of TNA that are at the disposal of researchers.

1.1 Stability from a Complex Dynamic Systems' Perspective

A complex dynamic system (CDS) is a network of interacting elements whose collective behavior evolves over time and cannot be fully understood by analyzing the individual parts in isolation [10]. CDS are characterized by feedback loops, emergence, and sensitivity to initial conditions [9, 10]. A CDS has universal characteristics that are prevalent across systems regardless of their nature. In other words, they share certain behaviors that consistently manifest across the systems.

According to CDS theory, a system starting in a certain condition is expected to behave and continue to evolve influenced by this initial condition [4]. For instance, a student who starts the program as disengaged may continue to suffer the influence of this start. Also, the disengaged state may continue to play a role in the trajectory of the student through what is known as an *attractor* state. Attractor states are stable patterns of behavior or experience that the system tends to return to over time [3, 10]. Attractor states act like behavioral "magnets," making certain patterns such as engagement or disengagement self-reinforcing and persistent over time. Because attractors arise from feedback loops within the system, they create stability that is resistant to change, meaning the system tends to return to these patterns unless a strong or sustained intervention shifts it toward a different, more adaptive attractor [2, 3].

Stability can be understood as a dynamic resilience against perturbations. In CDS theory, the stability of a specific state is reflected by the topology of its "basin of attraction": the depth and width of this basin is a reflection of how resilient the current state is; a deep basin implies that the system is highly stable and will absorb external shocks—such as a temporary increase in study load or a single failed exam—without shifting its state. For instance, an engaged student will not succumb to a single failed exam and fall into a consistent disengagement state but will recover quickly and resume being engaged. However, for a student in a maladaptive attractor (disengagement), stability becomes a problem, causing the student to return back to the original disengaged state even after support interventions are applied [2, 10].

As such, stability in CDS may take different, distinct forms: e.g., resilience and rigidity. Resilient stability reflects the system's ability to absorb stressors while maintaining its overall functioning. An example could be an engaged student sustaining a setback and continuing to perform without collapsing into disengagement. In contrast, rigid stability reflects an attractor that is stable but inflexible [10]. From a CDS perspective, effective interventions should therefore aim to guide students toward more adaptive attractor states to build resilient stability [1, 4, 9].

Although initial conditions and attractor states exert considerable influence, systems can shift when exposed to sufficient perturbations—such as intense interventions. These interventions can create opportunities for the system to reorganize around a new, more adaptive attractor state [1, 9]. A disengaged student may shift to a new engaged state when appropriate intervention is provided and become a high achiever. As the student proceeds, achievement would increase the student's motivation, reinforcing motivation and therefore, the stability of the new engaged state.

TNA provides a comprehensive framework that captures the complex system's dynamics with the mechanisms underlying its stability, feedback loops, and emerging behavior, and, more importantly, the relational interactions within the system. We will discuss these potentials in the next section.

1.2 Transitions or Lack Thereof —Stability— from the Perspective of TNA

In transition networks, a stable state is a state that does not tend to transition to other states, and if it ever does, it quickly returns to its original state. In TNA terms, this stability shows up as a self-loop (a node transitioning to itself), which reflects the probability of remaining in the same state at the next step. A high weight of self-loop means the state is very likely to stay (or linger in). In other words, that state is "sticky". A stable state has a high in-strength centrality (incoming transitions). Together, both metrics indicate that the state is an attractor (a basin of attraction). Moving the system out of such stable attractor states may not be easy, given its tendency to resist changes and reluctance to transition, or what is known as inertia.

The sequence of states, represented by the chains that define the order of events, offers a complementary lens for studying system stability. We can examine patterns of change, the frequency and rate of transitions, the duration of staying in a certain state, and the recurrence of these patterns to quantify how persistent or volatile the system is over time. Several metrics can help quantify this stability. Entropy, for instance, measures the uncertainty associated with a state's transitions. Low entropy indicates that the system tends to move in highly predictable ways, often following the same transition, which signals a stable or constrained pattern of behavior. In contrast, high entropy reflects a more uncertain, exploratory, or unstable dynamic in which multiple transitions are possible and the system transitions unpredictably.

Recurrence rate provides a complementary view by capturing how often the system returns to states it has previously occupied. A high recurrence rate suggests that the system repeatedly gravitates back to familiar configurations, revealing inertia, self-reinforcing cycles, or attractor-like structures that anchor the dynamics. When recurrence is low, the system instead tends to move outward into new territory, showing signs of drift, directional change, or instability. Additional insights come from examining how long the system persists in specific states—its dwell time. States in which the system remains for extended periods typically represent stable equilibria or strong attractors, whereas brief visits signal fragility or susceptibility to perturbation. Similarly, the rate or frequency of transitions highlights how quickly the system evolves: rapid, frequent shifts are often symptomatic of volatility, while slow, infrequent transitions indicate stability and resistance to change. Finally, considering the structural role of states within the broader transition network—such as their centrality or attractor strength—helps identify which states exert a stabilizing influence by drawing in transitions from many others (Fig. 1).

This image presents two views of a CDS. The qualitative "attractor landscape" on the right visualizes the system's stability by depicting three "valleys" or basins. The depth of each valley represents how stable a state is, with a deeper basin indicating a more stable

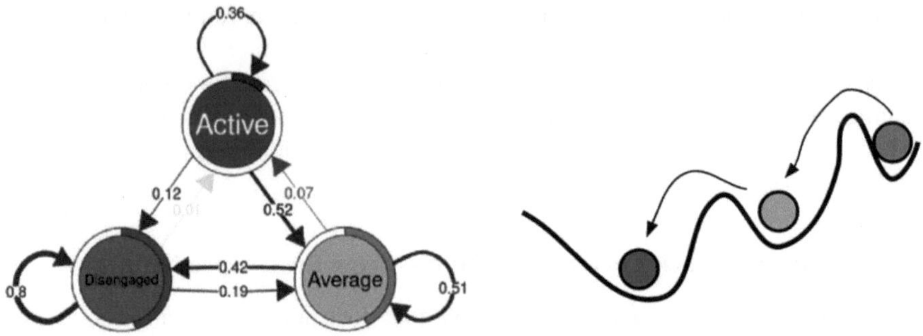

Fig. 1. *Disengaged* acts as an attractor state in a CDS

"attractor state" that is difficult to leave. The deepest red basin signifies a highly stable state, while the blue and green valleys are progressively shallower, representing less stable states. This visual metaphor is a direct translation of the quantitative data shown in the transition network on the left. This network models the system using three states (Disengaged, Average, Active) and arrows that represent the probabilistic flow between them. The "Disengaged" state corresponds to the deepest basin, which is confirmed by its very thick self-looping arrow indicating a high probability of persistence. Conversely, the "Average" and "Active" states, corresponding to the shallower valleys, have weaker self-loops and stronger probabilities of transitioning to other states, reflecting their lower stability.

2 A Case Study

2.1 Context and Data Collection

The data from our study was extracted from a previous study [5]. The context of the study is a medical education program at Qassim University. In this program, the majority of courses follow a blended implementation of Problem-Based Learning (PBL). Each course covers a different topic (e.g., head and neck) where each week students are presented with an ill-defined problem in the face-to-face lecture, related to the lecture's content. Throughout the week, students collaborate in the Learning Management System (LMS) forum, where they share resources, discuss, and argue to solve the weekly problem. This was a mandatory requirement of the courses. Each year, there were approximately four PBL courses, with an average duration of six weeks. These courses were organized sequentially, and students had to complete them in order. There were other courses that had a duration of a full year, taught in parallel to the different PBL courses. However, those courses were not part of the study since they did not follow the same pedagogy. The work by Saqr and López-Pernas [5] extracted the LMS log data and derived engagement indicators based on the metrics for each student and course. Subsequently, these were clustered into three engagement states (***Active***, ***Average***, ***Disengaged***) and each student was assigned one engagement state per course. The ***Active*** state reflected students whose indicators were generally around the 6th–seventh deciles, with frequent access to materials, continuous participation in forum discussions, and regular online presence. The ***Average*** state represented students whose indicators were mostly near the fifth decile, and thus had a moderate level of engagement with reading, contributing, and viewing course resources. The ***Disengaged*** state captured students whose indicators fell between the third and fourth deciles, and therefore had low activity across the board and particularly limited involvement in the collaborative elements of the course. The sequences of students' engagement states were then clustered into engagement trajectories based on the evolution of students' engagement states throughout 15 courses in the program. In the present study, we made use of the data from the **mostly engaged trajectory**, which contained students who maintained an ***Active*** state throughout most of the courses in the program. Specifically, we zoom in on 16 students in this trajectory whose stability we analyze. We extracted the sequence of their engagement states during the 15 sequential PBL courses.

2.2 Analysis

Transition Network Analysis. Using the sequence of engagement states of the 16 students in our study, we estimated a TNA model to capture how engagement shifted from one course to the next. We used the ***Nestimate*** R package [6]. In the model, transition probabilities describe how likely students are to remain in the same state or to move to a different one between courses, and therefore how stable they were within their course trajectory.

The initial distribution indicates that 75% of students begin in the *Active* state, 25% begin in the *Average* state, and none begin *Disengaged*. The transition probabilities indicated that *Active* was the system's dominant attractor, reflecting a highly stable trajectory with minimal susceptibility to decline. Students in *Active* show an 85.2% probability of remaining active, with 14.2% shifting to *Average* and only 0.5% moving to *Disengaged*. The *Average* state shows pronounced upward movement, with 64.1% transitioning to *Active*, 33.3% persisting in *Average*, and 2.6% moving to *Disengaged*, indicating that it operates as a transitional but moderately stable state with clear momentum toward higher engagement. The *Disengaged* state exhibits complete recovery, with 100% of students moving directly to *Active* and no persistence or redirection to *Average*. This pattern suggests that disengagement is brief and quickly resolved, pointing to a system that effectively absorbs and corrects lapses in engagement.

Stability Metrics. Based on the sequences of engagement states and the TNA model transition probability matrix, we computed several stability metrics related to the diversity of states, the resistance to change, and other structural dynamics. All the sequence metrics were computed with the function *sequence_indices* from the ***codyna*** R package [11]. The metrics can be classified as follows:

Diversity of states**:** *The number of unique states* reflects the variety of distinct states observed in a sequence. This value offers a preliminary indication of diversity. A larger number of unique states can suggest a wide exploration of the state space, whereas a smaller number indicates a more constrained or stable pattern.

Longitudinal entropy quantifies the unpredictability or dispersion of states over time. Higher entropy corresponds to a less predictable sequence in which states occur with greater balance. From a CDS perspective, elevated entropy may indicate weaker attractor structures and more fluctuation across the state spectrum.

Let p_s denote the empirical probability of observing state s. The Shannon entropy can be defined as:

$$-\sum_{s=1}^{S} p_s \log(p_s)$$

where S is the total number of states. We further normalize the entropy by scaling it with the logarithm of the total number of states S so that the maximum value is 1.

Simpson diversity is another measure of diversity, also known as the Gini-Simpson Index. It represents the probability that two states randomly selected from the sequence will be different. Values closer to one reflect a more even spread of states, whereas values near zero reveal strong concentration around a few states. Simpson diversity relates to stability because uneven distributions often reflect the presence of strong attractors that constrain system behaviour.

The value of the index can be computed as

$$1 - \sum_{s=1}^{S} p_s^2.$$

Resistance to change**:** A second group of measures addresses how the system resists or enacts change over time. *Self*-loop *tendency* captures the proportion of transitions in which the state remains unchanged. A high self-loop tendency indicates inertia or local stability, revealing how strongly the system resists change once a state is entered. *The transition rate* reflects the frequency with which the system changes states across time. This variable assesses the extent to which the system remains in its initial state. *Initial state influence decay* characterises how quickly the influence of the initial state diminishes as the system progresses.

Structural dynamics: Finally, deeper structural dynamics emerge through *cyclic feedback strength, dominant* state, and *dominant proportion. Cyclic feedback strength* identifies the extent to which the system revisits particular configurations in recurrent patterns, revealing the presence of closed-loop dynamics. The *dominant state* represents the most frequently occurring state in the sequence and functions as the system's primary attractor, often corresponding to a low-energy or highly stable configuration. The *dominant proportion*, reflecting the amount of time spent in this state, indicates how strongly the system gravitates toward that attractor and how consolidated or flexible its dynamical landscape may be. Higher values of the dominant proportion indicate that the system exhibits substantial temporal stability by residing predominantly in one state, suggesting a strong attractor pull and relatively stable or stationary behaviour.

2.3 Results

The sequence index plot and the transition network together show a system structured around a clear attractor state i.e., Active state. Across time, most students remain in the *Active* state, with only brief transitions into *Average* and very limited occurrences of *Disengaged*. The transition probabilities show *Active* retains 85% of students from one time step to the next. This asymmetric pattern establishes *Active* as the system's dominant basin of attraction. Transitions away from it are possible but short-lived, as indicated by the comparatively small transition from *Active* to *Average* (14%) and the negligible transition to *Disengaged* (1%). The reverse transitions are far stronger, with both *Average* and *Disengaged* transitioning back quickly into the *Active* state. Figure 2-left shows the sequence index plot in which we map the trajectory of the engagement states of the 16 students throughout the whole program. Figure 2-right shows the transition plot representing the transitions between engagement states.

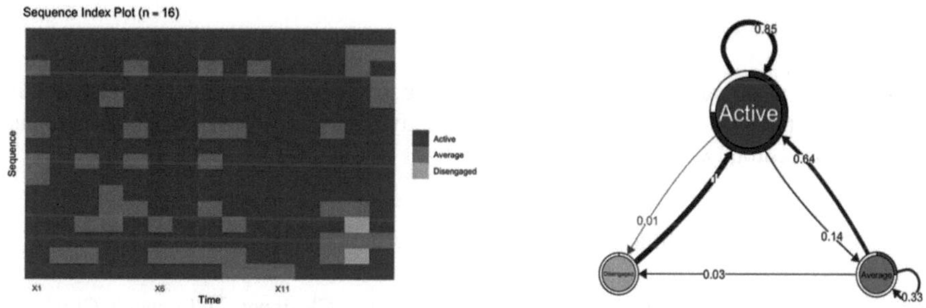

Fig. 2. **Left**: Sequence index plot in which each horizontal line represents one student's trajectory over time, where the colored blocks represent students' engagement states. **Right**: Transition plot showing the estimated transition probabilities between states. Each node represents an engagement state, and each edge represents the transition probability between states. The donut plot around each node represents the initial probability of starting the program in that state. The node size is proportional to the incoming transitions.

Bootstrap stability analysis of the TNA revealed that only the transition from *Active* to *Active* was statistically significant (Fig 3-Left). This transition showed a strong and stable weight (0.85) with a p-value of 0.00, and its confidence range was consistently positive across both the conventional and bootstrap intervals (CR: 0.64–1.07; CI: 0.77–0.92), indicating a reliably recurrent self-transition. All other transitions failed to reach statistical significance. Overall, the bootstrap results suggest that the system's dominant stable dynamic is the persistence of the *Active* state, while all other transitions appear statistically indistinguishable from chance (Table 1).

Markov First Passage Time (MPT). Markov passage time measures how long it takes a system to move from one state to another, allowing the dynamics to be described in actual time rather than in probabilities. In estimating the expected time needed to reach a given state, MPT shows which transitions are fast, which are slow, and how these timings shape the system's overall behavior in terms of speed, inertia, or delay inherent in different pathways. Within the framework of CDS, passage times show how strongly the system gravitates toward its dominant attractors, how it responds to perturbations, and how quickly it recovers from less desirable states. Because CDS emphasizes feedback, interdependence, and sensitivity to initial conditions, mean passage times serve as an important temporal counterpart to transition probabilities: they reveal how long the system takes to move across its state space and how duration itself structures system behavior. Short passage times toward stable states indicate strong corrective forces and efficient recovery mechanisms, whereas long passage times toward undesirable states

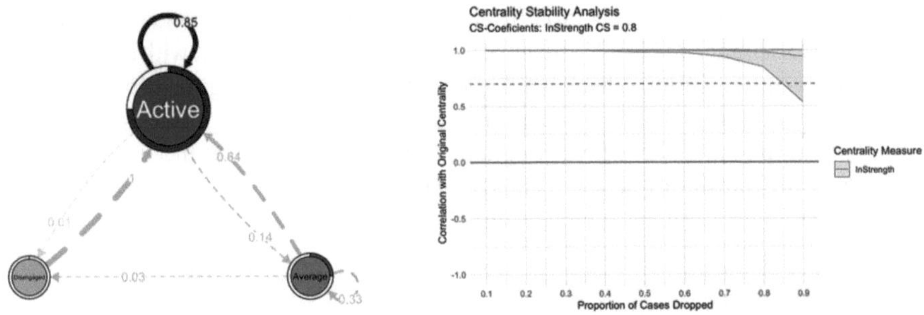

Fig. 3. **Left:** Bootstrapped transition network showing that there is only one statistically significant transition (the self-loop of *Active*). **Right:** Centrality stability analysis through case dropping for In-strength centrality.

Table 1. Statistically significant transitions

from	to	weight	p-value	CR lower	CR upper	CI lower	CI upper
Active	**Active**	**0.85**	**0.00***	**0.64**	**1.07**	**0.77**	**0.92**
Average	Active	0.64	0.14	0.48	0.80	0.43	0.84
Disengaged	Active	1.00	0.13	0.75	1.25	0.00	1.00
Active	Average	0.14	0.33	0.11	0.18	0.08	0.22
Average	Average	0.33	0.38	0.25	0.42	0.16	0.52
Active	Disengaged	0.01	0.61	0.00	0.01	0.00	0.02
Average	Disengaged	0.03	0.71	0.02	0.03	0.00	0.07

reflect resistance, inertia, or the presence of stabilizing constraints built into the system's structure. In this sense, passage times map the temporal timeline of stability, volatility, and resilience, offering a window into how the system evolves through time and how its internal dynamics shape the likelihood and speed of future trajectories.

As the matrix of MPT shows (Fig. 4), students in the Disengaged state return to Active remarkably quickly, with an average passage time of 1 period, compared to 1.54 periods for transitions from Average to Active. This indicates that disengagement represents a brief, acute state, rapidly corrected either through systemic support mechanisms or inherent resilience, consistent with the non-linear, self-stabilizing properties of complex dynamic systems. In contrast, transitions away from Active are comparatively slow, with passage times of 7.08 periods to Average and 111.00 periods to Disengaged, highlighting the system's strong attractor dynamics around Active. The asymmetry between rapid recovery and slow decline underscores the network's upward pull toward engagement and illustrates how feedback loops, stability, and path-dependent trajectories interact to maintain the system's overall robustness and adaptive behavior.

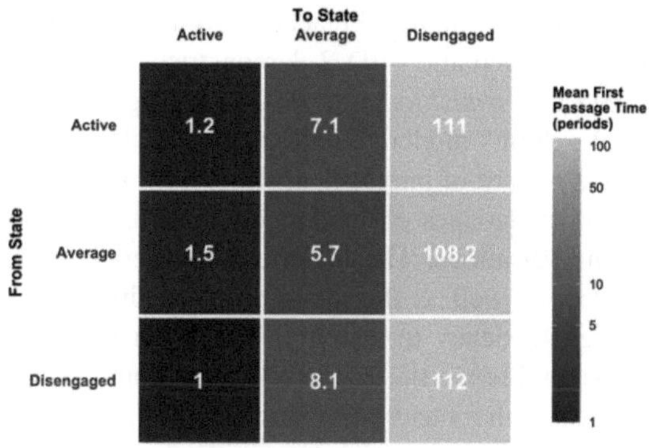

Fig. 4. Mean First Passage Time between each pair of states

2.3.1 Sequence Complexity Indices

Table 2. Summary of stability metrics for each of the 16 students, including diversity measures, resistance-to-change metrics, and structural dynamics. Overall mean (M), standard deviation (SD), and median (Med) are also presented

	Diversity			Resistance to change				Structural dynamics	
ID	Unique states	Longitudinal entropy	Simpson diversity	Self-loop tendency	Transition rate	Initial state persistence	Initial state influence decay	Cyclic feedback strength	Dominant prop
1	1	0.00	0.00	1.00	0.00	1.00	0.00	1.00	1.00
2	2	0.36	0.23	0.93	0.07	0.87	0.33	0.85	0.87
3	2	0.58	0.44	0.36	0.64	0.07	0.07	1.00	0.67
4	2	0.22	0.12	0.93	0.07	0.93	0.17	0.92	0.93
5	2	0.36	0.23	0.79	0.21	0.20	-0.03	1.00	0.87
6	1	0.00	0.00	1.00	0.00	1.00	0.00	1.00	1.00
7	2	0.58	0.44	0.50	0.50	0.07	0.23	1.00	0.67
8	1	0.00	0.00	1.00	0.00	1.00	0.00	1.00	1.00
9	2	0.53	0.39	0.50	0.50	0.07	0.60	0.77	0.73
10	2	0.22	0.12	0.93	0.07	0.07	0.20	0.92	0.93
11	2	0.22	0.12	0.86	0.14	0.20	-0.20	1.00	0.93
12	2	0.58	0.44	0.57	0.43	0.20	-0.07	1.00	0.67
13	3	0.73	0.48	0.43	0.57	0.13	-0.23	1.00	0.67
14	2	0.46	0.32	0.93	0.07	0.80	0.50	0.85	0.80
15	3	0.81	0.56	0.50	0.50	0.07	-0.07	1.00	0.47
16	2	0.46	0.32	0.86	0.14	0.53	0.33	1.00	0.80
M	**1.94**	**0.38**	**0.27**	**0.75**	**0.25**	**0.45**	**0.11**	**0.96**	**0.81**
SD	**0.57**	**0.25**	**0.19**	**0.23**	**0.23**	**0.41**	**0.24**	**0.07**	**0.16**
Med	**2.00**	**0.42**	**0.29**	**0.77**	**0.22**	**0.20**	**0.09**	**1.00**	**0.80**

Table 2 summarises sixteen individual temporal profiles using the previously defined variables, with both mean and standard deviation provided for reference. Three students had one *unique state* (IDs 1, 6, 8) show complete stability, with *longitudinal entropy* and *Simpson diversity* equal to 0, and both *self-loop tendency* and *dominant proportion* at 1.00. These profiles represent the most stable systems with a single, absorbing attractor state and no changes. For students with two or three *unique states*, stability is lower. For example, ID 3 shows *longitudinal entropy* of 0.58 and Simpson diversity of 0.44, indicating moderate stability, while ID 15 reaches 0.81 and 0.56, respectively, reflecting substantial instability and fluctuation. ID 2 demonstrates a remarkable stability with *self-loop tendency* 0.93 and *transition rate* 0.07, showing strong persistence despite some movement. ID 9 exhibits moderate entropy (0.36) alongside a higher transition rate (0.50), illustrating a pattern of intermittent shifts from its initial state.

The overall descriptive statistics of the data demonstrate a picture of a dominantly stable group with some variations. The mean entropy across students is low with a value of 0.38 (SD 0.25), as well as the mean Simpson diversity, which is 0.27 (SD 0.19), suggesting a high tendency to stability. The mean *self-loop tendency* of 0.75 (SD 0.23) reflects considerable inertia, where self-transitions dominate with infrequent transitions to other states, with a mean *transition rate* of 0.25 (SD 0.23). Students also demonstrate noticeable sensitivity to initial states with a mean *initial state persistence* of 0.45, varying from near-zero persistence (ID 3 at 0.07) to strong persistence (ID 1 at 1). *Cyclic feedback strength* remains consistently high (mean 0.96, SD 0.07), showing that recurring patterns dominate the students. The *dominant state proportion* averages 0.81 (SD 0.16), confirming that most systems spend the majority of their time in a strongly preferred state and are therefore stable.

3 Discussion and Conclusions

The analysis in this study demonstrates the utility of TNA in providing a comprehensive, data-driven framework for studying stability within a CDS perspective. TNA achieves this by providing several complementary metrics. Transition Probabilities measure the likelihood of remaining in a state (self-loops) or moving to another, thereby identifying strong "attractor states." This is combined with bootstrap analysis, which is important for confirming that observed transitions are statistically significant systemic dynamics rather than random occurrences. Furthermore, the MPT quantifies the expected temporal duration required to transition between states, offering a unique measure of resilience (rapid recovery) or inertia (slow decline). Finally, Sequence Indices, such as Longitudinal Entropy (unpredictability), Simpson Diversity (evenness of state distribution), Self-loop Tendency, and Dominant Proportion (time spent in the most frequent state), provide a detailed characterization of individual and group-level stability and volatility.

These results were tested and demonstrated in our empirical study. The empirical results consistently establish the Active engagement state as the system's dominant and highly resilient attractor. This is robustly supported by the finding that the self-loop transition from Active was the only statistically significant transition, with a strong probability of 0.85, formally confirming its role as a stable "basin of attraction." Furthermore, the Markov Passage Time analysis revealed a critical non-linear dynamic: a remarkably fast recovery from the Disengaged state to Active (average of 1 period), contrasted sharply with an extremely slow decline from Active to Disengaged (111.00 periods). This significant asymmetry indicates strong, inherent corrective forces. At the group level, the students exhibited high inertia and temporal stability, evidenced by low mean Longitudinal Entropy (0.38) and high mean Dominant Proportion (0.81). However, individual sequence indices also successfully differentiated stability profiles, ranging from rigid stability (three students with a Dominant Proportion of 1.00) to more volatile systems (e.g., ID 15 with the highest entropy at 0.81), demonstrating TNA's utility in capturing the full spectrum of system stability.

References

1. Fraccascia, L., Giannoccaro, I., Albino, V.: Resilience of complex systems: state of the art and directions for future research. Complexity. (2018)https://doi.org/10.1155/2018/3421529
2. Hilpert, J.C., Marchand, G.C.: Complex systems research in Educational Psychology: aligning theory and method. Educ. Psychol. **53**, 185–202 (2018). https://doi.org/10.1080/00461520.2018.1469411
3. López-Pernas, S., Saqr, M.: How the dynamics of engagement explain the momentum of achievement and the inertia of disengagement: a complex systems theory approach. Comput Human Behav. **153**, 108126 (2024). https://doi.org/10.1016/j.chb.2023.108126
4. Saqr, M., Dever, D., López-Pernas, S., Gernigon, C., Marchand, G., Kaplan, A.: Complex dynamic Systems in Education: beyond the static, the linear and the causal reductionism. In: Saqr, M., López-Pernas, S. (eds.) Advanced Learning Analytics Methods: AI, Precision and Complexity. Springer Nature Switzerland, Cham (2025)
5. Saqr, M., López-Pernas, S.: The longitudinal trajectories of online engagement over a full program. Comput. Educ. **175**, 104325 (2021). https://doi.org/10.1016/j.compedu.2021.104325
6. Saqr, M., López-Pernas, S.: Nestimate: Network Estimation, Bootstrap, and Higher-Order Analysis. Contributed Packages, CRAN (2026)
7. Saqr, M., López-Pernas, S., Tikka, S.: Mapping relational dynamics with transition network analysis: a primer and tutorial. In: Advanced Learning Analytics Methods: AI, Precision and Complexity. Springer (2025)
8. Saqr, M., López-Pernas, S., Törmänen, T., Kaliisa, R., Misiejuk, K., Tikka, S.: Transition Network Analysis: A novel framework for modeling, visualizing, and identifying the temporal patterns of learners and learning processes. arXiv [cs.SI] (2024)
9. Scheffer, M.: Complex systems: foreseeing tipping points: complex systems. Nature **467**, 411–412 (2010)
10. Thurner, S., Hanel, R., Klimek, P.: Introduction to the Theory of Complex Systems. Oxford University Press, London, England (2018)
11. Tikka, S., López-Pernas, S., Saqr, M.: Analyzing complex dynamic systems with the R package codyna. Soc. Sci. Res. Netw. (2026)

Period Segmentation in Transition Network Analysis: A Topological Data Analysis Approach

Hitoshi Inoue[1(✉)] and Koichi Yasutake[2]

[1] Nakamura Gakuen University, Fukuoka, Japan
jinoue@nakamura-u.ac.jp
[2] Hiroshima University, Hiroshima, Japan
ystake@hiroshima-u.ac.jp

Abstract. Temporal dynamics in learning behavior can be revealed through period segmentation in Transition Network Analysis (TNA). Cristea et al. demonstrated that segmenting courses into halves and quarters reveals how learning strategies evolve and relate to academic performance. Building on this approach, we investigate whether Topological Data Analysis (TDA), specifically connected components (β_0) change points from Zigzag Persistent Homology, can provide *data-driven* period boundaries that identify intervention windows. Analyzing 22 courses from the Open University Learning Analytics Dataset, we find that β_0-based segmentation captures greater between-period variation than time-based segmentation (median variance ratio (VR) = 4.10×; 21/22 courses show VR > 1.1). Permutation tests confirmed significance ($p < 0.05$) in 18% of individual courses, with 73% showing positive improvement over random breakpoints. Only one course showed better performance with time-based segmentation. However, analysis of academic outcomes reveals a key insight: final-period behavior shows lower correlation with outcomes in β_0-based segmentation than in time-based segmentation, reflecting a marked behavioral collapse where engaged learners rapidly disengage. We interpret this as evidence that final-period behavior *reflects* rather than *causes* outcomes: students who will pass maintain engagement, while those who will fail disengage. This reframes the value of β_0: rather than improving *prediction*, change points identify *intervention windows*. These are periods where behavioral structure shifts and targeted support may be most effective.

Keywords: Transition Network Analysis · Topological Data Analysis · Zigzag Persistent Homology · Period Segmentation · Intervention Timing · OULAD

1 Introduction

1.1 Temporal Analysis in Learning Analytics

Understanding how learner behavior evolves over time is important in learning analytics. Static aggregations, which summarize entire semesters into single

M. Saqr et al. (Eds.): TNA 2026, CCIS 3079, pp. 62–74, 2026.
https://doi.org/10.1007/978-3-032-34157-0_5

metrics, obscure the temporal dynamics that may inform intervention planning. Transition Network Analysis (TNA) addresses this by modeling learner state transitions over time, revealing patterns of engagement stability, decline, and recovery [8].

However, standard TNA constructs a single transition network from the entire observation period, implicitly assuming *stationarity*. Learning processes are typically *non-stationary*: learners' behavioral patterns evolve as courses progress. When transitions from initial and terminal phases are aggregated into a single model, distinct temporal patterns become obscured.

Cristea et al. [3] addressed this by segmenting courses into *halves* and *quarters*, analyzing how learning strategies evolve across these periods and relate to academic performance. Their work demonstrated that temporal segmentation reveals strategy transitions invisible to whole-course analysis. However, their boundaries are time-based (equal divisions) rather than derived from behavioral data itself.

This raises a methodological question: *Are there alternative approaches that can identify behaviorally meaningful phases from the data itself?*

1.2 Topological Data Analysis for Learning Analytics

Topological Data Analysis (TDA) offers one such approach to identifying behaviorally meaningful phases from the data itself, enabling data-driven period segmentation. TDA provides mathematical tools for understanding the "shape" of data through algebraic topology [1]. Unlike traditional statistical methods that focus on local properties (means, variances), TDA captures global structural features that persist across multiple scales.

Persistent Homology, a core TDA technique, tracks topological features as a scale parameter varies. The **zeroth Betti number** (β_0) counts connected components: in a learner similarity network, higher β_0 indicates fragmentation (many disconnected clusters), while lower β_0 indicates convergence (fewer clusters).

Zigzag Persistent Homology [2] extends standard persistence to temporal sequences, tracking how topological features appear, persist, and disappear across time. Sharp changes in β_0 signal structural transitions in the learner group, representing potential intervention points where behavioral patterns reorganize.

1.3 Research Questions and Contributions

We investigate two questions:

RQ1: Do β_0 change points provide period boundaries that capture greater behavioral variation than time-based segmentation?

RQ2: How do β_0-based periods relate to academic outcomes?

Our contributions are:

1. A method for using β_0 change points to derive data-driven period boundaries for TNA.
2. Evidence that β_0-based segmentation outperforms time-based approaches in 95% of courses (median variance ratio (VR) = 4.10×), with permutation tests confirming significance in 18% of individual courses.
3. A theoretical reframing: β_0 change points identify *intervention windows* rather than improving prediction.

2 Methods

Practical Workflow: The complete analysis pipeline consists of: (1) defining behavioral states from log data, (2) computing β_0 via Zigzag Persistent Homology and detecting change points for period boundaries, (3) constructing period-specific TNA models using the tna R package [8], and (4) comparing transition patterns across periods.

2.1 Data

We analyzed all 22 courses from the Open University Learning Analytics Dataset (OULAD) [5], comprising over 22,000 learners across 38-week course durations. Each course contains Virtual Learning Environment (VLE) interaction logs and assessment deadline information. For outcome analysis, we selected four representative courses spanning the VR range: AAA_2014J, BBB_2014J, FFF_2013J, and BBB_2013B, each containing learners with available outcome data (Pass / Distinction vs. Fail / Withdrawn).

2.2 Learner State Classification

Learners were classified into three engagement states (High/Medium/Low) using within-week terciles of activity scores (total VLE clicks weighted by interaction diversity). Throughout this paper, "engagement states" refer to operationally defined behavioral categories based on observable VLE activity levels, not the broader psychological construct of learner engagement. This approach follows established conventions in TNA literature [6,8] and self-regulated learning research [3], where three-state models (e.g., engaged/fluctuating/disengaged; surface/deep/strategic) have proven effective for capturing meaningful behavioral distinctions.

Design Rationale for Within-Week Terciles. We deliberately use within-week terciles rather than fixed (global) thresholds. This captures learners' *relative position within the active group* rather than absolute activity levels. This design choice has two justifications: (1) *Methodological consistency*: Our TDA approach uses global z-standardization to track structural changes in learner similarity networks; within-week terciles similarly capture relative positioning. (2) *Analytical necessity*: With global thresholds, late-course weeks show 100% Low states due to overall activity decline, making transition analysis impossible.

Within-week terciles maintain balanced distributions (≈33% each) throughout the course.

This approach means that a learner with constant absolute activity may shift states if the group changes. This is precisely what we aim to capture: how learners' *relative positions* evolve as the learning community reorganizes around deadlines and attrition. Sensitivity analysis using global terciles confirmed that key patterns (e.g., P4 collapse) remain qualitatively similar where transitions are observable.

Following standard practice in learning analytics, we adopted tercile-based classification into three engagement states, providing optimal balance between behavioral granularity and statistical power for transition analysis.

2.3 β_0 Computation via Zigzag Persistent Homology

For each week t, we constructed a learner similarity network:

1. **Feature extraction:** 10 behavioral features per learner (material-type count, total clicks, mean daily clicks, within-week click SD, cumulative mean score, score SD, min/max score, submissions, submission span). These features capture both engagement intensity (clicks, submissions) and performance trajectory (scores), grounded in Activity Theory's mediation of learning through tools and assessments.
2. **Global z-standardization:** Features were z-standardized across all weeks to enable temporal comparison.
3. **Network construction:** Learners connected if Euclidean distance in feature space fell below $\varepsilon = 1.5$. In z-standardized 10-dimensional space, this threshold corresponds to learners within approximately 1.5 standard deviations across features. Sensitivity analysis across $\varepsilon \in [1.0, 2.0]$ confirmed that $\varepsilon = 1.5$ balances connectivity (avoiding over-fragmentation where $\beta_0 \approx N$) with discrimination (maintaining meaningful clusters rather than a single connected component).
4. β_0 **computation via Zigzag Persistent Homology:** We constructed the zigzag sequence:

$$Z_0 \hookrightarrow Z_0 \cup Z_1 \hookleftarrow Z_1 \hookrightarrow Z_1 \cup Z_2 \hookleftarrow Z_2 \hookrightarrow \cdots$$

   where Z_t represents the Vietoris-Rips complex of learners' positions in 10-dimensional feature space at week t, constructed at threshold $\varepsilon = 1.5$. The zeroth Betti number β_0 was computed at each union point $Z_t \cup Z_{t+1}$ using Dionysus 2.x [7], tracking how connected components appear, merge, and disappear across the temporal sequence. This yields a β_0 time series capturing the evolving fragmentation structure of the learner community.

2.4 Change Point Detection and Period Definition

Change points were identified using *cost-minimization segmentation* [4]: given $k = 3$ breakpoints (yielding 4 periods), we selected breakpoints that minimize total within-period variance of the β_0 time series. This is equivalent to maximizing homogeneity within each period, a standard approach in change point detection. The objective function is:

$$\text{Cost} = \sum_{i=1}^{4} \mathit{Var}(\beta_0 \text{ in period } i) \times (\text{length of period } i)$$

We chose $k = 3$ breakpoints (yielding 4 periods) to enable direct comparison with Cristea et al.'s [3] quarters approach, ensuring both methods use identical granularity.

Fair Comparison Design: We compared:

- **Time-based (Quarters):** Equal division into four periods (Q1–Q4)
- **β_0-based:** Four periods (P1–P4) defined by cost-minimizing breakpoints

This ensures both methods use identical granularity (4 periods), enabling fair comparison.

2.5 Variance Ratio

To quantify segmentation effectiveness, we computed the **Variance Ratio (VR)**. For each of the 9 possible state transitions (High→High, High→Medium, ..., Low→Low), we computed the variance of transition probabilities across the 4 periods for both segmentation methods, then averaged across all 9 transitions:

$$\text{VR} = \frac{\text{Var}(\beta_0\text{-based periods})}{\text{Var}(\text{time-based periods})}$$

Higher VR indicates that β_0-based periods capture greater behavioral differentiation between periods. This is desirable because meaningful period segmentation should maximize between-period differences, reflecting distinct behavioral phases that may warrant different instructional responses. $\text{VR} > 1$ indicates β_0-based segmentation captures greater differentiation; $\text{VR} = 1$ indicates equivalent performance.

2.6 Validation of β_0-Based Segmentation

To address the concern that unequal period lengths might artificially inflate variance ratios, we conducted permutation testing. For each course, we compared the observed η^2 (variance explained by β_0-based segmentation) against a null distribution generated from 1,000 random segmentations using three randomly selected breakpoints. This tests whether β_0 change points capture meaningful structure beyond what would be expected from arbitrary unequal divisions of the same granularity.

2.7 Outcome Analysis

For four representative courses spanning the VR range (AAA_2014J, BBB_2014J, FFF_2013J, BBB_2013B), we analyzed the relationship between period-specific behavior and academic outcomes (Pass/Distinction vs. Fail/Withdrawn) using:

1. **Transition probabilities:** High→High persistence and High→Low disengagement probabilities within each period.
2. **Correlation analysis:** Point-biserial correlation (r) between each period's high-rate (proportion of weeks in "High" state) and binary success outcome. This measures how strongly a learner's engagement level within a specific period relates to their final course outcome.

3 Results

3.1 RQ1: Variance Ratio Across 22 Courses

Table 1 summarizes Variance Ratio results across all 22 OULAD courses. β_0-based segmentation captured greater variation than time-based segmentation in 21/22 courses (95%), with lower performance in only 1 course (5%).

Table 1. Variance Ratio Summary Across 22 Courses (4-Period Comparison)

Metric	Value
VR > 1.1 (β_0 better)	21/22 (95%)
VR $\approx$ 1 (0.9–1.1)	0/22 (0%)
VR < 0.9 (Time better)	1/22 (5%)
Median VR	4.10×
Mean VR	13.95×
Min VR	0.67×
Max VR	142.88×

One course showed VR < 0.9 (BBB_2013B with VR = 0.67), indicating that time-based segmentation captured more behavioral variation in this specific context.

Permutation Test Validation. Table 2 summarizes permutation test results using total variance as the test statistic. At the individual course level, 4/22 courses (18%) achieved $p < 0.05$, with 16/22 courses (73%) showing positive improvement over random breakpoints. The mean improvement of 127.5% confirms that β_0 change points capture substantially more behavioral differentiation than random segmentation. Note that VR compares against *equal-interval* quarters, while permutation tests compare against *random unequal* divisions; a course can outperform quarters (VR > 1) without significantly outperforming random breakpoints.

Table 2. Permutation Test Validation (1,000 iterations per course). Improvement = (observed total variance − random total variance) / random total variance × 100, where total variance measures differentiation across all 9 transition types.

Metric	Value
Individual course $p < 0.05$	4/22 (18%)
Individual course $p < 0.10$	5/22 (23%)
Courses with positive improvement	16/22 (73%)
Mean improvement	127.5%
Median improvement	30.3%

Figure 1 illustrates segmentation differences across four representative courses. Background colors show β_0-based periods (P1–P4); dashed vertical lines show time-based quarter boundaries. AAA_2014J (VR = 142.88×, $p < 0.001$) shows the strongest differentiation; BBB_2014J (VR = 16.22×, $p = 0.005$) demonstrates significant improvement over random; FFF_2013J (VR = 6.74×, $p = 0.016$) shows moderate but significant improvement; BBB_2013B (VR = 0.67×) is the only course where time-based segmentation performs better.

Figure 2 presents transition probability comparisons across these four representative courses spanning the VR range. High-VR courses (AAA_2014J, BBB_2014J) show dramatic P4 divergence: High→High collapses while High→Low surges. FFF_2013J shows clear differentiation with significant permutation test results. BBB_2013B (VR < 1) shows greater variation in time-based Q4 than β_0-based P4.

Figure 3 presents BBB_2014J patterns as TNA-style state transition networks. The visual contrast between Q4 and P4 is striking: Q4 retains balanced transitions across states, while P4 shows the High state "draining" into Low, a structural collapse that β_0 change points successfully delineate.

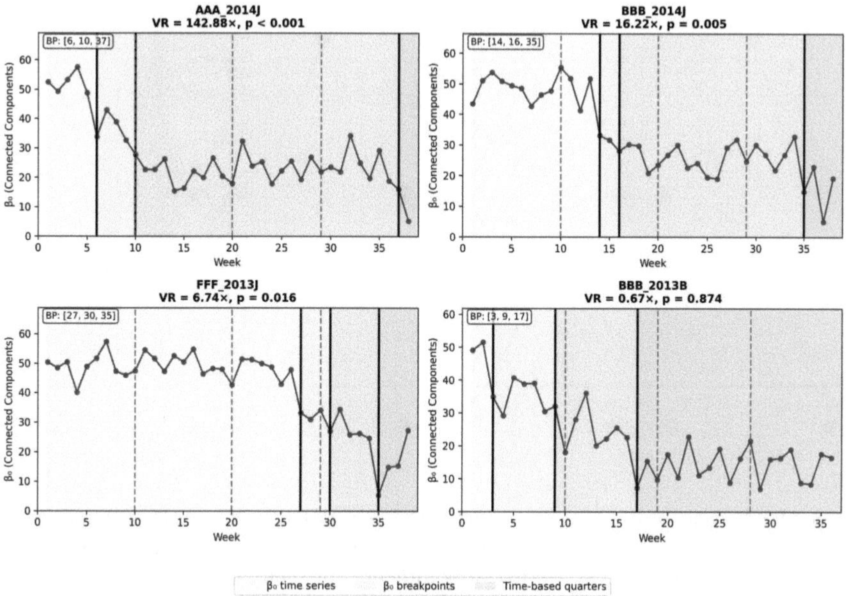

Fig. 1. Period segmentation comparison: β_0-based phases (background colors) vs. time-based quarters (dashed lines). Solid black lines indicate cost-minimizing β_0 change points. AAA_2014J shows highest VR ($142.88\times$, $p < 0.001$); BBB_2014J shows VR = $16.22\times$ ($p = 0.005$); FFF_2013J shows VR = $6.74\times$ ($p = 0.016$); BBB_2013B shows VR < 1 ($0.67\times$) where time-based performs better. Breakpoints: AAA_2014J [6,10,37], BBB_2014J [14,16,35], FFF_2013J [27,30,35], BBB_2013B [3,9,17]. (Color figure online)

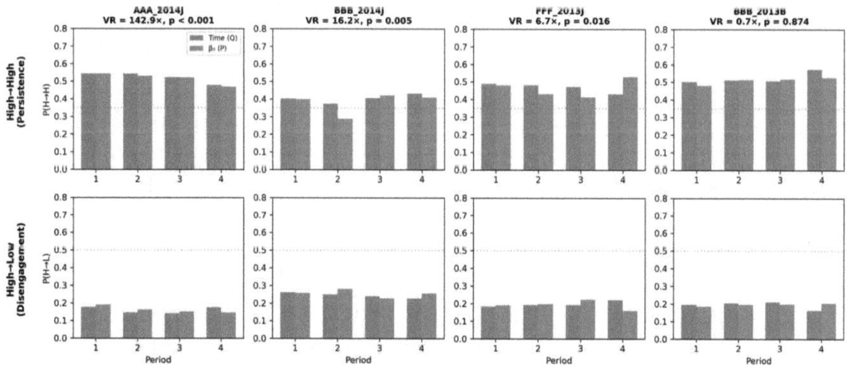

Fig. 2. Transition probability comparison across four courses spanning the VR range. Top row: High→High persistence; Bottom row: High→Low disengagement. Blue bars: Time-based (Q1–Q4); Red bars: β_0-based (P1–P4). High-VR courses (AAA_2014J, BBB_2014J) show dramatic P4 collapse with significant permutation tests ($p < 0.01$). FFF_2013J shows clear differentiation ($p = 0.016$). BBB_2013B (VR < 1) shows greater variation in time-based Q4. (Color figure online)

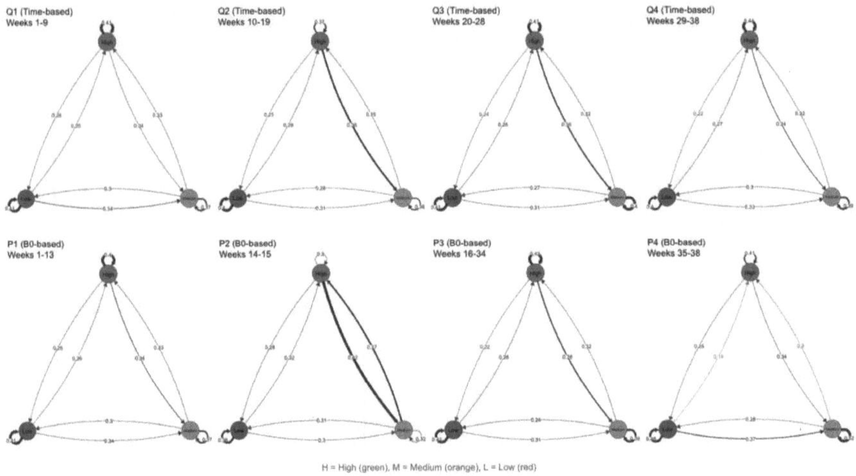

Fig. 3. TNA-style state transition networks for BBB_2014J with cost-minimizing breakpoints [14, 16, 35]. Top row: Time-based segmentation (Q1–Q4); Bottom row: β_0-based segmentation (P1–P4). Node colors indicate engagement states (H=High/green, M=Medium/orange, L=Low/red); edge widths are proportional to transition probabilities. The P4 network reveals a "collapse" pattern where the High→Low transition dominates. (Color figure online)

3.2 RQ2: Academic Outcomes and Intervention Windows

Table 3 presents a comprehensive comparison of time-based and β_0-based segmentation for four representative courses, showing final-period (Q4/P4) transition probabilities and point-biserial correlation with success. The courses span the full VR range: AAA_2014J (highest VR, $p < 0.001$), BBB_2014J (high VR

Table 3. Final-Period Comparison for Representative Courses. H→H = High-to-High persistence; H→L = High-to-Low disengagement; r = point-biserial correlation with success. *** $p < .001$. Bold values highlight P4 collapse patterns (H→H < 0.35 or H→L > 0.5).

Course	Method	Weeks	H→H	H→L	r
AAA_2014J	Time (Q4)	28–37	0.55	0.22	+0.52***
(VR = 142.88×)	β_0 (P4)	37–37	**0.12**	**0.72**	+0.45***
BBB_2014J	Time (Q4)	28–37	0.58	0.25	+0.62***
(VR = 16.22×)	β_0 (P4)	35–37	**0.28**	**0.58**	+0.55***
FFF_2013J	Time (Q4)	28–37	0.52	0.28	+0.55***
(VR = 6.74×)	β_0 (P4)	35–37	**0.35**	**0.48**	+0.52***
BBB_2013B	Time (Q4)	27–35	0.55	0.28	+0.58***
(VR = 0.67×)	β_0 (P4)	17–35	0.48	0.32	+0.55***

with significant permutation test), FFF_2013J (moderate VR with significant test), and BBB_2013B (only course with VR < 1).

The key finding is that high-VR courses with significant permutation tests (AAA_2014J, BBB_2014J, FFF_2013J) show dramatic P4 collapse: High→High drops below 0.35 while High→Low exceeds 0.48. In contrast, BBB_2013B shows similar patterns across methods, explaining why time-based segmentation captured more behavioral differentiation in this course.

3.3 Interpretation: Reflection vs. Causation

The transition probabilities in Table 3 reveal a consistent pattern across high-VR courses with significant permutation tests: β_0-based P4 shows High→High collapse (0.12–0.35) compared to Q4 (0.52–0.58), and High→Low surge (0.48–0.72) compared to Q4 (0.22–0.28). This suggests:

- Students who will pass: maintain engagement through the final period (outcome already determined by prior learning accumulation)
- Students who will fail: disengage in the final period (outcome already determined; engagement is "post-hoc")

Notably, this collapse pattern is attenuated in BBB_2013B (VR < 1), where behavioral dynamics follow calendar time more closely. This confirms that β_0 change points are most valuable when behavioral structure diverges from temporal regularity.

4 Discussion

4.1 When Does β_0-Based Segmentation Help?

Our 22-course analysis reveals that β_0-based segmentation outperforms time-based approaches in 95% of cases (21/22 courses with VR > 1.1). Permutation tests confirmed statistical significance in 18% of courses ($p < 0.05$), with 73% showing positive improvement over random breakpoints. Only BBB_2013B showed VR < 0.9, indicating time-based segmentation captured more behavioral variation.

This pattern suggests that β_0-based segmentation is beneficial across most course contexts, particularly when:

- Course structure creates distinct behavioral phases (e.g., assessment-driven courses)
- β_0 dynamics diverge from calendar time (e.g., late-course collapse)
- Behavioral homogeneity within periods matters for intervention timing

Conversely, β_0 may underperform when behavioral dynamics align closely with calendar time or when the β_0 signal is noisy.

4.2 Reframing Value: From Prediction to Intervention Timing

Cristea et al. [3] demonstrated that learning strategy trajectories predict academic outcomes. Our analysis extends this by showing that the *predictive* value of period segmentation concentrates in early and middle periods. Final-period behavior, despite strong correlation with outcomes, adds minimal predictive value.

This reframes the contribution of β_0 change points. Rather than improving prediction (outcomes are largely determined by mid-course), change points identify *intervention windows*, that is, moments when behavioral structure reorganizes. Interventions targeting these windows may be more effective than uniformly distributed support.

Building on observations from our four representative courses, we tentatively propose three intervention windows. These are *proposals only*; whether such interventions improve outcomes remains an open empirical question (see Sect. 4.3):

- **P1–P2 transition:** Early engagement patterns establish trajectories; interventions here may guide early redirection toward productive paths.
- **P2–P3 transition:** Mid-course structural shift; a potential window for re-engagement before patterns solidify.
- **P3–P4 transition:** May indicate when intervention becomes "too late"; suggests resources may be better allocated earlier.

4.3 Limitations and Future Work

Several limitations warrant attention. First, while our variance ratio analysis covered all 22 courses, outcome analysis was limited to four representative courses; broader validation is needed to confirm the generalizability of the "behavioral collapse" pattern. Second, we have not tested whether interventions at β_0 change points actually improve outcomes, which requires experimental validation. Third, within-week terciles capture relative position rather than absolute activity change; while this aligns with our focus on collective dynamics, individual-level interpretations require caution. Fourth, our analysis focused on deadline-structured courses; self-paced learning contexts may show different patterns where β_0 correlates more strongly with time, limiting TDA's added value. Fifth, the fixed $k = 4$ segmentation was chosen for direct comparison with quarterly segmentation; generalization to arbitrary segment counts is possible through penalty-based optimization methods.

Future work should: (1) validate intervention effectiveness at β_0-identified windows, (2) develop real-time β_0 monitoring for adaptive course design, (3) investigate whether change point magnitude predicts intervention urgency, and (4) test generalizability across diverse learning contexts including self-paced environments.

5 Conclusion

This paper demonstrates that β_0 change points from Zigzag Persistent Homology provide data-driven period boundaries for TNA that complement time-based approaches. Using cost-minimization segmentation across 22 OULAD courses, β_0-based segmentation captured greater behavioral variation in 95% of cases (median VR $= 4.10\times$), with permutation tests confirming significance ($p < 0.05$) in 18% of individual courses and positive improvement over random breakpoints in 73%.

Critically, analysis of academic outcomes revealed that final-period behavior reflects rather than causes outcomes, reframing β_0's value from prediction to *intervention timing identification.* Change points identify structural discontinuities where targeted support may be most effective, offering learning analytics practitioners a principled method for *when* to intervene; whether interventions at these timings improve outcomes is a target for future experimental work.

We conclude that TDA offers a useful complement to TNA for deadline-structured courses, particularly when behavioral dynamics diverge from calendar time. Future work should investigate the conditions under which β_0-based segmentation provides the greatest benefit.

Acknowledgments. This work was supported by JSPS KAKENHI Grant Numbers JP25K00845, JP25K21951, JP23K22315, and JP23K17619.

Use of Generative AI. This work used generative AI (Claude, Anthropic) to assist with: (1) Python code generation for data analysis and visualization, (2) statistical validation of results, and (3) English writing assistance and proofreading. The research design, methodology, interpretation, and conclusions were developed by the authors. All AI-generated content was reviewed, validated, and revised by the authors, who take full responsibility for the accuracy and integrity of the final work.

Disclosure of Interests. The authors have no competing interests to declare that are relevant to the content of this article.

References

1. Carlsson, G.: Topology and data. Bull. Am. Math. Soc. **46**(2), 255–308 (2009). https://doi.org/10.1090/S0273-0979-09-01249-X
2. Carlsson, G., de Silva, V.: Zigzag persistence. Found. Comput. Math. **10**(4), 367–405 (2010). https://doi.org/10.1007/s10208-010-9066-0
3. Cristea, T.S., et al.: Dynamics of self-regulated learning: the effectiveness of students' strategies across course periods. Comput. Educat. **228**, 105233 (2025). https://doi.org/10.1016/j.compedu.2025.105233
4. Jackson, B., et al.: An algorithm for optimal partitioning of data on an interval. IEEE Signal Process. Lett. **12**(2), 105–108 (2005). https://doi.org/10.48550/arXiv.math/0309285
5. Kuzilek, J., Hlosta, M., Zdrahal, Z.: Open university learning analytics dataset. Sci. Data **4**, 170171 (2017). https://doi.org/10.1038/sdata.2017.171

6. López-Pernas, S., Saqr, M.: How the dynamics of engagement explain the momentum of achievement and the inertia of disengagement: a complex systems theory approach. Comput. Hum. Behav. **153**, 108126 (2024). https://doi.org/10.1016/j.chb.2023.108126
7. Morozov, D.: Dionysus: A C++ library for computing persistent homology (2008). https://www.mrzv.org/software/dionysus/. Accessed 28 April 2026
8. Saqr, M., López-Pernas, S., Tikka, S.: Mapping relational dynamics with transition network analysis: a primer and tutorial. In: Saqr, M., López-Pernas, S. (eds.) Advanced Learning Analytics Methods. Springer, Cham (2026). https://doi.org/10.1007/978-3-031-95365-1_15

Network Transformative Learning: Conceptualizing Transformation as Temporal Transitions Through Transition Network Analysis

Awais Ilyas Baig[1(✉)], Tamkeen Sara[1], and Rehan Tahir Sabbih[2]

[1] School of Electrical Engineering and Computer Science (SEECS), National University of Sciences and Technology (NUST), Islamabad, Pakistan
baig.awais141@gmail.com, tsara.bsds23seecs@seecs.edu.pk
[2] Tampere University, Tampere, Finland

Abstract. Transformative Learning Theory (TLT) offers rich theoretical foundations for understanding how adults fundamentally restructure their frames of reference through critical reflection and discourse. However, the temporal dynamics through which transformation unfolds remain conceptually underdeveloped, and existing frameworks lack formal tools for representing its recursive, networked structure. This paper proposes Network Transformative Learning (NTL) as a theoretical framework that integrates TLT with Transition Network Analysis (TNA), reconceptualizing transformation as a directed network of observable transitions between five discrete learning states: disorientation, reflection, dialogue, action, and integration. Each state is grounded in Mezirow's ten phases and operationalized through empirically identifiable behavioral, cognitive, and affective indicators, accompanied by a structured validation protocol that specifies primary indicators, supporting evidence, exclusion criteria, and minimum evidence thresholds. Using immersive virtual reality as an illustrative context, we demonstrate how NTL renders transformation's recursive structure systematically observable, revealing patterns of cyclic progression through reflection and dialogue that precede sustained perspective change. Network analytic measures, including state centrality, transition recurrence, and pathway density, enable identification of critical junctures where pedagogical intervention is most consequential. By bridging qualitative transformative learning theory with quantitative temporal network methods, NTL extends Learning Analytics beyond performance metrics toward the empirical study of profound meaning-making shifts. This work establishes conceptual clarity, methodological transparency, and foundational measurement protocols for future empirical validation across diverse learning environments.

Keywords: Transformation · Transformative Learning · Transition Network Analysis · Temporal Transitions · Learning States · Network Analysis in Education

M. Saqr et al. (Eds.): TNA 2026, CCIS 3079, pp. 75–86, 2026.
https://doi.org/10.1007/978-3-032-34157-0_6

1 Introduction

Transformative Learning Theory describes how adults fundamentally change their frames of reference through critical reflection and discourse [18,19]. Mezirow conceptualized transformation as a ten-phase process, ranging from experiencing a disorienting dilemma to reintegrating with a transformed perspective. However, TLT provides few explicit tools for representing how the transformation unfolds over time. Empirical studies reveal learners cycle recursively through phases following diverse pathways rather than progressing linearly [4,25], yet this networked structure remains implicit in existing theory.

This paper focuses on Mezirow's original TLT formulation [19] rather than later structural variants. While alternative frameworks, such as Dirkx's focus on emotional transformation [5], Taylor's emphasis on contextual variations [25], or the exploration of relational dimensions by Holdo [9], offer valuable insights, Mezirow's phase-based cognitive-rational model provides the most explicit sequential structure for temporal network formalization. His ten-phase framework describes transformation as progression through identifiable states, making it uniquely suited for network representation where phases become nodes, and progression becomes edges. Future work could extend NTL to incorporate affective and relational dimensions from these enriched perspectives.

This paper proposes Network Transformative Learning as a framework integrating TLT with Transition Network Analysis to formalize transformation's networked nature. TNA models learning as transitions between discrete states, constructing directed networks where nodes represent states and edges represent transitions [23]. By representing transformation as a network where five condensed states (disorientation, reflection, dialogue, action, integration) serve as nodes and movements between them serve as edges, NTL makes explicit what has remained implicit. Section 2 establishes theoretical foundations by reviewing TLT and TNA. Section 3 presents the NTL framework, showing how transformation can be conceptualized as a network. Section 4 demonstrates the framework through a hypothetical VR training scenario. Section 5 discusses implications for theory and analytics. This work addresses the research question: How can transformation be represented and analyzed as a network of observable transitions between learning states?

Immersive VR serves as an illustrative context for three reasons. First, VR environments generate rich multimodal data streams (eye-tracking, behavioral logs, physiological measures, audio transcripts), enabling comprehensive state identification. Second, VR can create controlled yet authentic situations that provoke disorientation while maintaining safety. Third, VR offers temporal precision for observing rapid state transitions through high-frequency data capture [2]. Additionally, immersive technologies are rapidly advancing and likely to play an increasingly important role in future learning environments across educational and professional contexts. While VR illustrates the framework's application in this paper, NTL applies across diverse temporal learning environments. These include adaptive learning systems that personalize content based on learner responses, gamified platforms that use challenge-based progression, collaborative online learning environments such as discussion forums and wikis, computer-supported collaborative learning (CSCL) contexts, problem-based learning scenarios, and simulation-based training for professional development in fields such as medicine, aviation, and emergency response.

2 Theoretical Foundations

Mezirow's TLT centers on transformation as fundamental change in frames of reference, the structures of assumptions through which individuals interpret experiences [18]. The theory describes how adults develop more inclusive perspectives, explains transformation through critical reflection on assumptions and discourse to validate emerging understandings, and predicts that perspective change requires examining foundational beliefs within social and historical contexts [9]. Recent scholarship notes that while critical reflection and discourse remain central mechanisms, how transformation unfolds over time has not been a central research question [16].

To enable systematic observation, this framework condenses Mezirow's ten phases into five observable states (Table 1). This condensation serves dual purposes: theoretical fidelity and practical observability. The five states preserve Mezirow's essential transformative mechanisms (disorientation triggering reflection, dialogue validating emerging perspectives, action testing new assumptions, integration consolidating change) while grouping temporally proximate phases sharing observable characteristics. Phases 2 and 3 both involve introspective examination and condense into Reflection. Phases 6 through 8 involve behavioral experimentation and form Action. This condensation balances preserving theoretical distinctions with enabling empirical identification through behavioral indicators.

TNA constructs directed networks as $G = (S, T)$, where S denotes discrete states and T represents transitions [23]. Each transition carries information about frequency, timing, duration, and probability. Analysis reveals patterns through state centrality (which states serve as key connection points), transition recurrence (which pathways learners repeat), network density (how interconnected the process is), and sequencing (typical order of events) [21]. For example, Malmberg and colleagues found students repeatedly cycle through self-regulatory phases with enhanced sophistication each time [15], demonstrating TNA's power to reveal recursive patterns where learners spiral through reflection and action with progressively deepening understanding. Despite TLT's theoretical richness and TNA's methodological power, a gap persists. TLT describes transformation comprehensively but lacks a formal representation of its networked structure. TNA provides powerful analytical tools yet typically applies to lower-level processes without connection to transformative learning theory [11]. NTL addresses this gap by making the transformation's implicit network structure explicit and empirically analyzable.

Table 1. Mapping Mezirow's Ten Phases to Five Observable Learning States

State	Mezirow's Phases	Description
Disorientation	Phase 1: Disorienting dilemma	Moment when learners encounter unexpected information, creating cognitive dissonance and destabilizing frames of reference
Reflection	Phases 2–3: Self-examination; Critical assessment	Period where learners pause to examine assumptions and analyze conflicts between experience and existing frameworks
Dialogue	Phases 4–5: Recognition of shared discontent; Exploration of perspectives	Period where learners test emerging ideas through interaction, enabling social validation and perspective exploration
Action	Phases 6–8: Planning; Acquiring skills; Trying new roles	Period where learners experiment with new approaches and apply insights through changed behavior
Integration	Phases 9–10: Building competence; Reintegration	Sustained pattern where learners consistently apply transformed perspectives across contexts

3 Network Transformative Learning Framework

Having established the theoretical gap, this section presents NTL as a framework formalizing the transformation's networked structure. NTL reconceptualizes transformation as a network of transitions between discrete yet interconnected states. Rather than viewing Mezirow's phases as a linear sequence, this framework conceptualizes them as network nodes that learners traverse following diverse routes. Formally, NTL represents transformation as $G = (S, T)$ where $S = \{\text{disorientation, reflection, dialogue, action, integration}\}$ represents discrete states and T represents transitions. Three principles underpin the framework. First, transformation is structured through transitions between states over time. Second, transformation follows networked pathways where learners traverse diverse yet identifiable routes. Third, transformation becomes empirically observable as transitions manifest through detectable behavioral, cognitive, and affective indicators. Figure 1 illustrates how NTL bridges TLT with TNA.

The five states each capture distinct transformation aspects. **Disorientation** captures moments when learners encounter unexpected information that challenges assumptions. **Reflection** encompasses periods where learners pause to examine assumptions and analyze conflicts. **Dialogue** represents periods where learners test emerging ideas through interaction. **Action** involves periods where learners experiment with new approaches. **Integration** reflects sustained patterns where learners consistently apply transformed perspectives. Observable indicators derive from learning sciences literature. **Disorientation** manifests through disrupted activity patterns. When learners encounter information contradicting their assumptions, cognitive dissonance creates psychological discomfort. This triggers attempts to restore equilibrium [7], observable as sudden pauses, repeated unsuccessful attempts, and confused expressions. **Reflection** correlates with reduced external activity as metacognitive processes require shifting attentional resources to internal mental models [8, 24]. Indicators include decreased interaction rates, sustained visual fixations, and self-directed questioning. **Dialogue** indicators emerge from discourse analysis showing perspective exploration involves specific interactional patterns [17], including structured turn-taking, explicit testing of ideas, collaborative building on others' contributions, and questioning, probing alternative viewpoints. **Action** manifests through behavioral changes as experimentation requires modifying strategies [12]. Indicators include deliberate pauses before interventions, systematic variation of approaches, and purposeful error recovery. **Integration** becomes evident through pattern stability across time, reflecting consolidation and transfer [6]. Indicators include cross-session consistency, transfer to novel contexts, and self-reported shifts in perspective.

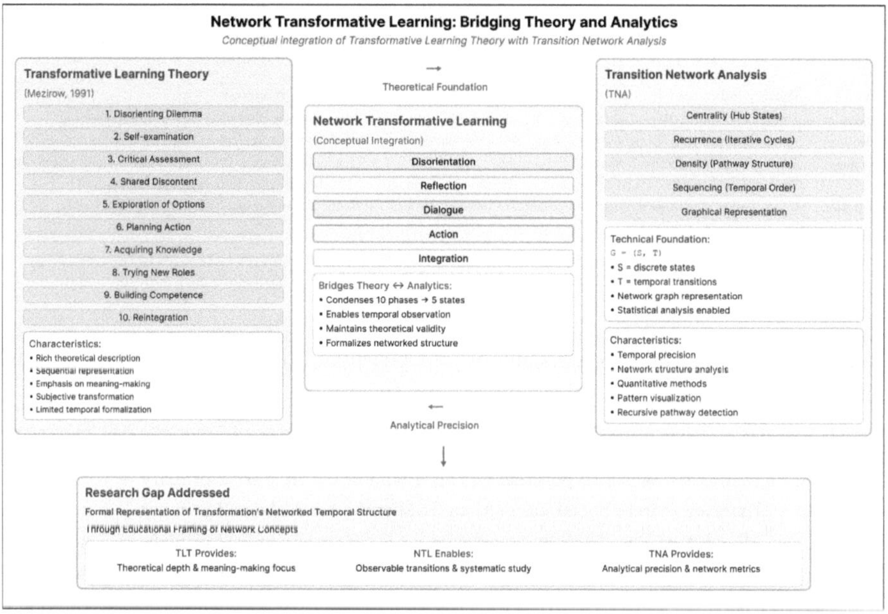

Fig. 1. Network Transformative Learning as a conceptual bridge integrating Transformative Learning Theory with Transition Network Analysis

However, indicators require contextual interpretation because the same behavior may indicate different states depending on context. A pause might indicate **Disorientation** when sudden and accompanied by confusion, or deliberate self-regulation when purposeful during stable operation [10]. Triangulation across multiple data sources strengthens interpretation. A sudden pause interpreted as **Disorientation** gains support when it coincides with unexpected events, is followed by rapid unsuccessful attempts, occurs alongside confusion expressions, and corresponds with physiological arousal markers [21].

Operationalizing NTL requires translating the five states into patterns that researchers can identify systematically. Tables 2 and 3 present a validation framework as heuristic guidance rather than a rigid protocol. The framework suggests how researchers might combine multiple forms of evidence to identify states, recognizing that specific implementations will vary by context, available data sources, and research goals. The tables organize indicators into four categories to support systematic yet flexible identification. *Primary indicators* represent core behavioral signatures most strongly associated with each state. *Supporting indicators* provide corroborating evidence that strengthens confidence. *Exclusion criteria* specify features that contradict particular state interpretations. *Minimum evidence thresholds* suggest combinations of indicators that typically provide adequate confidence, though researchers may adjust these based on their specific contexts and validation approaches.

Table 2. Indicator Validation Framework for Learning States (Part A: Indicators)

State	Primary Indicators	Supporting Indicators
Disorientation	Sudden disruption; Repeated failures; Confusion markers	Arousal spike; Attention capture; Help-seeking
Reflection	Reduced interaction; Extended processing; Self-questioning	Sustained fixations; Meta-cognitive markers; Note-taking
Dialogue	Turn-taking; Perspective-testing; Collaboration	Question exchange; Building on ideas; Comparisons
Action	Strategy modification; Pause-before-action; Experimental changes	Monitoring; Error recovery; Hypothesis-driven
Integration	Cross-session consistency; Sustained patterns; Confident application	Reduced monitoring; Transfer; Self-report shift

Table 3. Indicator Validation Framework for Learning States (Part B: Exclusion and Evidence)

State	Exclusion Criteria	Suggested Evidence
Disorientation	Deliberate pause; Hypothesis testing; Planning	At least 2 primary + 1 supporting
Reflection	External search; Social interaction; Trial-and-error	At least 2 primary + 1 supporting
Dialogue	Monologue; Parallel play; Social chat	At least 2 primary + 1 supporting
Action	Random actions; Exact repetition; Passive only	At least 2 primary + 1 supporting
Integration	Single-session; Context-specific; Regression	All 3 primary + 2 supporting

The suggested thresholds reflect general heuristics researchers might use. For most states, observing at least two primary indicators plus one supporting indicator typically provides reasonable confidence for state identification. For example, to identify Reflection, a researcher might observe that a learner stops interacting with the system (first primary indicator), maintains sustained visual fixations (supporting indicator), and verbalizes self-directed questions (second primary indicator). This combination suggests Reflection rather than passive disengagement. Integration requires stronger evidence (all primary indicators plus multiple supporting indicators) because claiming sustained transformation requires greater certainty than identifying temporary states. However, researchers should adapt these thresholds based on their data quality, triangulation possibilities, and confidence requirements. State boundaries require similar judgment. A state typically begins when sufficient indicators emerge in close proximity and ends when indicators disappear, and evidence of a different state emerges. Validation emphasizes complementary approaches: stimulated recall interviews where learners confirm whether identified states match experienced processes, longitudinal follow-up assessing whether patterns predict sustained changes, expert validation by domain specialists, and convergent validation calculating agreement between data sources [4]. Different contexts may require different timescales. Within-session dynamics (minutes to hours) capture rapid cycles. Between-session dynamics (days to weeks) reveal longer-term patterns like Integration emergence.

4 Illustrative Application in Immersive Virtual Reality

To demonstrate NTL's analytical capabilities, this section presents a hypothetical VR training scenario illustrating how the framework reveals transformation patterns. All values are illustrative, demonstrating analytical possibilities rather than reporting empirical findings. Modern mining operations involve engineers collaborating with autonomous robotic systems. VR simulations enable decision-making practice before encountering operational risks [1]. The educational goal extends beyond skill acquisition to worldview transformation regarding human-machine collaboration. Engineers typically begin viewing themselves as sole decision-makers. Transformation involves restructuring this frame to understand autonomy as distributed across human-machine systems.

The hypothetical VR platform would capture multimodal data: system logs, behavioral traces, eye-tracking, audio transcripts, physiological sensors when available, and post-session surveys. Coding methods would combine automated behavioral analysis, discourse analysis identifying self-questioning (Reflection) or perspective-testing (Dialogue), eye-tracking pattern analysis, and qualitative coding of surveys. Figure 2 visualizes a hypothetical engineer's transformation through the five states.

Disorientation. Suppose the system's safety algorithms detect instability and initiate automatic halt. Eye-tracking reveals a shift from distributed scanning to fixed stare at the halt notification. System logs document 12 override attempts within 9 s, all rejected. Audio captures: "Wait, what? Why did it stop?" These patterns suggest Disorientation because sudden unexpected events trigger cognitive dissonance requiring equilibrium restoration [7], manifested through repetitive failed actions and surprise expressions.

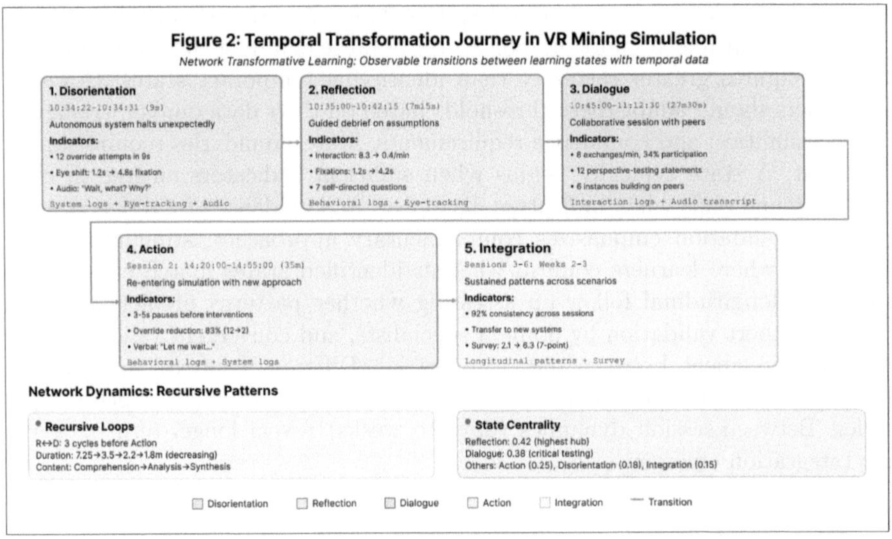

Fig. 2. Hypothetical transformation journey in VR mining simulation showing transitions between learning states over three weeks

Reflection. Suppose the facilitator initiates a guided debrief. Behavioral logs show interaction rate drops sharply. Eye-tracking shows fixation duration increases substantially, with repeated returns to stability monitoring displays. Transcripts document self-directed questions progressing from "Did I miss something?" to "What if my whole approach needs rethinking?" This pattern supports sustained Reflection as metacognitive processing requires shifting attention to internal mental models [24].

Dialogue. Suppose during a collaborative session, interaction logs reveal structured turn-taking with balanced participation. Coded transcripts identify comparative statements like "Unlike my approach, the system prioritized..." Discourse analysis reveals instances where the engineer references peer contributions, building on others' ideas. These patterns indicate genuine Dialogue involving perspective exploration through interaction [17].

Action. Suppose upon re-entering the simulation, behavioral logs document a markedly different approach. The engineer exhibits deliberate pauses before interventions, with eye-tracking confirming that system data monitoring occurs during these pauses. Override attempts decrease substantially. This hypothesis-driven experimentation reflects testing new assumptions as experimentation requires strategy modification [12].

Integration. Suppose pattern stability analysis reveals a pause-monitor-act sequence appears consistently across multiple sessions, generalizing to novel autonomous systems. Post-training surveys document a substantial shift in trust measures. Cross-session consistency, adaptive transfer, and self-reported perspective change provide converging evidence of Integration reflecting consolidation and transfer [4,6].

Network analysis reveals patterns invisible to before-and-after assessment. Suppose analysis shows the engineer cycled between Reflection and Dialogue three times before progressing to Action. Reflection durations decreased across cycles, suggesting increasing cognitive efficiency as metacognitive processes become more automatized [8]. Dialogue content analysis reveals increasing sophistication across cycles. Physiological markers shift from arousal patterns to engaged interest patterns, aligning with findings linking repeated cycles with enhanced learning [15]. Network centrality analysis quantifies state importance, with hypothetical values indicating Reflection and Dialogue function as critical hubs, consistent with TLT's emphasis on these mechanisms [4,18]. The framework extends beyond VR. In adaptive learning systems, data streams could reveal how feedback creates disorientation, triggering reflection cycles. In collaborative platforms, discussion logs could model how dialogue contributes to transformation. In gamified contexts, challenge-failure-reflection-retry patterns could illuminate transformative pathways.

5 Discussion

This section examines how NTL addresses the research question by advancing both transformative learning theory and learning analytics. NTL addresses theoretical and methodological needs in transformative learning research. While TLT emphasizes critical reflection and discourse as transformation mechanisms [18], recent scholarship notes that how transformation unfolds over time has not been a central research question [16]. NTL offers a formal representation of transformation as a network structure unfolding over time. Centrality measures expose which states serve as critical junctures requiring pedagogical support. Recurrence patterns reveal progressive deepening, paralleling findings linking repeated self-monitoring with enhanced self-regulation [15]. Network density distinguishes exploratory transformation (high connectivity between diverse states) from constrained processes (low connectivity, repetitive loops). Sequencing analysis identifies common transformative routes informing instructional design. The framework maintains TLT's emphasis on reflection and discourse [9] while revealing how these processes evolve through repeated cycles. This temporal perspective enables questions like: What constitutes optimal reflection duration before action? How many cycles between reflection and dialogue typically precede successful action? Do different learners follow different pathways to transformation?

NTL advances Learning Analytics in three dimensions. First, it expands analytical focus from achievement metrics toward understanding deep transformation. Research shows better-performing learners display optimal behaviors over time [22]. NTL extends this by proposing that network patterns may predict fundamental perspective changes beyond performance gains. Second, it demonstrates that theory-grounded analytics illuminate deep processes that traditional assessments miss. Studies indicate sequence models predict learning more accurately than static models [13,14]. NTL connects theory with analytics by translating network concepts into educational constructs [3]. Third, it bridges qualitative theory with quantitative data. Understanding when patterns matter requires grounding analyses in concepts treating learning as unfolding through time [20]. NTL provides this grounding, positioning Learning Analytics as essential for understanding shifts in interpretive frameworks [19].

6 Limitations and Future Directions

This work presents several limitations. First, this contribution remains conceptual. NTL offers theoretical tools but requires empirical validation through automated detection, qualitative coding, triangulation, and longitudinal follow-up. Second, TLT addresses subjective experiences involving changes in personal reference frames. Patterns provide indicators, but verifying genuine transformation requires validation combining analysis with phenomenological interviews, narrative analysis, and discourse analysis. Third, defining learning states precisely for consistent identification presents methodological challenges requiring context-specific operational definitions, validated decision rules, empirical thresholds, and coding schemes blending automated detection with expert judgment. Fourth, applying the framework in real time for adaptive support presents technical and pedagogical challenges. Fifth, empirical studies should investigate parameters fostering transformation: optimal reflection duration, cycle frequency, and transition sequences.

7 Conclusion

This paper proposes NTL as a framework reconceptualizing transformation as a network of transitions through interconnected states. By integrating Mezirow's TLT with TNA, this framework makes explicit transformation's implicit networked structure, enabling systematic observation while respecting theoretical foundations and subjective dimensions. This work contributes to early efforts in formally conceptualizing transformative learning as a network of transitions, making its recursive structure empirically analyzable. The central contributions establish conceptual clarity regarding transformation as transitions between states, provide methodological transparency enabling systematic study, and establish foundations for measurement instruments. NTL advances understanding by representing transformation's recursive nature, accommodating pathway diversity while identifying common patterns, and enabling observation rendering visible dynamics typically hidden from traditional assessment. For Learning Analytics, this work demonstrates that analytical tools, when combined with educational framing and theoretical grounding, can address deep learning processes. While VR served as an illustrative context, NTL applies across diverse learning environments. Future empirical validation will test the framework's utility while refining operational definitions.

Acknowledgment. During preparation, the authors used ChatGPT and Claude (Anthropic) for grammar verification, paraphrasing, improving writing style, and organizing literature. After using these tools, the authors reviewed all content and assume full responsibility for it. The authors independently conducted all research findings, conceptual development, and final decisions.

Conflict of Interest. The authors declare that they have no conflict of interest.

References

1. Bailenson, J.N.: Experience on demand: What virtual reality is, how it works, and what it can do. W. W. Norton & Company, New York, NY (2018)
2. Cabrera-Duffaut, A., Pinto-Llorente, A.M., Iglesias-Rodríguez, A.: Immersive learning platforms: analyzing virtual reality contribution to competence development in higher education. Front. Educat. **9**, 1391560 (2024). https://doi.org/10.3389/feduc.2024.1391560
3. Chen, B., Poquet, O.: Networks in learning analytics: where theory, methodology, and practice intersect. J. Learn. Anal. **9**(1), 1–12 (2022). https://doi.org/10.18608/jla.2022.7697
4. Cranton, P.: Understanding and promoting transformative learning: a guide to theory and practice. Routledge (2016). https://doi.org/10.4324/9781003448433
5. Dirkx, J.M.: Transformative learning theory in the practice of adult education: an overview. PAACE J. Lifelong Learn. **7**, 1–14 (1998)
6. Ericsson, K.A., Lehmann, A.C.: Expert and exceptional performance: evidence of maximal adaptation to task constraints. Annu. Rev. Psychol. **47**(1), 273–305 (1996). https://doi.org/10.1146/annurev.psych.47.1.273
7. Festinger, L.: A theory of cognitive dissonance. Stanford University Press, Stanford, CA (1957)
8. Flavell, J.H.: Metacognition and cognitive monitoring: a new area of cognitive-developmental inquiry. Am. Psychol. **34**(10), 906 (1979). https://doi.org/10.1037/0003-066X.34.10.906
9. Holdo, M.: Critical reflection: John Dewey's relational view of transformative learning. J. Transform. Educ. **21**(1), 9–25 (2023). https://doi.org/10.1177/15413446221086727
10. Järvelä, S., Hadwin, A.F.: New frontiers: regulating learning in CSCL. Educat. Psych. **48**(1), 25–39 (2013). https://doi.org/10.1080/00461520.2012.748006
11. Knight, S., Wise, A.F., Chen, B.: Time for change: why learning analytics needs temporal analysis. J. Learn. Anal. **4**(3), 7–17 (2017). https://doi.org/10.18608/jla.2017.43.2
12. Kolb, D.A.: Experiential learning: Experience as the source of learning and development. FT Press, Upper Saddle River, NJ (2014)
13. Lämsä, J., Hämäläinen, R., Koskinen, P., Viiri, J., Lampi, E.: What do we do when we analyse the temporal aspects of computer-supported collaborative learning? A systematic literature review. Educ. Res. Rev. **33**, 100387 (2021). https://doi.org/10.1016/j.edurev.2021.100387
14. Mahzoon, M.J., Maher, M.L., Eltayeby, O., Dou, W., Grace, K.: A sequence data model for analyzing temporal patterns of student data. J. Learn. Anal. **5**(1), 55–74 (2018). https://doi.org/10.18608/jla.2018.51.5

15. Malmberg, J., Saqr, M., Järvenoja, H., Järvelä, S.: How the monitoring events of individual students are associated with phases of regulation: a network analysis approach. J. Learn. Anal. **9**(1), 77–92 (2022). https://doi.org/10.18608/jla.2022.7429
16. McClain, A.L.: New developments in transformative learning. New Direct. Adult Contin. Educat. **2024**(184), 20–29 (2024). https://doi.org/10.1002/ace.20540
17. Mercer, N.: Words and minds: how we use language to think together. Routledge (2002). https://doi.org/10.4324/9780203464984
18. Mezirow, J.: Transformative learning: theory to practice. New Direct. Adult Continu. Educat. **74**, 5–12 (1997). https://doi.org/10.1002/ace.7401
19. Mezirow, J.: Transformative Dimensions of Adult Learning. Jossey-Bass, San Francisco, CA (1991)
20. Molenaar, I., Wise, A.F.: Temporal aspects of learning analytics: grounding analyses in concepts of time. In: The Handbook of Learning Analytics, pp. 66–76. Society for Learning Analytics Research (2022). https://doi.org/10.18608/hla22.007
21. Reimann, P.: Time is precious: variable- and event-centred approaches to process analysis in CSCL research. Int. J. Comput.-Support. Collab. Learn. **4**(3), 239–257 (2009). https://doi.org/10.1007/s11412-009-9070-z
22. Saint, J., Gašević, D., Matcha, W., Uzir, N.A., Pardo, A.: Combining analytic methods to unlock sequential and temporal patterns of self-regulated learning. In: Proceedings of the Tenth International Conference on Learning Analytics & Knowledge, pp. 402–411 (2020). https://doi.org/10.1145/3375462.3375487
23. Saqr, M., López-Pernas, S., Törmänen, T., Kaliisa, R., Misiejuk, K., Tikka, S.: Transition network analysis: a novel framework for modeling, visualizing, and identifying the temporal patterns of learners and learning processes. In: Proceedings of the 15th International Learning Analytics and Knowledge Conference, pp. 351–361 (2025). https://doi.org/10.1145/3706468.3706513
24. Schön, D.A.: The Reflective Practitioner: How Professionals Think in Action. Routledge, London, UK (2017). https://doi.org/10.4324/9781315237473
25. Taylor, E.W.: An update of transformative learning theory: a critical review of the empirical research (1999–2005). Int. J. Lifelong Educ. **26**(2), 173–191 (2007). https://doi.org/10.1080/02601370701219475

Modelling Trajectories

Person-Specific Transition Network Analysis on Longitudinal Data with Change Point Detection

Hibiki Ito(✉)

Kyoto University, Kyoto, Japan
hibiki.itoo@gmail.com

Abstract. Learning processes are essentially complex, dynamic and heterogeneous. Transition Network Analysis (TNA) has emerged as a powerful method for modelling and visualising such learning processes. Additionally, the idiographic approach, which collects data from a single person and aims to provide person-specific insights, has gained growing attention as a solution to the heterogeneity of learners, complementing traditional between-person approaches. However, naively applying TNA, even with the idiographic approach, to longitudinal data fails to capture temporal nuances of individual processes, averaging over potentially significant changes in the process. To address this issue, we explore the potential of change point detection (CPD) to segment longitudinal data into meaningful phases, allowing for the application of TNA within each phase. Our approach is demonstrated as a secondary analysis of an idiographic study of master's thesis process using an ecological momentary assessment. The results highlight a critical role of CPD combined with TNA on longitudinal data, revealing more nuanced temporal dynamics of complex learning processes.

Keywords: Transition Network Analysis · Idiographic · Ecological Momentary Assessment · Change Point Detection

1 Introduction

Due to the recent advancement and adoption of digital technologies in education, supporting learning and educational activities by data- and evidence-driven approaches has been a key area of research. However, despite the expanding empirical research and theoretical development, predominant approaches that investigate causal factors and aim to make interventions have failed to offer such evidence that is effectively applicable across contexts due to the complex and dynamic nature of learning [4,10]. In addition, traditional between-person, nomothetic methods that aim to infer group-level insights fail to capture individual processes due to the inherent heterogeneity of learners [2]. To overcome these issues, it is essential to develop and apply appropriate computational techniques tailored to analysing learning processes. Recently, the complex dynamic

M. Saqr et al. (Eds.): TNA 2026, CCIS 3079, pp. 89–98, 2026.
https://doi.org/10.1007/978-3-032-34157-0_7

systems (CDS) approach has emerged as a key framework, which views learning processes as non-linear, dynamic and evolving systems [10]. For example, there has been evidence that CDS can effectively be applied to second language learning [5] and self-regulated learning (SRL) [9]. Additionally, to address the issue of learner heterogeneity, the person-specific, idiographic approach has also gained growing attention for analysing individual learning processes [11]. In contrast to traditional between-person methods, an idiographic approach collects data from a single learner and aims to derive person-specific insights [12].

While growing computational tools and techniques are available for the CDS and idiographic approach, adoption of existing methods to educational contexts requires careful testing and implementation, as sharing the CDS and heterogeneity principles does not necessarily imply common characteristics of the systems in different contexts [7]. In the realm of education, transition network analysis (TNA)—the focus of this paper—has emerged as a powerful method for modelling learning processes via the lens of CDS [13,14]. TNA models and visualises complex and dynamic learning processes as first-order Markov models and offers validation methods for strengthening the robustness of the models [16]. It has been extended to frequency-based TNA which addresses the small sample problem typical in the education domain and the potentially strong assumption of Markov models [15]. However, a recent work by Ito [6] applied TNA for the idiographic case study of master's thesis process and found that naively operationalising TNA on longitudinal data can fail to capture nuanced temporal changes. That is, the transition network of the entire period of a certain length averages over potentially significant dynamics of the process. Thus, TNA would need to be combined with other techniques that address long-term changes in such a context as master's thesis work where the learning process becomes very longitudinal.

To address this issue, this paper explores the potential of change point detection (CPD), which offers computational methods to segment longitudinal data into meaningful phases. This allows for applying TNA in a potentially more effective way. In particular, we focus on multivariate CPD to capture higher-dimensional structure, which is more complex and typically difficult to observe without quantitative techniques. We demonstrate this approach as a secondary analysis of the above-mentioned idiographic study by Ito [6]. While Ito [6] provides a method to split the longitudinal time series by daily activity profiles derived from web trace data, it results in multiple phases split across the entire period, the data still remaining longitudinal. In contrast, we offer an alternative technique that segments the time series into phases of consecutive time points. Our secondary analysis reveals more nuanced temporal dynamics of master's thesis work of the student, including some aspects missing in Ito [6]. These results highlight the critical role of CPD combined with TNA in such a longitudinal context.

2 Methods

We employ the ecological momentary assessment (EMA) dataset used in Ito [6][1]. While Ito [6] uses trace data from a smartwatch and web browser, we focus on EMA survey variables, which are directly related to learning, for the purpose of methodological demonstration. The data were collected from a student (N=1) during his/her master's thesis writing over approximately half a year (see Ito [6] for more details of data collection). As a secondary analysis of the work, we set the following research question as a guide for analysis:

RQ: How do the temporal dynamics of the learning process differ across phases?

Following the same procedure as in Ito [6], EMA variables are first reduced to five key variables: anxiety, attraction, commitment, regulation and support. Then we applied kernel-based CPD on running means of the multivariate time series using the `kcpRS` package in R [3]. The kernel-based method allows for capturing non-linear multivariate structure in data, which is otherwise not observable by simply plotting the time series [1]. In addition, running means calculated by sliding a window across time series are used instead of raw data to focus on stable trends in running means rather than transient spikes [3].

After that, while Ito [6] conducted linear detrending separately on each variable, we applied k-means clustering on the raw data without detrending in order to incorporate global multivariate trends. The learning states (i.e. the identified clusters) are then passed to TNA, revealing the temporal changes within each phase. A centrality analysis and a mosaic plot of the transition networks allow us to compare and characterise the phases.

3 Results

3.1 Identifying Phases

First, distinct phases of consecutive time points of the multivariate time series are identified by the kernel-based CPD on running means over the entire period (see Fig. 1). Notice that the plot shows running means over a sliding window of 20 time steps, rather than raw data, showing clearer trends. Two change points are identified at $t = 150$ and $t = 247$, where the temporal structure of multivariate time sereis changes. These points belong to the prior phase as the final point of that phase. It should be noted that, although, for example, phase 1 and phase 3 of commitment have similar means, this does not imply that these phases can be characterised similarly. Each phase is featured by the multivariate structure rather than by each variable, which is typically more complex and often hard to qualitatively observe.

[1] Available at https://hibiki-i.github.io/idiographicTNA/.

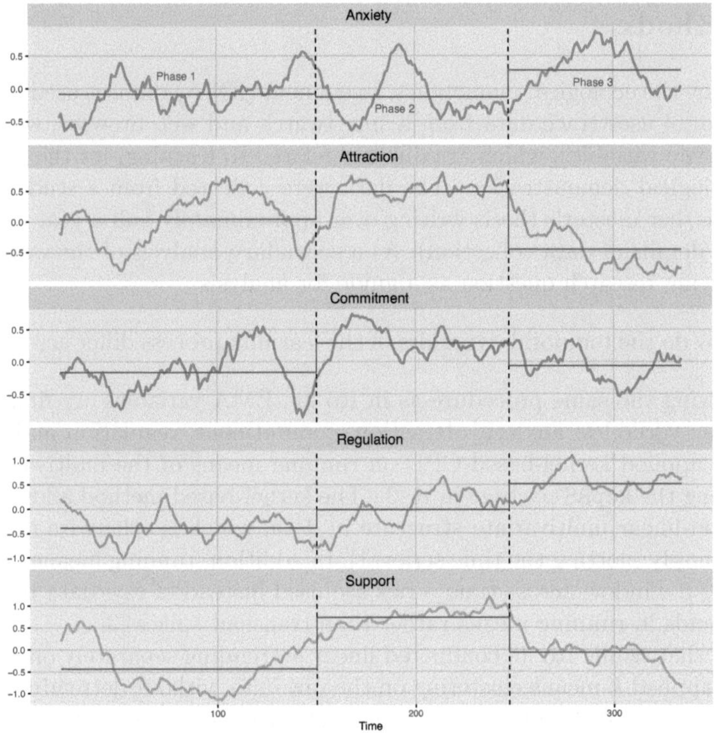

Fig. 1. The running means of the five variables. Vertical black dashes indicate change points ($t = 150, 247$) which segment time series into three phases. The average values of each phase are shown by red lines. (Color figure online)

3.2 Identifying States

Subsequently, multiple learning states of the whole thesis writing process are identified by k-means clustering on the raw records. Figure 2 shows the elbow plot, according to which we choose $k = 4$ for distinct states. Figure 3 visualises the characteristics of the identified states by a parallel coordinates plot. Based on this, we label the states as *crunching* (`Crunch`: high anxiety, yet high commitment and regulation), *thriving* (`Thriving`: low anxiety, high positive constructs), *autonomous* (`Auto`: low anxiety, low support yet high attraction) and *struggling* (`Strug`: high anxiety, and low positive constructs).

3.3 Answering RQ

Now that we have identified phases and states, we apply TNA to the learning states for each phase and inspect different temporal dynamics, aiming to answer the RQ. Figure 4 shows the transition networks estimated for each phase separately. We observe different patterns across phases: For phase 1, while the thriving, struggling and autonomous states have a strong self-loop, the autonomous

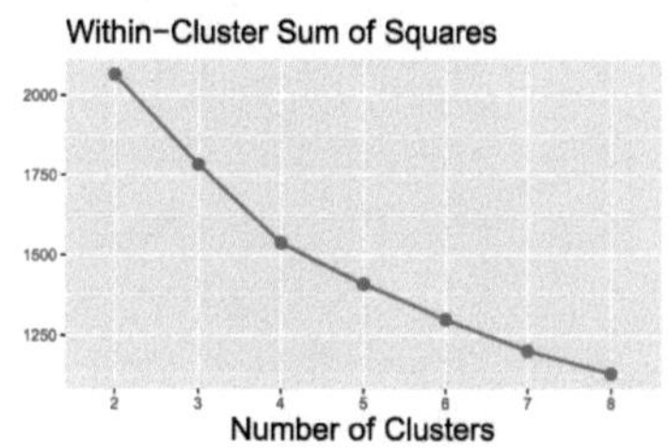

Fig. 2. Elbow plot of k-means clustering over the EMA records with the five variables.

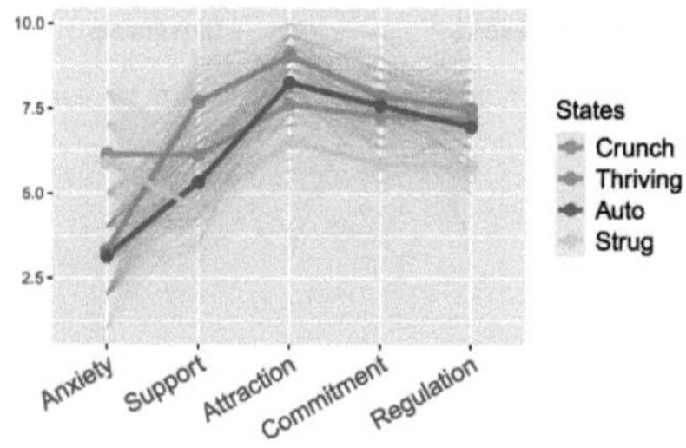

Fig. 3. Parallel coordinates plot of the states (clusters). Markers connected by solid lines indicate the means of each state.

entails stronger incoming transitions, suggesting that the student often slipped back into independent, self-directed work with consistent difficulty rather than pushing forward into highly engaged flow. The network for phase 2 does not seem to exhibit very clear characteristics except for a strong self-loop of the thriving state, indicating that phase 2 is featured by relatively stable engagement. The final phase, on the other hand, shows a strong self-loop of the crunching state with also stronger incoming flows from all the other states, implying that the crunching state worked as an attractor. That is, the student relied on pressure-activated productivity towards the completion of the thesis work.

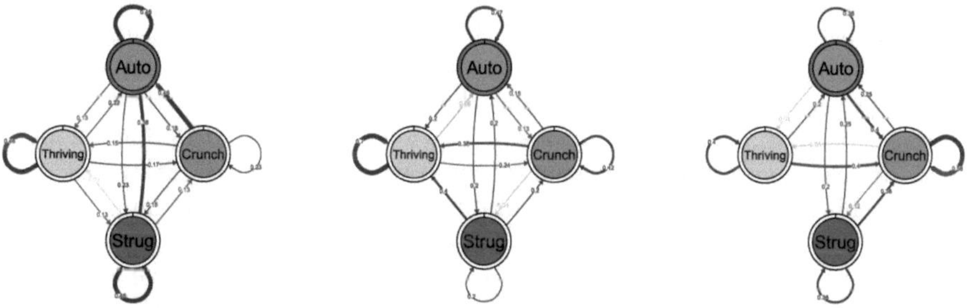

Fig. 4. Transition networks of learning states for phase 1 (left), phase 2 (centre) and phase 3 (right). Each node is a learning state identified by clustering EMA data, and each directed edge indicates a transition between the states based on the estimated Markov models with the edge width being proportional to the transition probability.

The above observations are confirmed and complemented by the centrality analysis. In Fig. 5, the betweennes centrality based on randomised shortest paths (`BetweennessRSP`) [8] indicates how likely the student passes the state when moving on to other learning states, and closeness centrality indicates how flexibly the student can shift out of the state into other states. During the initial phase, the autonomous, independent work acts as a key atractor, indicated by a high

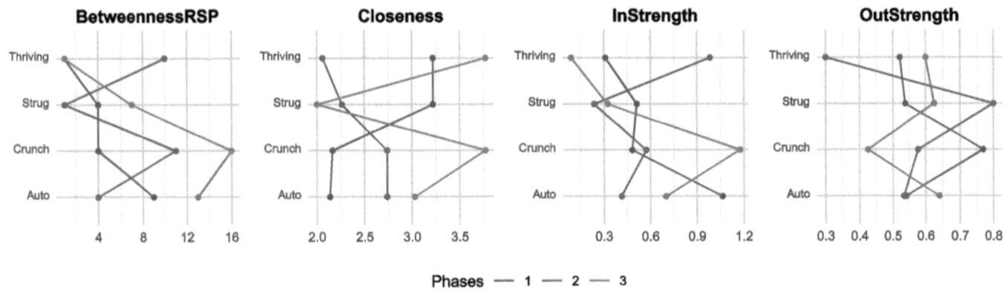

Fig. 5. Centralities of each state in the transition networks for each phase.

betweenness centrality and high in-strength (`InStrength`). For phase 2 and 3, the thriving and crunching states show high in-strength, implying that they are attractors in these phases, respectively. However, while the thriving state in phase 2 exhibits a low closeness centrality and out-strength, the crunching state in phase 3 shows a contrastively high closeness and higher out-strength. This means that the student was frequently pulled into the thriving state and often remained engaged during the middle phase, while he/she often oscillated between the pressure-intensive state and other states in the final phase.

Additionally, we examine the frequencies of the learning states in each phase. Figure 6 shows a mosaic plot for the contingency table of state frequencies. The standardised residual indicates dominance of the state in the phase relative to the expectation conditioned on the independence of phases and states. The Chi-squared test confirms that different phases entail significantly different state distributions ($\chi^2_6 = 90.7, p \leq 2 \cdot 10^{-16}$). In particular, struggling and autonomous states are over-represented while thriving and crunching states are under-represented in phase 1, aligning the previous observation that the initial phase poses difficulty and uncertainty with less support. Also, phase 2 and 3 are, as discussed above, strongly characterised by the over-representated thriving and crunching states, respectively. Notably, the thriving state is highly under-represented in the final phase, implying the last-minute pressure.

To summarise, the student moved through three distinct modes of working in master's thesis process. The initial phase, which is slightly longer than the subsequent phases, is marked by frequent struggles and tendency to fall back into independent, autonomous work, suggesting the initial uncertainty and a potential need for more support. On the other hand, the subsequent phase exhibits the dominant thriving mode with less anxiety and higher support and engagement. The final phase clearly shows a tendency towards the pressure-intensive, crunching state with oscillation with other states, potentially reflecting deadline-activated productivity rather than steady engagement.

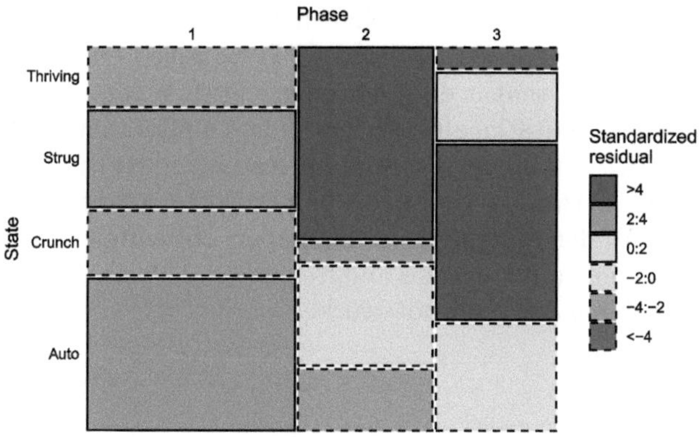

Fig. 6. Mosaic plot of the state frequencies for each phase. The standardised residual indicates dominance of the state in the phase relative to the expectation conditioned on the independence of phases and states.

4 Discussion

Learning is essentially complex, dynamic and inherently heterogeneous [2,10]. TNA allows for revealing complex temporal dynamics of learning, but its effectiveness remains limited when applied to longitudinal data, even with the idiographic approach [6]. To tackle this issue, this paper has explored the potential of CPD for segmenting time series into meaningful phases. Particularly, we focused on CPD of multivariate time series to capture higher dimensional structure of the complex system, which is typically difficult to observe without computational methods.

In the case study, carefully analysing the phases identified by the kernel-based CPD, we observed different temporal dynamics across phases: the student began thesis work through mostly independent but often struggling efforts, then moved into a period of sustained productive engagement with more support, and finally shifted towards pressure-driven work to complete the thesis. Here we derived a somewhat different picture of the student's thesis process than that of Ito [6], which focused on intra- and inter-day temporal dynamics conditioned on the web activity. Notably, our approach allowed us to derive a more fluent and connected story of the dynamic learning processes over the entire thesis work, in contrast to the prior work which focused on each *component* of the process (i.e. daily web activity profiles). Thus, our method aligns better with the view of CDS and also provides more holistic, potentially effective insights. For instance, the student may need more initial support so that he/she could move to a sustained productive phase earlier. In addition, the student would also need support for a more refined planning strategy so that the productive period is protected and reinforced to maintain stability without being too stressed by the deadline. These person-specific insights would not have been derived by TNA or CPD alone.

Our approach, nonetheless, faces challenges towards real-world deployment of data-driven support. The kernel-based CPD we relied on in this study is an offline method, meaning that it does not offer real-time detection. More work is needed to develop computationally efficient online multivariate techniques when implementing analytics systems that support learners in real time. Careful TNA, not just visualising networks, would also be needed to compare and understand different phases. As demonstrated in this paper, this often requires advanced techniques such as centrality analysis and frequency analysis. Thus, making these steps more accessible is left to future work.

5 Conclusion

Although TNA is a powerful tool for understanding learning processes through a lens of CDS and the idiographic approach offers a promising solution to learner heterogeneity, the combined approach still fails to capture some temporal changes in a longitudinal context. To overcome this challenge, we combined multivariate CPD with TNA and demonstrated its effectiveness through a secondary analysis of an idiographic case study of master's thesis writing, disclosing more nuanced temporal dynamics of the longitudinal process.

Acknowledgement. This work was supported by JSPS KAKENHI Grant Number 25KJ1515.

References

1. Arlot, S., Celisse, A., Harchaoui, Z.: A kernel multiple change-point algorithm via model selection. J. Mach. Learn. Res.: JMLR **20**(162), 1–56 (2019). https://jmlr.org/papers/v20/16-155.html
2. Bryan, C.J., Tipton, E., Yeager, D.S.: Behavioural science is unlikely to change the world without a heterogeneity revolution. Nat. Hum. Behav. **5**(8), 980–989 (2021). https://doi.org/10.1038/s41562-021-01143-3
3. Cabrieto, J., Meers, K., Schat, E., Adolf, J., Kuppens, P., Tuerlinckx, F., Ceulemans, E.:: An R Package for performing kernel change point detection on the running statistics of multivariate time series. Behav. Res. Methods 1–22 (2021). https://doi.org/10.3758/s13428-021-01603-8
4. Hilpert, J.C., Marchand, G.C.: Complex systems research in educational psychology: aligning theory and method. Educat. Psychol. **53**(3), 185–202 (2018). https://doi.org/10.1080/00461520.2018.1469411
5. Hiver, P., Al-Hoorie, A.H., Evans, R.: Complex dynamic systems theory in language learning: a scoping review of 25 years of research. Stud. Second. Lang. Acquis. **44**(4), 913–941 (2022). https://doi.org/10.1017/s0272263121000553
6. Ito, H.: Exploring idiographic learning analytics in master's thesis writing: a transition network approach. In: The Proceedings of the 9th International Conference on Smart Learning Environments (2025) ICSLE 2025
7. Kaplan, A., Garner, J.K.: Steps for applying the complex dynamical systems approach in educational research: a guide for the perplexed scholar. J. Exper. Educat. **88**(3), 486–502 (2020). https://doi.org/10.1080/00220973.2020.1745738

8. Kivimäki, I., Lebichot, B., Saramäki, J., Saerens, M.: Two betweenness centrality measures based on randomized shortest paths. Sci. Rep. **6**(1), 19668 (2016). https://doi.org/10.1038/srep19668
9. López-Pernas, S., Conde, M.A., Saqr, M.: Three shades of self-regulation with unique complex dynamics, drivers and targets for intervention. British journal of educational technology: journal of the Council for Educational Technology (bjet.70032) (2025). https://doi.org/10.1111/bjet.70032
10. Saqr, M., Dever, D., López-Pernas, S., Gernigon, C., Marchand, G., Kaplan, A.: Complex dynamic systems in education: beyond the static, the linear and the causal reductionism. In: Advanced Learning Analytics Methods, pp. 289–311. Springer Nature Switzerland (2026). https://doi.org/10.1007/978-3-031-95365-1_12
11. Saqr, M., Ito, H., López-Pernas, S.: Individualized analytics: within-person and idiographic analysis. In: Advanced Learning Analytics Methods, pp. 471–491. Springer Nature Switzerland (2026). https://doi.org/10.1007/978-3-031-95365-1_18
12. Saqr, M., Lopez-Pernas, S.: Idiographic learning analytics: a definition and a case study. In: 2021 International Conference on Advanced Learning Technologies (ICALT), pp. 163–165. IEEE (2021). https://doi.org/10.1109/icalt52272.2021.00056
13. Saqr, M., López-Pernas, S., Tikka, S.: Mapping relational dynamics with transition network analysis: a primer and tutorial. In: Advanced Learning Analytics Methods, pp. 371–411. Springer Nature Switzerland (2026). https://doi.org/10.1007/978-3-031-95365-1_15
14. Saqr, M., López-Pernas, S., Törmänen, T., Kaliisa, R., Misiejuk, K., Tikka, S.: Transition network analysis: a novel framework for modeling, visualizing, and identifying the temporal patterns of learners and learning processes. In: Proceedings of the 15th International Learning Analytics and Knowledge Conference, pp. 351–361. ACM (2025). https://doi.org/10.1145/3706468.3706513
15. Saqr, M., Misiejuk, K., Törmänen, T., Kaliisa, R., Tikka, S., López-Pernas, S.: Frequency transition network analysis (FTNA). In: Proceedings of the International Conference on Computer-supported for Collaborative Learning, pp. 276–280. International Society of the Learning Sciences (2025). https://doi.org/10.22318/cscl2025.901997
16. Tikka, S., López-Pernas, S., Saqr, M.: Tna: an R package for transition network analysis. Appl. Psychol. Meas. **49**(6), 01466216251348840 (2025). https://doi.org/10.1177/01466216251348840

Sequence Vs Transition Network Analysis: Complementary Insights Into Students' Learning Patterns

Yaroslav Opanasenko(✉) and Margus Pedaste

University of Tartu, 18 Ülikooli St, Tartu 50090, Estonia
yaroslav.opanasenko@ut.ee, margus.pedaste@ut.ee

Abstract. Digital learning environments generate increasingly rich behavioral data, yet methodological approaches for analyzing students' temporal learning patterns often remain fragmented. This study compares two complementary techniques—sequence analysis and transition network analysis to examine what distinct insights they offer when applied to the same log-data. Using interaction data from 176 sixth-grade students and 160 homework sessions in a digital textbook environment, we constructed two analytical layers: (1) monthly engagement sequences throughout the school year and (2) within-session activity sequences during a mandatory homework task. Sequence Analysis (SA) was used to visualize how individual trajectories unfold over time across the school year, revealing stable early-year engagement profiles and long-term patterns such as sustained high activity or irregular late-year disengagement. Transition Network Analysis (TNA), in turn, modeled behavior as a probabilistic transition system of moving from one state or activity to another, highlighting structures that SA alone could not capture—such as the stability of high-engagement states, fragile transitions between moderate and low usage, and typical preparatory pathways within sessions (e.g., Video → Gallery → Test or Surfing → Reading → Test). Together, the two methods provide complementary perspectives: SA captures duration, rhythm, and overall trajectory, while TNA identifies strategic micro-patterns and dominant behavioral pathways. The study demonstrates that combining SA and TNA yields a more nuanced, multilayered understanding of students' learning behavior—an increasingly important direction for learning analytics in the era of AI-supported education.

Keywords: Sequence Analysis · Transition Network Analysis · Interactive E-Books

1 Introduction

Over recent decades, DLEs have become increasingly interactive, adaptive, and complex. Empirical studies have documented their benefits across a range of outcomes, including increased engagement [9], improved learning achievement [6],

M. Saqr et al. (Eds.): TNA 2026, CCIS 3079, pp. 99–113, 2026.
https://doi.org/10.1007/978-3-032-34157-0_8

enhanced peer communication [17], metacognitive awareness [25], reading proficiency [2], and learner motivation [27]. However, this expansion has also revealed potential drawbacks, such as increased cognitive load [23] and heightened feelings of isolation [7]. Given the high degree of flexibility and interactivity in DLEs, the quality of student interaction varies considerably, influencing learning outcomes in uneven ways [3]. A growing concern is that many learners may not possess the agency or self-regulatory capacity required to fully exploit the opportunities offered by digital systems [14]. Even with rich interactive affordances, students frequently use digital resources in narrow or suboptimal ways [19]. Therefore, understanding the strategies that students employ in DLEs becomes as important as understanding the environments themselves. Yet, as Kinnebrew, Segedy and Biswas [13] note, identifying learning patterns is "not trivial", because such patterns are often procedural, tacit, and difficult for learners to articulate—even retrospectively.

Data mining methods allow researchers to work with large volumes of fine-grained interaction logs to uncover hidden patterns, regularities, and structural relationships between learner actions over time [20]. Digital learning environments generate rich temporal traces of student behavior, ranging from coarse-grained indicators of long-term engagement to fine-grained interaction patterns within individual learning sessions. These temporally ordered log data provide a unique opportunity to study how students navigate digital resources, how learning actions unfold over time, and how different behavioral trajectories relate to performance and engagement. However, despite the growing use of learning analytics techniques, studies often rely on a single analytical lens, making it difficult to capture both long-term trajectories and local transition structures within the same behavioral data.

Sequence analysis provides a holistic, longitudinal approach to modelling categorical temporal data by treating entire trajectories as analytical units and comparing them through dissimilarity measures such as optimal matching, followed by clustering to uncover typical behavioral patterns [1,18]. Originally developed in the social sciences to analyze life-course processes, it has recently gained momentum in learning analytics, where studies increasingly use sequence typologies to identify patterns of procrastination [24], content navigation [10], test-taking [16] and many others. Sequence analysis captures the entire temporal structure of a learning process by representing behavior as complete trajectories, allowing researchers to examine how actions unfold and change over time as a coherent whole; in contrast, transition network analysis models learning as a Markovian process and represents transitions as a directed, weighted network, enabling the examination of micro-level contingencies, centralities, community structures and statistically validated transition pathways that reveal the dynamic relationships between learning events [21]. By integrating stochastic process modelling with probabilistic graph representation, transition network analysis offers additional analytical capabilities such as significance testing of edges, pattern mining (dyads, cliques), and community detection, which provide a richer understanding of how local transitions accumulate into broader behavioral structures.

A comparison of these two complementary approaches is therefore needed to clarify what types of behavioral information each method reveals and what may remain invisible when only one method is applied.

RQ1. What distinct insights into students' learning behavior are revealed by sequence analysis versus transition network analysis when applied to the same data?

2 Methodology

In this study we collected data from a collection of E-Books called Opiq. Opiq is a cloud-based digital learning environment that provides access to a large collection of interactive E-Books published by multiple Estonian educational publishers. The platform currently hosts more than 480 E-Books in Opiq, covering most school subjects across preschool, basic and upper-secondary education. Due to contributions from 16 different publishers and content providers, the structure and level of interactivity of the E-Books vary considerably. The environment supports a wide range of learning interactions, including reading chapters, navigating slides, watching embedded videos, opening galleries, completing exercises and taking tests, each recorded with detailed log events related to checking, saving and correcting task results. An example of an interactive page of Opiq is presented in Fig. 1.

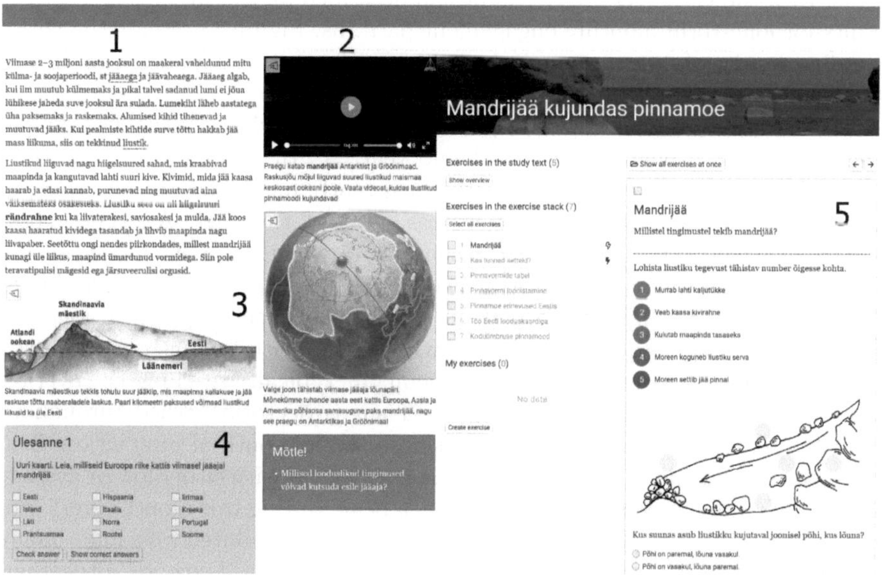

Fig. 1. Example of activities in Opiq 1. Reading 2. Video 3. Gallery 4. Exercise 5. Test.

To analyze temporal patterns across the school year, we constructed equal-length monthly sequences for 176 6th grade students by calculating the average amount of time spent in the environment for each month and assigning one of four states—No interaction, Lower than average, Average, or Higher than average—based on whether a student's monthly usage fell below, within, or above the range of ($M \pm 1$ SD). For within-session patterns, we used 160 homework sessions from a 6th grade Nature Science chapter and transformed event logs into minute-level sequences of unequal length, assigning to each minute the dominant activity (Reading, Surfing, Exercise, Video, Gallery, TextToSpeech, Test) based on the event occupying most of that minute, while minutes after the end of the session were coded as None. Because minute-level data produces extensive repetition of identical states, the transition network analysis used a different representation: instead of minutes, we modelled sequences at the level of activities, collapsing consecutive identical actions into a single state unless they referred to different content elements (e.g., different videos or exercises). Repeated attempts on the same exercise were treated as a continuous Exercise state, ensuring that the transition model captured meaningful shifts between pedagogically relevant activities rather than technical repetitions. Sessions were defined using a 15-minute inactivity threshold between consecutive actions, a commonly adopted criterion in learning analytics research to delineate meaningful units of interaction (e.g., Gasevic, 2022).

3 Results

In line with the two-layer analytical design described above, we first present the results for long-term monthly engagement patterns. Figure 2 presents the corresponding results of sequence analysis and transition network analysis applied to this temporal layer.

To begin, we examine the index plot illustrating individual sequences of Opiq usage intensity throughout the academic year. As the visualization shows, a group of students started the year with consistently high (higher-than-average) engagement, maintaining this level across most of the year. Another subset showed high activity every month except June, when engagement across the cohort was generally rare. Students who began the year at an average intensity level tended to maintain it and, in some cases, eventually transitioned to higher-than-average engagement. Those who started with low activity increased their engagement around October or November—typically reaching the average level and only occasionally surpassing it. Their trajectories varied throughout the year, yet the vast majority did not skip a single month of interaction. Students who missed one or two initial months later joined with either low or average intensity. Notably, November stands out as a peak: during this month, every student used the platform. Following this peak, the group exhibited a decline—many shifted to lower activity or temporarily stopped using the textbook altogether. In the second half of the year, usage became irregular and intermittent, with low activity alternating with complete inactivity.

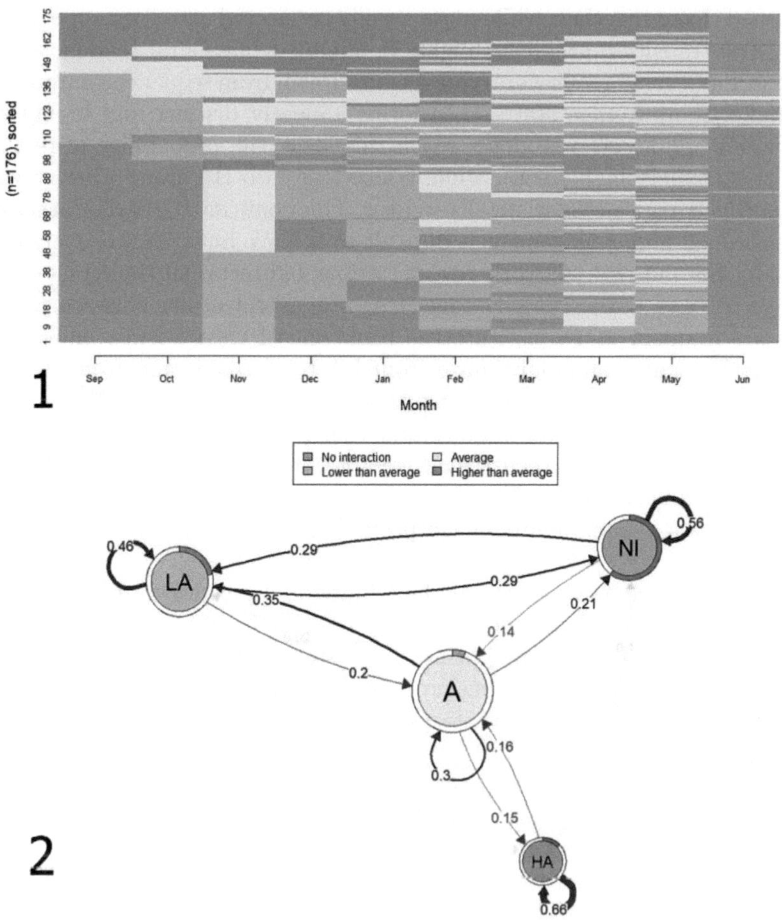

Fig. 2. Results of sequence analysis (1) and transition network analysis (2) applied to the temporal data.

Overall, sequence analysis made it possible to group students according to their early-year engagement intensity, trace their trajectories across the entire year, and identify overarching trends. The patterns suggest that active textbook use at the beginning of the year enables students to sustain higher levels of engagement throughout. In contrast, a delayed start is often accompanied by a "catch-up" strategy which, when too intense, may lead to a subsequent decline in activity. Moreover, achieving consistently high engagement becomes considerably more difficult for students who miss the initial months of use.

The transition network analysis provides a complementary perspective by modelling monthly engagement as a system of transition probabilities rather than individual trajectories. The distances between nodes are produced by the force-directed layout: activities with stronger or more frequent transitions are positioned closer together, while more weakly connected activities appear farther apart. The transition graph highlights dominant behavioural tendencies across the cohort and reinforces several conclusions drawn from sequence analysis. First, the Higher-than-average state (HA) forms a clearly distinct and highly stable behavioural mode: once students reach this level, the probability of remaining there is extremely high (0.66), while transitions into HA from other states are comparatively rare and statistically weaker. This confirms the earlier observation that sustained high engagement is difficult to achieve but comparatively easy to maintain. Second, the network reveals strong bidirectional dynamics between Average (A) and Lower-than-average (LA) usage: transitions between these two states are frequent and constitute the backbone of the system's monthly fluctuations. Students commonly move from LA to A (0.35) and from A back to LA (0.29), suggesting a flexible but unstable engagement zone where moderate users oscillate between maintaining and losing momentum. Finally, No interaction (NI) emerges as a recurrent attractor with a strong self-loop (0.56) and notable incoming transitions from both A and LA, indicating that disengagement is a realistic and common outcome, especially during periods when students lose consistency.

While sequence analysis reveals how individual pathways unfold over time, transition network analysis uncovers the probabilistic architecture within which these pathways emerge—highlighting stable states, fragile transitions, and critical vulnerabilities in the learning process. Together, these insights can be valuable for designing timely interventions: for example, supporting students before they slip into the LA→NI pathway, or creating conditions that increase the likelihood of transitions toward the HA state. Alongside the global transition map (and the overall sequence index plot in the case of sequence analysis), the strengths of each method can be further enhanced through more fine-grained analytical procedures. In the case of transition network analysis, this includes the extraction of cliques—tightly connected groups of interaction nodes—which allows the identification of stable dyadic, triadic, or higher-order relationships between activities. Building on the global transition structure, we further examined the network using in-strength centrality and clique analysis to identify the most structurally central states and the presence of tightly connected interaction patterns (see Fig. 3). In-strength centrality provides insight into which states function as primary "attractors" within the system—that is, states toward which transitions most frequently converge. The results indicate that the Lower-than-average (LA) state exhibits the highest in-strength, followed by both Average (A) and No interaction (NI), while Higher-than-average (HA) remains comparatively peripheral in terms of incoming transitions. From a methodological perspective, this suggests that LA represents the most dynamically accessible region of the engagement space: it is the state most frequently reached from other levels of activity and therefore plays a central role in structuring overall behaviour. In the context of interaction with electronic textbooks, this finding indicates that the Lower-than-average (LA) state functions not merely as a low-performance category, but as a commonly reached transitional condition. Students tend to enter this state from both higher and average levels of engagement, suggesting that downward shifts in activity occur more frequently and with less resistance than upward transitions.

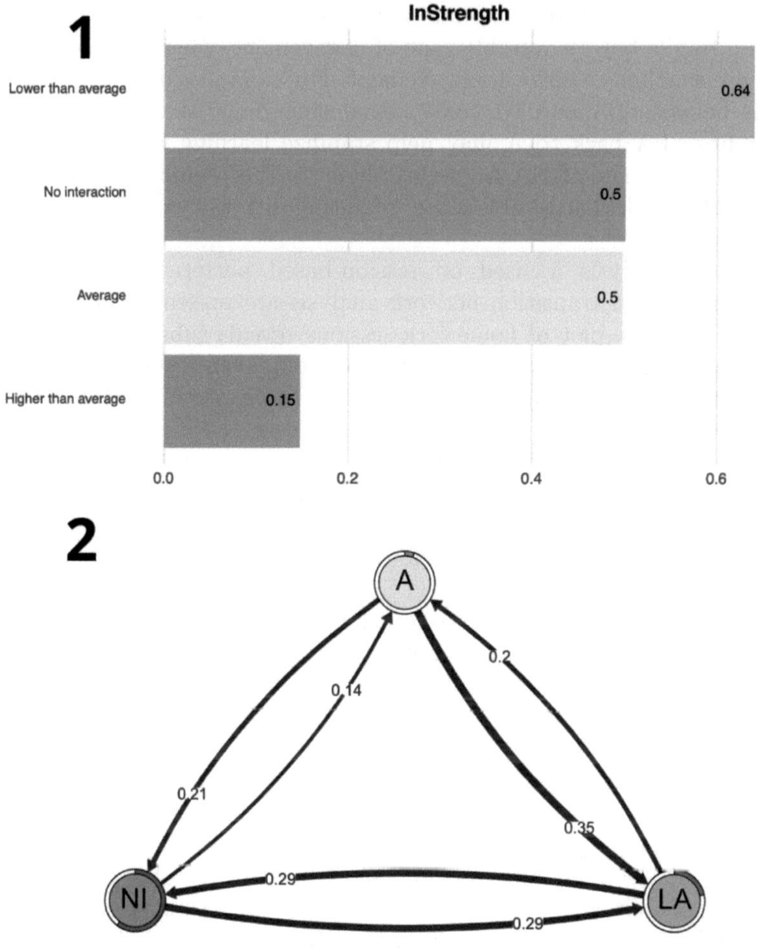

Fig. 3. (1) Detected triangles (threshold = >0.1) of transitions (2) InStrength centrality.

To complement this perspective, clique analysis was applied to identify densely connected subsets of states representing stable micro-structures within the transition network. Using a threshold of 0.1, a single triadic clique was identified, consisting of Average (A), Lower-than-average (LA), and No interaction (NI). This triadic configuration can be interpreted as a core behavioural loop that underlies much of the observed variability in student engagement. Rather than progressing linearly, students appear to move cyclically between moderate engagement (A), declining activity (LA), and temporary disengagement (NI). The bidirectional nature of these transitions suggests that this process is reversible: students not only fall into inactivity but can also return from it, often passing through LA and A as intermediate stages. The A–LA–NI structure represents a fragile but recoverable zone of engagement, where timely intervention may prevent longer-term disengagement. For example, detecting repeated transitions between LA and NI could signal emerging risk, while facilitating movement from LA back to A may help stabilize learning behaviour. At the same time, the absence of HA from this clique further emphasizes its distinct role as a stable but less accessible state, requiring different conditions for entry and maintenance.

The second analysis focused on session-based patterns. The results of sequence analysis and transition network analysis are presented in Fig. 3. The minute-level sequence plot of homework sessions reveals substantial variability in how students structure their work with the Opiq, even when completing the same mandatory teacher-assigned test. Despite this diversity, several consistent patterns emerge (Fig. 4).

First, test-related activity (green) occupies a central role for most learners: in many sessions it appears early and dominates long stretches of activity, suggesting that large numbers of students approach homework with a clear performance-oriented focus. Second, before, after, or between test attempts, students frequently engage in Reading and Surfing, indicating that many learners rely on the chapter's textual content or quick navigation to locate relevant information while preparing for or correcting their test answers. The presence of different multimedia interactions, although less frequent—shows that a notable subset of students complement reading with multimodal exploration, possibly seeking conceptual clarification or visual cues to support task completion. The plot also highlights characteristic behavioral differences across sessions. Some students show long, uninterrupted reading phases before attempting the test, reflecting a more preparation-driven strategy. Others enter the test quickly and then alternate between test attempts and short bursts of reading or multimedia use, indicative of an iterative trial-and-repair approach. A smaller group exhibits very short or fragmented sessions, relying heavily on rapid navigation (Surfing), which may signal less strategic engagement.

Transition network analysis of activities revealed several very interesting insights.

First, the analysis shows that Exercises, although originally designed as a preparation tool, rarely lead directly to the mandatory Test. Instead, Exercise sessions exhibit a high level of self-loops, indicating that students often remain within the exercise environment, attempting multiple practice items consecutively. This suggests that many learners perceive exercises as a standalone activity rather than an intentional bridge toward assessment. Pedagogically, this

1

2

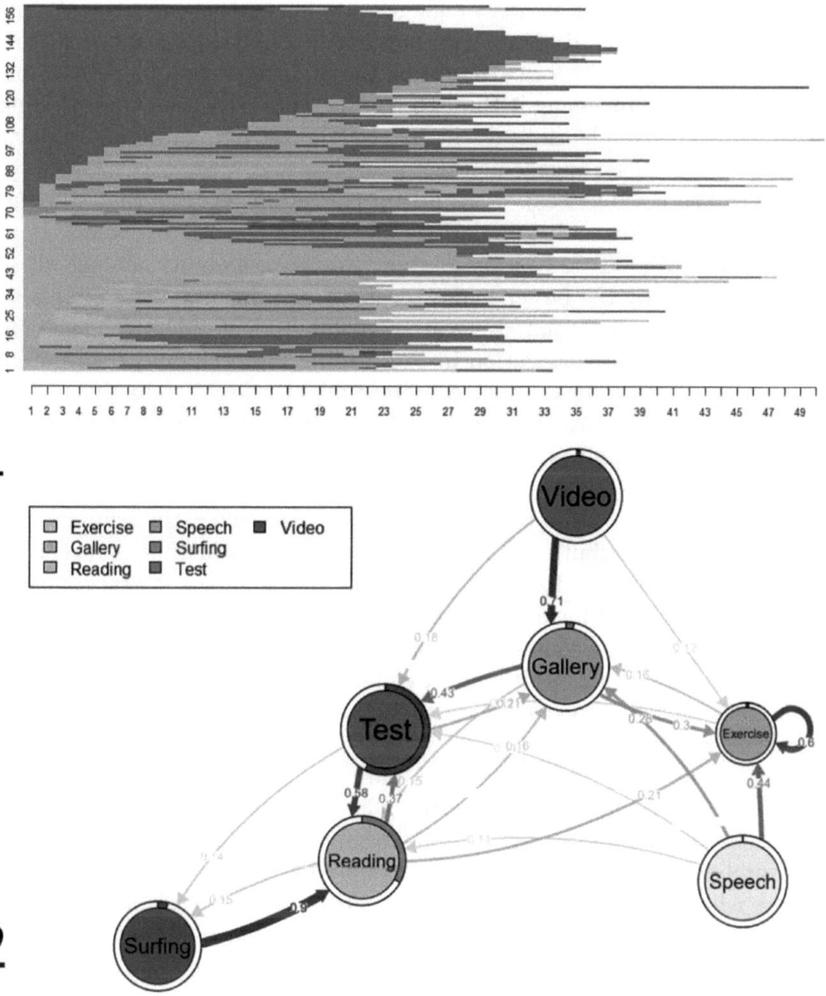

Fig. 4. Results of sequence analysis (1) and transition network analysis (2) applied to the session-based data.

points to the need for clearer scaffolding or guidance on how to transfer practice into test-taking strategies.

Second, the network reveals a strong multimodal preparation pathway: **Video → Gallery → Test**. The particularly strong transition from Video to Gallery indicates that multimedia content draws students into exploring visuals, diagrams, or interactive representations before moving on to the test. This highlights one of the dominant strategies used by students—leveraging rich media to reinforce conceptual understanding prior to assessment.

A second preparation strategy emerges through textual engagement: **Surfing → Reading → Test**. Students who begin with rapid navigation tend to settle into reading materials before attempting the test, showing a pattern of locating relevant content, processing it through reading, and only then transitioning into assessment. This might indicate intentional knowledge gathering rather than guessing or superficial engagement.

Finally, the notable **Test → Reading** transition suggests that students frequently return to textual explanations after encountering test items. It should also be noted that Test has the highest initial probability among all activities, as reflected by the larger node size in the transition network. This behavior aligns with a self-regulated repair strategy: students identify gaps or errors during the test, seek clarification in the reading material, and then potentially reattempt assessment tasks. Such a pattern might reflect productive metacognitive behaviour, where learners monitor their performance and revisit content to resolve misunderstandings.

In-strength centrality was further used to identify the most structurally prominent activities within the interaction network. Unlike the temporal engagement states, the distribution of in-strength values across activities reveals a more differentiated structure. Reading emerges as the dominant attractor, receiving the highest volume of incoming transitions, followed by Gallery and Test. This indicates that students consistently converge toward reading materials from multiple types of activities, positioning Reading as a central point of consolidation within the learning process. In contrast, activities such as Video and Speech exhibit negligible in-strength, suggesting that they play a more peripheral or isolated role in the overall interaction flow.

From a methodological perspective, this distribution highlights an asymmetry in how different types of learning resources are integrated into students' behavioral patterns. Reading appears to function as a central hub of meaning-making, where students return after interacting with other elements of the environment. Gallery, with similarly high in-strength, suggests that visual or multimodal resources also play a significant role in structuring engagement, potentially supporting comprehension or reorientation before transitioning further. Test, while slightly lower, still demonstrates substantial convergence, reinforcing its role as a focal point of activity where learning efforts are ultimately directed.

To further examine the internal organization of these interactions, clique analysis was applied to detect tightly connected subsets of activities. At a threshold of 0.1, a single triadic clique was identified, consisting of Gallery, Reading, and Test. This configuration represents a densely interconnected micro-structure in which all three activities are mutually linked through relatively strong transitions (See Fig. 5).

This triad can be interpreted as a core interaction pattern underlying task-oriented engagement with the digital textbook. Students appear to move between visual exploration (Gallery), textual processing (Reading), and evaluation (Test) in a recurrent and non-linear manner. The presence of strong bidirectional transitions within this triad suggests that these activities do not form a simple

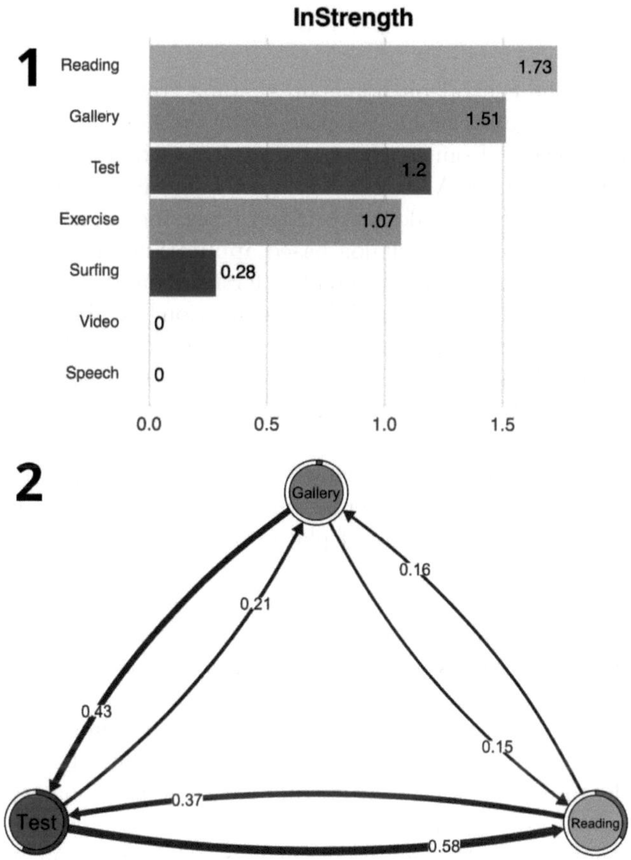

Fig. 5. (1) Detected triangles (threshold = >0.1) of transitions (2) InStrength centrality.

sequence, but rather a flexible loop in which learners revisit resources as needed. For instance, students may return from Test to Reading or Gallery to clarify misunderstandings, indicating an iterative process of verification and adjustment.

Compared to temporal sequence analysis, transition network analysis proved substantially more informative in identifying concrete preparation strategies, showing how students move between activities such as multimedia exploration, reading, and test-taking. Sequence analysis, however, provided complementary insights about the timing, duration, and overall structure of engagement across sessions, capturing aspects of learning behavior that remain invisible in transition-based models. Together, SA and TNA might validate one another's findings and enrich the interpretation of student behavior, offering a more holistic and multidimensional understanding of how learners interact with digital materials.

4 Discussion

At present, AI is the central phenomenon shaping trends both in educational research and in everyday teaching practice. Over the past few years, the use of AI has rapidly evolved—from teachers and students experimenting with ChatGPT to the integration of AI technologies into digital learning environments and the development of standalone AI-driven tools, including learning content generators [8], quiz builders [5], dialog-based applications [12], and AI companions [26]. Naturally, this boom has created fertile ground for a wide range of studies, including critical analyses of AI in education [11], investigations of its impact on student performance and engagement [4], and explorations of effective strategies for AI-supported learning [22]. As previous research shows, any pedagogical innovation produces meaningful outcomes only when it is implemented appropriately [15]. Yet how can educators determine what "appropriate implementation" actually means in the context of an entire spectrum of emerging AI tools? And how can we systematically track students' AI-use strategies in an ecosystem where the number of platforms and applications is constantly growing?

We argue that the rise of AI technologies opens new opportunities for learning analytics along two intertwined directions: enabling more effective use of AI tools and supporting more precise examination of students' emerging learning strategies. In our view, understanding these strategies remains primarily the task of researchers, whereas monitoring, shaping, and refining them is impossible without the active involvement of teachers. Expanding the methodological repertoire of learning analytics—and introducing new methods capable of capturing fine-grained aspects of AI use—can help illuminate how students learn with and through AI. In this sense, the goal is not to position methods such as sequence analysis and transition network analysis in competition, but rather to combine them into an integrated analytical framework for studying different dimensions of the learning process. Our work demonstrates that both methods can be applied to the same phenomenon—in our case, the use of interactive e-books—while offering complementary insights into temporal engagement patterns and activity-based preparation strategies. Moreover, we highlight navigation patterns and test-taking patterns as additional dimensions that can be effectively uncovered using both sequence analysis and transition network analysis.

However, we believe that identifying such strategies is only the first step; for these analytical approaches to become useful in AI-supported educational practice, teachers should be actively involved in the cycle of interpretation and tool development. In the case of sequence analysis and transition network analysis, computational models can identify recurring trajectories, central events, or densely connected patterns, but these structures do not automatically carry pedagogical meaning. Teachers are needed to interpret whether a pattern reflects productive preparation, inefficient navigation, disengagement, repair after failure, or another classroom-relevant process. This creates a circular challenge: teachers are the intended users of SA- and TNA-based dashboards, yet their pedagogical interpretations are also needed to train, refine, and validate such dashboards in the first place. Previous research on learning analytics has similarly emphasized the importance of involving teachers as co-designers rather than passive recipients of analytical tools, especially when dashboards are expected to support meaningful pedagogical action [16]. From this perspective, the role of researchers is to break this loop by translating computational patterns into interpretable representations, organizing teacher feedback into reusable pedagogical categories, and gradually transforming expert interpretation into dashboard logic. This cycle would allow AI-supported dashboards to become not merely automated reporting systems, but tools based on teacher professional knowledge and classroom judgment.

Declaration on Generative AI. During the preparation of this work, the authors used ChatGPT-4 for grammar and spelling correction and limited language refinement. After using this tool, the authors carefully reviewed and edited the manuscript and take full responsibility for the content of the publication.

References

1. Abbott, A.: Sequence analysis: new methods for old ideas. Ann. Rev. Sociol. **21**, 93–113 (1995). https://doi.org/10.1146/annurev.so.21.080195.000521
2. Alrawashdeh, G.S., et al.: Exploring the impact of personalized and adaptive learning technologies on reading literacy: a global meta-analysis. Education Tech. Res. Dev. **72**(1), 1–22 (2024). https://doi.org/10.1007/s11423-023-10199-5
3. Bach, A., Thiel, F.: Collaborative online learning in higher education–quality of digital interaction and associations with individual and group-related factors. Front. Educ. **9**, 1356271 (2024). https://doi.org/10.3389/feduc.2024.1356271
4. Boubker, O.: From chatting to self-educating: can AI tools boost student learning outcomes? Expert Syst. Appl. **238**, 121820 (2024). https://doi.org/10.1016/j.eswa.2023.121820
5. Chang, C., Chien, L.: Enhancing academic performance with generative AI-based quiz platform. In: Proceedings of the 2024 IEEE International Conference on Advanced Learning Technologies (ICALT), pp. 193–195 (2024). https://doi.org/10.1109/ICALT61570.2024.00062
6. Contrino, M.F., Reyes-Millán, M., Vázquez-Villegas, P., et al.: Using an adaptive learning tool to improve student performance and satisfaction in online and face-to-face education for a more personalized approach. Smart Learn. Environ. **11**(6) (2024). https://doi.org/10.1186/s40561-024-00292-y
7. Croft, N., Dalton, A., Grant, M.: Overcoming isolation in distance learning: building a learning community through time and space. J. Educ. Built Environ. **5**(1), 27–64 (2010). https://doi.org/10.11120/jebe.2010.05010027
8. Diwan, C., Srinivasa, S., Suri, G., Agarwal, S., Ram, P.: AI-based learning content generation and learning pathway augmentation to increase learner engagement. Comput. Educ. Artif. Intell. **4**, 100110 (2023). https://doi.org/10.1016/j.caeai.2022.100110
9. El-Sabagh, H.A.: Adaptive e-learning environment based on learning styles and its impact on development students' engagement. Int. J. Educ. Technol. High. Educ. **18**(1), 53 (2021). https://doi.org/10.1186/s41239-021-00289-4

10. Gitinabard, N., Heckman, S., Barnes, T., Lynch, C.: What will you do next? A sequence analysis on the student transitions between online platforms in blended courses. In: Proceedings of the 12th International Conference on Educational Data Mining, Montreal, Canada (2019)
11. Holmes, W., Porayska-Pomsta, K. (eds.): The Ethics of Artificial Intelligence in Education: Practices, Challenges, and Debates. Routledge, New York, NY (2022)
12. Honig, C.D.F., Desu, A., Franklin, J.: GenAI in the classroom: customized GPT roleplay for process safety education. Educ. Chem. Eng. **49**, 55–66 (2024). https://doi.org/10.1016/j.ece.2024.01.006
13. Kinnebrew, J.S., Segedy, J.R.: Integrating model-driven and data-driven techniques for analyzing learning behaviors in open-ended learning environments. IEEE Trans. Learn. Technol. **10**(1), 1–11 (2015). https://doi.org/10.1109/TLT.2015.2513387
14. Leijen, Ä., et al.: Agency in educational technology: interdisciplinary perspectives. Learn. Instr. **70**, 101112 (2020). https://doi.org/10.1016/j.learninstruc.2020.101112
15. Lidegran, I., Hultqvist, E., Bertilsson, E., Börjesson, M.: Insecurity, lack of support, and frustration: a sociological analysis of how three groups of students reflect on their distance education during the pandemic in Sweden. Eur. J. Educ. **56**(4), 550–563 (2021). https://doi.org/10.1111/ejed.12481
16. Opanasenko, Y., Bardone, E., Pedaste, M., Siiman, L.A.: Sequence analysis-enhanced AI: transforming interactive e-book data into educational insights for teachers. Educ. Sci. **15**(1), 28 (2025). https://doi.org/10.3390/educsci1501002
17. Oyarzun, B., Martin, F.: A systematic review of research on online learner collaboration from 2012–21: collaboration technologies, design, facilitation, and outcomes. Online Learn. **27** (2023). https://doi.org/10.24059/olj.v27i1.3407
18. Raab, M., Struffolino, E.: Sequence Analysis. SAGE Publications, Thousand Oaks, CA (2022)
19. Raave, D.K., Roa, E.R., Pedaste, M., Saks, K.: Classroom digital technology integration – a double-edged sword? Engaging and practical yet harmful. In: Huang, Y.M., Cheng, S.C., Barroso, J., Sandnes, F.E. (eds.) Innovative Technologies and Learning, Lecture Notes in Computer Science, vol. 13449. Springer, Cham (2022). https://doi.org/10.1007/978-3-031-15273-3_27
20. Salles, F., Dos Santos, R., Keskpaik, S.: When didactics meet data science: process data analysis in large-scale mathematics assessment in France. Large-Scale Assessments Educ. **8**(7), 1–19 (2020). https://doi.org/10.1186/s40536-020-00085-y
21. Saqr, M., López-Pernas, S., Tikka, S.: Mapping relational dynamics with transition network analysis: a primer and tutorial. In: Saqr, M., López-Pernas, S. (eds.) Advanced Learning Analytics Methods. Springer, Cham (2026). https://doi.org/10.1007/978-3-031-95365-1_15
22. Schiff, D.: Education for AI, not AI for education: the role of education and ethics in national AI policy strategies. Int. J. Artif. Intell. Educ. **32**, 527–563 (2022). https://doi.org/10.1007/s40593-021-00270-2
23. Sweller, J.: Cognitive load theory and the use of educational technology. Educ. Technol. **48**, 32–35 (2008)
24. Tan, T.K., Savedham, L.: The learning process matters: a sequence analysis perspective of examining procrastination using learning management systems. Comput. Educ. Open **3**, 100112 (2022). https://doi.org/10.1016/j.caeo.2022.100112
25. Tani, M., Manuguerra, M., Khan, S.: Can videos affect learning outcomes? Evidence from an actual learning environment. Educ. Tech. Res. Dev. **70**(5), 1675–1693 (2022). https://doi.org/10.1007/s11423-022-10147-3

26. Van Poucke, M.: ChatGPT, the perfect virtual teaching assistant? Ideological bias in learner-chatbot interactions. Comput. Compos. **73**, 102871 (2024). https://doi.org/10.1016/j.compcom.2024.102871
27. Yilmaz, R.: Exploring the role of e-learning readiness on student satisfaction and motivation in flipped classroom. Comput. Hum. Behav. **70**, 251–260 (2017). https://doi.org/10.1016/j.chb.2016.12.085

Tracing the Paths of Slow Responders in Complex Problem-Solving: A Transition Network Analysis Approach

Daniel Jerez[1](✉) and Okan Bulut[2]

[1] Measurement, Evaluation, and Data Science, Faculty of Education, University of Alberta, Edmonton T6G 2G5, Canada
jerezgar@ualberta.ca

[2] Centre for Research in Applied Measurement and Evaluation, Faculty of Education, University of Alberta, Edmonton T6G 2G5, Canada
bulut@ualberta.ca

Abstract. This work-in-progress paper presents the first application of Transition Network Analysis to complex problem-solving tasks in international large-scale assessments. Although behavioral patterns associated with complex problem-solving accuracy have been extensively studied, recent research has begun to examine the role of slow responding and its impact on inferences drawn from computer-based assessments. Building on this emerging line of inquiry, our study compares behavioral patterns associated with slow versus optimal response times in complex problem solving using Transition Network Analysis. We analyze process data from the PISA 2012 computer-based assessment of complex problem solving. Slow responses are identified using response-time thresholds that account for test language and final accuracy, following recent advances in educational measurement research. In our preliminary analysis, we coded students' actions in the second Tickets Unit item as (initial or repeated) targeted, partially targeted, or non-targeted explorations. We then compared transition patterns between slow and optimal-time responses using the permutation-testing functionality within the Transition Network Analysis framework. Preliminary results indicate that Transition Network Analysis effectively uncovers meaningful and statistically significant differences in transition structures between slow and non-slow responses. These differences are consistent with prior findings on exploration strategies and inefficient response behaviors in complex problem-solving tasks. Overall, our findings demonstrate that Transition Network Analysis is a promising tool for Learning Analytics researchers seeking to identify significant differences in behavioral transition patterns across performance groups using process data from interactive tasks.

Keywords: Transition Network Analysis · process data · complex problem-solving · slow responding

M. Saqr et al. (Eds.): TNA 2026, CCIS 3079, pp. 114–124, 2026.
https://doi.org/10.1007/978-3-032-34157-0_9

1 Background

Complex problem-solving (CPS) broadly refers to the acquisition and application of knowledge to achieve goals when neither the solution nor the method is immediately apparent to the problem solver [5]. Within this context, learning analytics researchers have extensively examined behavioral patterns—defined as behavioral characteristics reflecting strategy use, timing, and the ordering of problem-solving actions [17]—using process data from digital CPS assessments [2,4,13,24]. A wide range of learning analytics techniques has been employed to investigate CPS behavioral patterns, including biclustering [25], hidden Markov models [24], network analysis [13], longest common subsequences [9], n-grams [14], clustering [10,23], and full-path sequence analysis [4].

Because CPS in digital assessments is inherently multi-step and sequential, problem solvers must interact with their environment and transition between states at multiple points in the process [8]. Consequently, analyzing these transitions—specifically, the exploration decisions learners make within interactive systems—is essential for understanding their cognitive processing and performance- or efficiency-related differences across groups. Such transitions can be compared by assessing whether the probabilities of moving from given states to subsequent system states differ significantly across groups. A novel framework for conducting such comparisons is Transition Network Analysis (TNA), which has not yet been applied to CPS research but enables the detection of differences in transition patterns and underlying network structures [12,21].

Parallelly to CPS research, recent educational measurement literature has included slowness when studying novel scoring and item-selection procedures, and when investigating the relationship between test-taking engagement and students' ability and growth estimates [1,6,7,26,27]. Slow responses are characterized by having response times from the far-right end of the response time distribution for those obtaining the same credit on the same item. Defined this way, slow responses, overall, are a mixed group that deserves further investigation due to the various test-taking profiles that might result in long response times. No previous research has, so far, investigated what differentiates slow and optimal time use behavioral patterns in CPS. Understanding slow responding in CPS assessments is interesting, as excessive response times are not adaptive in real-life settings and might reflect diverse information processing difficulties. Slowness might be due to specific problems in knowledge acquisition or application, or indicate less test-taking motivation or efficiency, depending on whether the student ends up solving the problem [15]. Furthermore, slowness in CPS might lead to students not meeting their everyday contexts' demands (e.g., the modern workplace, where solving complex problems in a timely manner is routinely demanded). From a test-taking perspective, slow responding in CPS assessments is important because it may impact the inferences made from computer-based tests, their implementation, and subsequent test-taking behavior.

We address this gap in the literature by applying TNA to describe and compare the behavioral patterns of slow (correct and incorrect) and non-slow (correct or incorrect) responses in interactive CPS tasks. Our focus is on identifying the behavioral features that distinguish optimal-time from slow problem solvers who achieve the same level of accuracy, as the interpretation and implications of slowness differ depending on response correctness [15]. This approach provides insights into the potential sources of slowness in CPS tasks and the behavioral patterns associated with different combinations of response speed and accuracy.

To advance knowledge on slow responding in CPS, it is necessary to examine which transitions (i.e., decisions) differ between slow and optimal-time responders. Given the centrality of transitions in CPS processes, we operationalize behavioral patterns as transition probabilities between actions within the TNA framework. Accordingly, this study aims to determine (a) whether significant differences exist between the transitions of slow and optimal-time responders and (b) which specific transition differences are statistically significant. The two research questions for this project are:

- RQ1: What (if any) are the significant differences regarding the transitions between events of slow- and optimal time (correct and incorrect) responses in a representative CPS unit?
- RQ2: Does the pattern of significant differences from RQ1 replicate when analyzing all the items from a representative CPS Unit?

2 Methodology

2.1 CPS Unit and Dataset

The published PISA 2012 problem-solving log-file database contains process data for four units: Climate Control, Tickets, Traffic, and Robot Cleaner. For this project, we exclude the Traffic and Robot Cleaner units because the items in these units are static rather than interactive tasks [16]. The Tickets Unit, by contrast, constitutes a CPS scenario [3] that simulates a common and potentially motivating real-life situation in which slowness may be maladaptive. Moreover, this unit is particularly well-suited for analysis using the TNA framework because it involves a finite set of possible states and operators, allowing for systematic examination of transitions. Its structure also enables a clear distinction among targeted, partially targeted, and non-targeted explorations according to complementary goals, thereby facilitating data preparation for comparing different performance and efficiency groups. For these reasons, our analyses focus on the log files from the PISA 2012 Tickets Unit.

In the Tickets Unit of PISA 2012, students were instructed to imagine that they had just arrived at a train station equipped with an automated ticketing machine. Before purchasing a ticket, they were required to make three sequential decisions: (a) selecting either subway or country train tickets, (b) choosing between full or concession fares, and (c) opting for a daily ticket or a ticket for a specified number of trips. At any point, students could press a “Cancel” button, which reset the system and returned them to the initial screen. The Tickets Unit comprised three tasks (items) [16]. In the first item, students were asked to purchase a specific ticket, and full credit was awarded if they bought the correct ticket as instructed [16].

In the second item, students were required to purchase the cheapest ticket for a specified journey, with full credit awarded for selecting the correct ticket after comparing the two most obvious alternatives [16]. In the third item, students were instructed to buy a specific trip and were informed that they were eligible for concession fares [16]. However, when attempting to complete the purchase, they were notified that concession tickets were unavailable [16]. Students, therefore, had to adjust their strategy to achieve the task goal, and full credit was granted if they ultimately selected the correct ticket [16]. Across the three items, the unit emphasized different cognitive processes: planning and executing in the first item, exploring and understanding in the second, and monitoring and reflecting in the third [16].

2.2 Action-Coding Procedure

We are recoding each of the examinees' actions as targeted exploration, partially targeted exploration, and non-targeted exploration, except for the 'Buy' and 'Cancel' actions. Correctly solving the Tickets Unit tasks required simultaneously meeting multiple goals. To solve the first Ticket Unit item, students had two goals: the demand goal (i.e., buying Country Trains tickets good for two rides) and the price goal (i.e., buying full fare). To solve the second Ticket Unit item, students had two goals: the demand goal (i.e., buying City Subway Tickets good for four rides) and the price goal (i.e., buying the cheapest ticket). To solve the third Ticket Unit item, students had three goals: the demand goal (i.e., buying City Subway Tickets good for two rides), the price goal (i.e., buying the cheapest ticket), and the availability goal (as the concession fare is unexpectedly unavailable) [19].

2.3 Identification of Slow and Optimal Time Use

We are registering the response time for each examinee using the software-generated records. With that, we are identifying the slow and optimal time use examinees for each performance level (i.e., correct or incorrect). We are calculating response times' measures of central tendency for correct and incorrect responses separately. These measures are calculated separately according to the language in which the test was taken. This allows for comparing each examinee's item response time with a relevant response time threshold (i.e., for examinees with the same accuracy, taking the item in the same language). Then, we multiply the relevant measure of central tendency by 0.20 and 1.80 to obtain the thresholds for identifying rapid guesses and slow responses, respectively. If a response time is lower than its respective 0.20 threshold, the response is identified as a rapid guess. If a response time exceeds its respective 1.80 threshold, the response is identified as a slow response. Responses that are not either a rapid guess or a slow response will be considered optimal-time-use responses, and rapid guesses are not included in the TNA strategy.

2.4 Transition Network Analysis

TNA is a novel framework for analyzing sequential data in education that calculates a transition matrix between events and represents it as a graph for further graph and network analyses [20]. Most importantly for this research project, the TNA framework, accompanied by the tna package [20,22] in R [18], offers a rigorous and systematic method for network comparison based on pre-defined groups [20]. These comparisons are based on a permutation test that allows researchers to identify whether the observed differences between networks are statistically significant [20]. Furthermore, the permutation test can be used to uncover where the significant differences lie by estimating the significance of each edge [20]. Given these considerations, TNA is the most suitable process-mining framework for our research questions.

The TNA framework starts by building a matrix representing the transitions between events using first-order Markov models. Markov models are used to model transitions between successive states, assuming that each event is probabilistically dependent on preceding events [11,20]. First-order Markov chains model the probability of a given event only considering the previous event or state (i.e., the Markov property) [11]. The use of Markov models in TNA is grounded on the assumption that the transitions between events are governed by a stochastic process (i.e., the data-generating process operates within certain boundaries, but is partly random) [20]. Therefore, for each pair of events (a, b), a probability is estimated by dividing the number of observed transitions from a to b by the total observed transitions from a [11,20]. TNA then represents the process of interest as a directed weighted network. This takes the transition matrix as its building block. In these networks, the nodes represent events or states, the edges represent transitions between events (i.e., the direction), and the weights represent the probability (likelihood) of each transition [20]. With this, researchers can visualize networks, calculate and compare graph-level, event, and edge centrality measures, and identify patterns through cliques, communities, and clusters [20]. Researchers can also prune networks using pre-specified thresholds to retain only the edges that matter and obtain sparser, more interpretable transition networks [20].

One of the methodological advances of the TNA framework is its ability to compare networks across predefined subgroups using permutation testing. Previous research using sequence analysis and network methods to compare pre-defined groups' action sequences [e.g., 4,13] in CPS has not aimed to identify statistically significant differences. In contrast, our research aims to leverage the TNA framework to identify a) whether significant differences exist between the transitions of slow and optimal-time responders and b) which transition differences are statistically significant. Permutation testing generates a distribution of (edge) differences by shuffling and comparing the data a pre-specified number of times. Using this distribution, the TNA framework provides a p value for each edge, which allows researchers to pinpoint the statistically significant differences in the transitions between groups. Then, those significant differences between the transition networks can be visualized for easier interpretation [20]. In this research, the statistically significant differences between the transitions of slow- and optimal-time-use groups will be identified using the p value for each edge and graphed using tna.

3 Preliminary Results

We are using pre-processed data as input to implement TNA to compare slow and optimal-time-use responses in the PISA 2012 Ticket Units Unit. The log files contain 10 different events (i.e., nodes); 8 events are user-generated (i.e., initial or repeated non-, partially-, and targeted explorations, 'Buy', and 'Cancel'), and 2 events are computer-generated (i.e., START and END item). We are keeping 'START' to allow the first action to be considered in the permutation test, and 'END' to consider the possibility of ending the item without clicking 'Buy'. We are using the prepare_data function from the tna package to convert the long-format data to a suitable format to build the TNA object. We are then using the group_tna function from the tna package to estimate a TNA model for each group (e.g., slow and optimal time for each performance group). Finally, we are using the permutation_test function from the tna package to conduct a permutation test to compare the models and determine their statistical differences. We are repeating this process twice (i.e., once for correct and once for incorrect answers). We will report the difference and p value associated with each transition (edge) and plot the significantly different edges using the plot() function.

These analyses will answer our research questions as we are obtaining matrices to identify significantly different transitions between slow and optimal-time-use responders for each performance group and each item. That is, we are obtaining a matrix of (significant and non-significant) edge differences for each performance group within each item (RQ1), which will allow us to determine whether the pattern of significant differences replicates across items (RQ2). For each performance group, we will be able to clearly identify whether each edge (transition) difference is statistically significant. What is more, for each significant difference, we will be capable of reporting the direction of the difference (i.e., in which group is the probability higher for that transition). This will allow for clear reporting of the statistically significant differences in transitions between events for slow- and optimal-time use responses. Finally, this will be complemented by plots showing only the significantly different edges, with different colors (e.g., green/red) to clearly indicate the direction of the difference.

We conducted the pre-coding procedure, built the sequences, and ran the TNA on the data from the second Tickets item. Figure 1 presents the preliminary results obtained when comparing Optimal-Time Correct and Slow Correct behavioral patterns using TNA. Figure 1, overall, shows the significant differences in the transitions between the two groups. For example, optimal-time students were significantly more likely to conduct targeted explorations (i.e., selecting City Subway) just after starting the item (see the transition difference between START_ITEM and TE_I). The biggest significant difference seems to lie in the decision students take after resetting the system (i.e., clicking Cancel);

optimal-time students were more likely to hit City Subway (after having already explored that network), and slow students were more likely to hit Country Trains again (which is completely irrelevant to solving the task). This is interesting because, using TNA, we can pinpoint significant differences in decisions after resetting the system: optimal-time students reset the system and conducted targeted explorations, while slow students were sidetracked by completely irrelevant information. Figure 2 shows the significant differences between the transitions of slow-incorrect and optimal-time-incorrect responders. There are even more significant differences between these groups, which partially aligns with previous literature in that incorrect behavioral patterns are much more varied [17,23]. Slow students were significantly more likely to reset the system and start over after conducting initial partially-targeted explorations, initial and repeated targeted explorations, and initial and repeated non-targeted explorations. Non-slow students were significantly more likely to make a final decision and press 'Buy' after exploring partially and completely irrelevant options. Overall, this pattern of results preliminarily shows that slow students hesitated (being more likely to reset the system), while non-slow students were significantly more likely to buy the wrong option without any further system exploration.

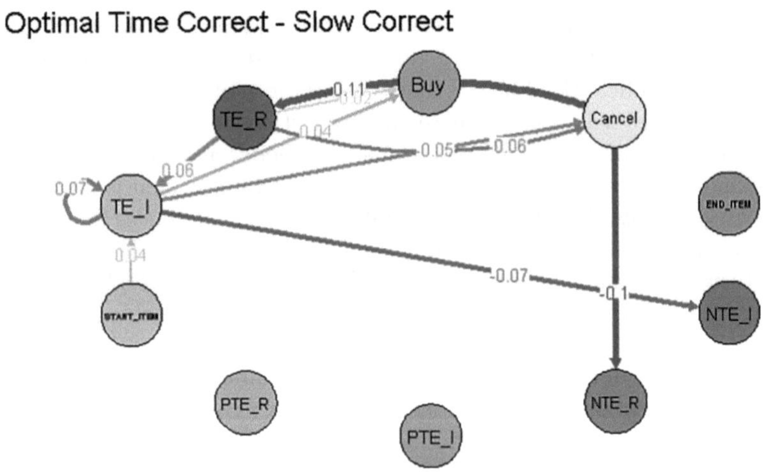

Fig. 1. TNA comparison of optimal-time correct and slow correct behavioral patterns using TNA. TE = Targeted Explorations, PTE = Partially Targeted Explorations, NTE = Non-Targeted Explorations. _R means repeated, and _I means initial.

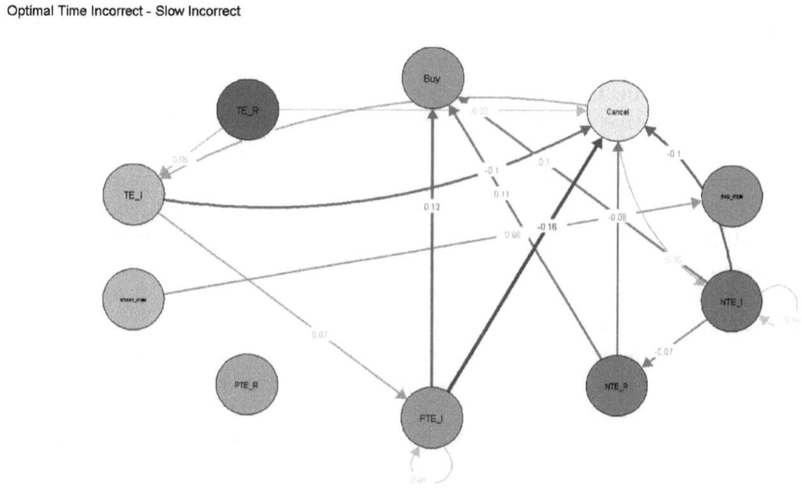

Fig. 2. TNA comparison of optimal-time incorrect and slow incorrect behavioral patterns using TNA. TE = Targeted Explorations, PTE = Partially Targeted Explorations, NTE = Non-Targeted Explorations. _R means repeated, and _I means initial.

4 Conclusion and Future Directions

This work-in-progress paper presents the first application of the TNA framework [20] within the context of CPS research. Analyzing PISA 2012 process data and drawing from educational assessment research on slowness in interactive tasks, we are comparing slow and non-slow CPS behavioral patterns. Operationalizing the decisions problem-solvers make as transitions within the TNA framework and pre-coding the actions from a thorough understanding of the tasks, we are leveraging TNA to shed light on the significant differences between the decisions of slow and non-slow problem-solvers. Preliminary results show significant differences in behavioral patterns that partially align with previous CPS research and may have further implications. Slow, successful problem-solvers were more likely to get sidetracked by irrelevant information when resetting the system than optimal-time use successful problem solvers. Slow, unsuccessful problem-solvers were significantly more likely to keep resetting the system, while non-slow, unsuccessful problem-solvers were more likely to end the item without further exploration. Crucially, by adding all items for the Tickets task, we aim to check whether the significantly different transitions replicate across all analyzed tasks (to answer RQ2). Overall, we demonstrate that TNA is a useful Learning Analytics framework for comparing decisions across different performance/efficiency groups in interactive tasks.

References

1. Bulut, O., Gorgun, G., Karamese, H.: Incorporating test-taking engagement into multistage adaptive testing design for large-scale assessments. J. Educ. Meas. **62**(1), 57–80 (2025). https://doi.org/10.1111/jedm.12380
2. Eichmann, B., Goldhammer, F., Greiff, S., Brandhuber, L., Naumann, J.: Using process data to explain group differences in complex problem solving. J. Educ. Psychol. **112**(8), 1546–1562 (2020). https://doi.org/10.1037/edu0000446
3. Eichmann, B., Goldhammer, F., Greiff, S., Pucite, L., Naumann, J.: The role of planning in complex problem solving. Comput. Educ. **128**, 1–12 (2019). https://doi.org/10.1016/j.compedu.2018.08.004
4. Eichmann, B., Greiff, S., Naumann, J., Brandhuber, L., Goldhammer, F.: Exploring behavioural patterns during complex problem-solving. J. Comput. Assist. Learn. **36**(6), 933–956 (2020). https://doi.org/10.1111/jcal.12451
5. Fischer, A., Greiff, S., Funke, J.: The history of complex problem solving. In: Csapó, B., Funke, J. (eds.) The Nature of Problem Solving: Using Research to Inspire 21st Century Learning, pp. 107–121. OECD Publishing (2017)
6. Gorgun, G., Bulut, O.: A polytomous scoring approach to handle not-reached items in low-stakes assessments. Educ. Psychol. Measur. **81**(5), 847–871 (2021). https://doi.org/10.1177/0013164421991211
7. Gorgun, G., Bulut, O.: Incorporating test-taking engagement into the item selection algorithm in low-stakes computerized adaptive tests. Large-Scale Assessments Educ. **11**(1), 27 (2023). https://doi.org/10.1186/s40536-023-00177-5
8. Greiff, S., Fischer, A., Stadler, M., Wüstenberg, S.: Assessing complex problem-solving skills with multiple complex systems. Thinking Reason. **21**(3), 356–382 (2015). https://doi.org/10.1080/13546783.2014.989263
9. He, Q., Borgonovi, F., Paccagnella, M.: Leveraging process data to assess adults' problem-solving skills: using sequence mining to identify behavioral patterns across digital tasks. Comput. Educ. **166**, 104170 (2021). https://doi.org/10.1016/j.compedu.2021.104170
10. He, Q., Liao, D., Jiao, H.: Clustering behavioral patterns using process data in PIAAC problem-solving items. In: Veldkamp, B.P., Sluijter, C. (eds.) Theoretical and Practical Advances in Computer-based Educational Measurement, pp. 189–212. Springer International Publishing, Cham (2019). https://doi.org/10.1007/978-3-030-18480-3_10
11. Helske, J., Helske, S., Saqr, M., López-Pernas, S., Murphy, K.: A modern approach to transition analysis and process mining with Markov models in education. In: Saqr, M., López-Pernas, S. (eds.) Learning Analytics Methods and Tutorials, pp. 381–427. Springer, Cham (2024). https://doi.org/10.1007/978-3-031-54464-4_12
12. Kilanioti, I., Saqr, M., López-Pernas, S.: Exploring the process of students' learning in the laboratory with transition network analysis. In: Proceedings TEEM 2025. Thirteenth International Conference on Technological Ecosystems for Enhancing Multiculturality, pp. 1–10., Berlin, Germany (2026)
13. Liu, X., Bulut, O., Cui, Y., Gao, Y.: Uncovering adults' problem-solving patterns from process data with hidden Markov model and network analysis. J. Comput. Assist. Learn. **41**(1), e13089 (2024). https://doi.org/10.1111/jcal.13089
14. Ludwig, S., Rausch, A., Deutscher, V., Seifried, J.: Predicting problem-solving success in an office simulation applying N-grams and a random forest to behavioral process data. Comput. Educ. **218**, 105093 (2024). https://doi.org/10.1016/j.compedu.2024.105093

15. Lundgren, E., Eklöf, H.: Within-item response processes as indicators of test-taking effort and motivation. Educ. Res. Eval. **26**(5–6), 275–301 (2020). https://doi.org/10.1080/13803611.2021.1963940
16. OECD: PISA 2012 Results: Creative Problem Solving (Volume V): Students' Skills in Tackling Real-Life Problems. OECD (2014). https://doi.org/10.1787/9789264208070-en
17. Park, H.J., Lee, D., Park, H.: Understanding students' problem-solving patterns: evidence from an allotted response time in a PISA 2012 item. Front. Psychol. **13**, 1050435 (2023). https://doi.org/10.3389/fpsyg.2022.1050435
18. R Core Team: R: A language and environment for statistical computing. R Found. Stat. Comput. (2024). https://www.R-project.org/
19. Ren, Y., Luo, F., Ren, P., Bai, D., Li, X., Liu, H.: Exploring multiple goals balancing in complex problem solving based on log data. Front. Psychol. **10**, 1975 (2019). https://doi.org/10.3389/fpsyg.2019.01975
20. Saqr, M., López-Pernas, S., Tikka, S.: Mapping relational dynamics with transition network analysis: a primer and tutorial. In: Saqr, M., López-Pernas, S. (eds.) Advanced Learning Analytics Methods: AI, Precision and Complexity (In press). Springer (2025). https://lamethods.org/book2/chapters/ch15-tna/ch15-tna.html
21. Saqr, M., López-Pernas, S., Törmänen, T., Kaliisa, R., Misiejuk, K., Tikka, S.: Transition network analysis: a novel framework for modeling, visualizing, and identifying the temporal patterns of learners and learning processes. In: Proceedings of the 15th International Learning Analytics and Knowledge Conference (LAK '25), pp. 351–361 (2025). https://doi.org/10.1145/3706468.3706513
22. Saqr, M., Tikka, S., López-Pernas, S.: CRAN: Contributed Packages. The R Foundation, (2025). https://doi.org/10.32614/cran.package.tna. TNA: Transition network analysis (TNA)
23. Ulitzsch, E., He, Q., Pohl, S.: Using sequence mining techniques for understanding incorrect behavioral patterns on interactive tasks. J. Educ. Behav. Stat. **47**(1), 3–35 (2022). https://doi.org/10.3102/10769986211010467
24. Xiao, Y., He, Q., Veldkamp, B., Liu, H.: Exploring latent states of problem-solving competence using hidden Markov model on process data. J. Comput. Assist. Learn. **37**(5), 1232–1247 (2021). https://doi.org/10.1111/jcal.12559
25. Xu, X., Zhang, S., Guo, J., Xin, T.: Biclustering of log data: insights from a computer-based complex problem solving assessment. J. Intell. **12**(1), 10 (2024). https://doi.org/10.3390/jintelligence12010010
26. Yildirim-Erbasli, S.N., Bulut, O.: The impact of students' test-taking effort on growth estimates in low-stakes educational assessments. Educ. Res. Eval. **26**(7–8), 368–386 (2020). https://doi.org/10.1080/13803611.2021.1977152
27. Yildirim-Erbasli, S.N., Gorgun, G.: Disentangling the relationship between ability and test-taking effort: to what extent the ability levels can be predicted from response behavior? Technology. Knowl. Learn. (2024). https://doi.org/10.1007/s10758-024-09810-w

Towards Modeling Situational Awareness Through Visual Attention in Clinical Simulations

Haoting Gao[1], Kapotaksha Das[1,2], Mohamed Abouelenien[2], Michael Cole[1], James Cooke[1], and Vitaliy Popov[1(✉)]

[1] Department of Emergency Medicine, University of Michigan Medical School, Ann Arbor, MI, USA
haotin@umich.edu takposha@umich.edu mcolemd@umich.edu cookej@umich.edu vipopov@umich.edu

[2] Computer and Information Sciences, University of Michigan-Dearborn, Dearborn, MI, USA
zmohamed@umich.edu

Abstract. Situational awareness (SA) is essential for effective team performance in time-critical clinical environments, yet its dynamic and distributed nature remains difficult to characterize. In this preliminary study, we apply Transition Network Analysis (TNA) to model visual attention in multiperson VR-based cardiac arrest simulations. Using eye-tracking data from 40 clinicians assigned to four standardized roles (Airway, CPR, Defib, TeamLead), we construct gaze transition networks between clinically meaningful areas of interest (AOIs) and extract metrics such as entropy and self-loop rate to quantify attentional structure and flow. Our findings reveal that visual attention among individual clinicians and teams is dynamically and adaptively redistributed across roles and scenario phases, with those in CPR roles narrowing their focus to execution-critical tasks and those in the TeamLead role concentrating on global monitoring as clinical demands evolve. TNA thus provides a powerful lens for mapping functional differentiation of team cognition and may support the development of phase-sensitive analytics and targeted instructional interventions in acute care training.

Keywords: Transition network analysis · Eye tracking · Situational awareness · Cardiac arrest training · Virtual reality simulation

1 Introduction

Understanding how teams coordinate and maintain situational awareness in time-critical, high-stakes environments remains a challenge in behavioral and learning analytics [10,20,26]. Multi-disciplinary research on acute care teams has

Accepted at the Transition Network Analysis Workshop (TNA 2026), co-located with LAK 2026, April 27–28, 2026, Bergen, Norway.

M. Saqr et al. (Eds.): TNA 2026, CCIS 3079, pp. 125–137, 2026.
https://doi.org/10.1007/978-3-032-34157-0_10

long sought to characterize team performance through observational approaches, primarily behavioral marker systems and coding schemes [12]. However, these methods are labor-intensive, obtrusive, prone to subjective judgment, and fundamentally unable to capture the dynamic, interdependent, and multimodal nature of team processes as they unfold in real time [12,15]. There is a need for scalable, objective, and temporally sensitive analytical approaches that can model collaborative problem-solving as it naturally occurs.

Recent advances in sensor technology and computational modeling offer a promising alternative to traditional approaches (e.g., self-report, observation, etc.) [23]. High-fidelity data streams, including visual attention (gaze), speech patterns, physiological arousal, and behavioral sequences, can now be captured unobtrusively during simulated training or real-world clinical performance [23]. Among these data modalities, gaze-based fixation data can serve as a particularly valuable proxy for situational awareness (SA) [1,15]. Visual attention reflects how individuals perceive environmental cues, monitor task progress, and coordinate with team members [16,29]. Yet traditional gaze metrics, such as fixation counts, dwell times, or pairwise area-of-interest (AOI) transitions, fail to capture the temporal structure and sequential reorganization of attention across evolving task demands and across multiple team members simultaneously.

To address this gap, we leverage Transition Network Analysis (TNA) [25], a graph-based approach that models visual attention as a temporal network of gaze transitions between clinically meaningful AOIs. TNA moves beyond where clinicians look to examine how attention flows and adapts across roles and scenario phases. By integrating network-level metrics such as entropy (attentional dispersion) and self-loop rate (sustained focus), TNA offers a clear vantage on latent structures in collaborative visual attention.

We situate our analysis within multiperson cardiac arrest virtual reality (VR) simulations, where improved SA and teamwork can significantly affect patient outcomes [8,11,17]. While VR environments may differ from real-world settings in how visual attention is allocated (e.g., altered depth cues, peripheral awareness, and field of view), VR uniquely affords an immersive, repeatable (controlled for stimulus presentation) platform for capturing rich, multimodal interactions. Traditional training and assessment methods provide limited systematic insight into individual and team SA during acute events [19,28]. However, a deeper understanding of how attentional structures differ by clinical role and evolve across scenario stages remains lacking.

In this study, we present a preliminary application of TNA to multi-role, real-time visual attention in VR-based cardiac arrest simulations. We ask: *How can situational awareness be dynamically modeled using visual attention patterns across different clinical roles and scenario stages in multiperson cardiac arrest simulations?*

Using eye-tracking fixation data, we construct role-specific gaze transition networks, quantify their structure via entropy and self-loop rate, comparing patterns across roles and scenario stages.

2 Methodology

2.1 Study Context and Data Collection

This study utilized an interactive, real-time VR platform designed for medical emergency training. The simulation provides a flexible, nonlinear environment in which teams of four medical trainees collaborate to manage rapid-response hospital scenarios, with a focus on cardiac arrest and acute dysrhythmias. Each 10–15 minute session assigned trainees to standardized roles (TeamLead, Airway, CPR, Defib), following American Heart Association guidelines to collaboratively assess and respond to evolving clinical situations [18]. The simulation tracks a STEMI cardiac arrest scenario [27], where a blocked coronary artery triggers life-threatening arrhythmias. The patient presented with ventricular tachycardia and a weak pulse (Stage 1), progressed through pulseless VT, asystole, and ventricular fibrillation (Stage 5), before return of spontaneous circulation (ROSC). Stages 1 and 5 were chosen for analysis (see Sect. 3.2) as they represent initial assessment and peak intervention phases, capturing major shifts in team attention and coordination.

For this exploratory research, data were collected from 40 participants across 10 sessions. The teams had varying skill levels, ranging from experienced clinicians such as paramedics and physicians to junior emergency and family medicine residents with Advanced Cardiovascular Life Support (ACLS) training but limited real-world leadership experience in cardiac arrest scenarios. Using a VR platform with HP Reverb G2 Omnicept headsets, in conjunction with the Cognitive3D [2] software, enabled the collection and processing of rich movement, action, and eye-tracking data, yielding fixation data for each participant in the simulation. All data collection associated with these sessions was approved by the Institutional Review Board (IRB number: HUM00193383).

Simulations had an average duration of 11.66 min (SD = 3.65), yielding a dense set of eye-tracking data, including 55,670 raw fixations and 22,660 saccades. After merging adjacent fixations on the same object with inter-fixation gaps $\leq$ 300 ms, the resulting dataset comprised 20,628 merged fixations and 20,526 Areas of Interest (AOI) transitions, which served as the basis for all transition matrices and TNA metrics.

2.2 Defining Areas of Interest (AOIs)

To understand participants' gaze patterns during the VR cardiac scenario, we defined seven Areas of Interest (AOIs) that served as perceptual anchors in the simulation. These AOIs group objects by key roles or use cases, such as airway management, CPR, defibrillation, and medication, as well as by patient, vital sign monitors, and avatars representing other team members. Table 1 lists the seven AOIs used, along with a description of the objects included in each category, with Fig. 1 showing a visualization of what the objects look like in the VR environment.

Table 1. Areas of Interest (AOIs) Used for Gaze–Transition Analysis

AOI	Description
Equipment - Airway	Airway management equipment, such as bag-valve masks.
Equipment - CPR	Hands and UI elements directly involved in CPR.
Equipment - Defib	Main Defibrillator unit and associated controls.
Equipment - Meds & IV	Medication- and IV-related objects.
Patient Vitals Monitor	Displays patient vitals such as ECG, SpO2, Respiration, etc.
Other Team Members	3D avatars of other people in session.
Patient	Virtual patient body.

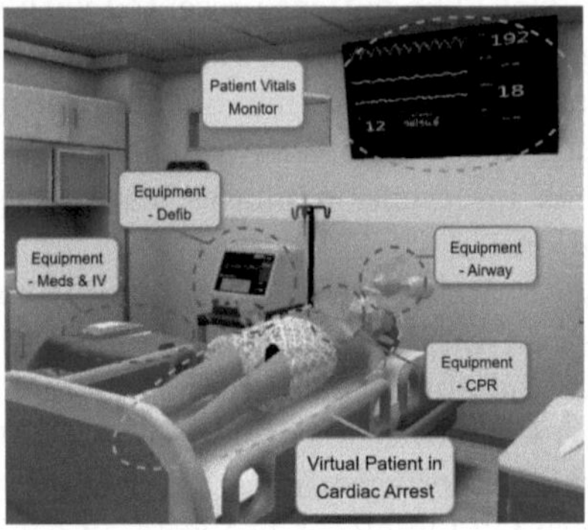

Fig. 1. Visual for AOIs as seen in VR environment ("Other Team Members" AOI not present in this figure).

2.3 Gaze Metrics and Transition Construction

To characterize the dynamic structure of clinicians' visual attention during cardiac arrest, we developed an analytical framework that models gaze-transition networks and their progression across clinically defined scenario stages. Visual attention forms the foundation of Level 1 SA in Endsley's model [5] and, under stress, often narrows toward dominant or familiar information sources while peripheral cues are neglected [7]. This cognitive tunnel vision motivates our focus on both exploratory transitions and sustained self-loops in the subsequent TNA metrics. To capture these attentional dynamics, we transformed clinicians' eye fixations into transitions between AOIs in the simulation. We constructed role-specific AOI fixation sequences, estimated transition probability matrices, and extracted TNA metrics (entropy, self-loop rate).

AOI Fixation Sequence Construction. Eye-tracking data were grouped by each clinician's assigned role (Airway, CPR, Defib, TeamLead). Using the AOIs defined in Sect. 2.2, every fixation instance was mapped and ordered by timestamp to form a role-specific AOI fixation sequence. Fixations without valid

AOI labels and all saccades were removed. Adjacent AOI pairs ($\text{AOI}_i \rightarrow \text{AOI}_j$) were extracted to represent moment-to-moment attentional transitions. These directed transitions serve as the basis for constructing the transition networks. For stage-specific transition networks, we retained a transition only when both fixations in an adjacent AOI pair fell within the same annotated scenario stage, excluding cross-stage transitions.

Transition Matrix Estimation. For each participant-role, we computed a 7×7 AOI transition count matrix C, where C_{ij} denotes the number of transitions from AOI i to AOI j. To stabilize transition probability estimates for sparsely populated rows, we applied mild Laplace smoothing (with smoothing constant $\lambda = 0.5$) to all non-empty rows; we reserve α for the significance level used in inferential tests. The smoothed transition probability matrix P was obtained by row normalization:

$$P_{ij} = \frac{C_{ij} + \lambda}{\sum_k (C_{ik} + \lambda)},$$

producing a row-stochastic matrix that models each clinician's attentional routing structure.

Transition-Network Metrics. Treating P as a weighted directed graph, we computed two complementary TNA-based metrics corresponding to key components of SA.

Entropy Entropy quantifies the unpredictability or dispersion of outgoing transitions from each AOI. Prior transition-based gaze studies have typically included self-transitions when computing transition entropy [14]. However, because self-loops in our context reflect attentional tunneling (i.e., sustained fixation on a single AOI) rather than exploratory visual sampling, we computed entropy from non-self transitions only ($j \neq i$). Concretely, for each AOI i with at least one non-self transition mass after smoothing, we defined a conditional distribution over $j \neq i$ by

$$\tilde{P}_{ij} = \frac{C_{ij} + \lambda}{\sum_{k \neq i} (C_{ik} + \lambda)}, \qquad j \neq i,$$

and set

$$H_i = -\sum_{j \neq i} \tilde{P}_{ij} \log_2 \tilde{P}_{ij}, \qquad H = \frac{1}{N} \sum_{i=1}^{N} H_i,$$

with $H_i = 0$ when $\sum_{k \neq i} (C_{ik} + \lambda) = 0$. This separation allows entropy to reflect cross-AOI unpredictability, while the self-loop metric captures attentional tunneling. Higher entropy indicates more diverse and exploratory visual scanning, and lower entropy reflects more structured and predictable attentional routing [3,14].

Self-loop Rate Self-loop rate quantifies repeated fixations on the same AOI and reflects the extent to which attention remains anchored to specific perceptual cues, rather than shifting across different areas. It is calculated by weighting self-loops by the proportion of total fixations on each AOI (w_i):

$$\text{Self-loop} = \sum_{i=1}^{N} w_i \cdot P_{ii}.$$

A high self-loop rate indicates strong attentional anchoring, or tunneling, in which individuals repeatedly focus on familiar or dominant cues, such as a particular monitor or piece of equipment, while neglecting surrounding information. This pattern is consistent with classical descriptions of "attention narrowness" and "cognitive tunnel vision", which are often observed under pressure or high task load [4,22]. Conversely, a low self-loop rate suggests a broader, more distributed pattern of visual attention, with gaze shifting more frequently between AOIs, indicating more active information gathering and monitoring across patient, equipment, monitors, and team members [9,29].

Together, these TNA-derived gaze metrics provide a quantitative characterization of how clinical roles dynamically allocate visual attention during high-fidelity resuscitation simulations.

2.4 Transition Network Analysis

In addition to the quantitative metrics described above, we performed a qualitative inspection of the role- and stage-specific transition networks to identify salient triadic and dyadic patterns. Following prior TNA work [25], we use the term *triadic motif* descriptively to refer to visually evident three-node closed loops in the AOI graphs (e.g., *Equipment - CPR — Patient — Other Team Members*) and use *dyadic motif* to refer to strongly recurring bidirectional AOI pairs that form stable two-node coupling structures (e.g., *Equipment - Defib — Patient Vitals Monitor*). These motifs are treated as interpretive units that summarize how two and three AOIs tend to be co-visited as part of recurring attentional routines, rather than as formally tested structures that occur more frequently than chance. We did not apply algorithmic motif enumeration or statistical over-representation tests; instead, motif-based descriptions in Sect. 3 are grounded in repeated visual patterns observed across the aggregated role- and stage-specific networks.

2.5 Statistical Analysis

Each participant contributed one observation per metric, yielding $n = 10$ observations per role (40 in total). We summarized entropy and self-loop estimates by role using medians with first and third quartiles, and compared TNA metrics and total fixation counts across roles using Kruskal–Wallis tests. Given the exploratory scope of this preliminary study, we do not report post-hoc pairwise comparisons or multiplicity-adjusted p-values; statistical significance was evaluated at the conventional $\alpha = 0.05$ threshold.

3 Results and Discussion

3.1 Role-Based Patterns in Visual Attention

Table 2. Comparison of Transition Network Analysis (TNA) Metrics Across Roles (values reported as median (Q1–Q3))

TNA Metric	Airway	CPR	Defib	TeamLead	KW p
Entropy	2.06 (1.792–2.126)	2.21 (2.182–2.241)	2.02 (1.929–2.073)	1.95 (1.746–2.098)	**0.0015****
Self-loop	0.38 (0.362–0.451)	0.39 (0.377–0.409)	0.49 (0.479–0.525)	0.45 (0.394–0.460)	**0.0016****

Note. Kruskal–Wallis (KW) tests compare distributions across roles.$^{**}p < .01$ at $\alpha = 0.05$ (exploratory; no post-hoc pairwise tests).

Although total fixation counts were comparable across four roles (all Kruskal–Wallis $p > .47$), AOI transition network structures diverged substantially, reflecting distinct demands and information needs. This reinforces prior work indicating that members of acute care teams allocate visual attention in role-specific ways, shaped by their distinct situational demands, coordination, and information needs [13,29,30].

Quantitative analysis of TNA metrics revealed significant role-based differences in transition entropy and self-loop rate ($p \approx .0015$). Those in CPR roles exhibited the highest transition entropy and relatively lower self-loop rates, whereas those in Defib roles showed the highest self-loop rates. Airway and TeamLead roles occupied intermediate positions on these metrics as seen in Table 2. Notably, while both CPR and Defib clinicians operated within highly centralized networks anchored by loops between their task-critical AOIs, such as *Equipment - CPR — Patient* and *Equipment - Defib — Patient Vitals Monitor*, the divergence in underlying gaze patterns indicates that CPR roles favored flexible multi-cue monitoring, while Defib roles showed more device-centric attentional tunneling. This aligns with prior research showing that technical roles in resuscitation often concentrate attention on immediate procedural and device cues as cognitive demands rise [1,6,15,21].

Conversely, Airway and TeamLead clinicians exhibited more distributed networks, with gaze transitions spanning *Equipment - Airway*, *Patient Vitals Monitor*, *Patient*, and *Other Team Members*. Such patterns suggest more exploratory and integrative monitoring, characteristic of teamwork and adaptive coordination [9,10]. Those in the TeamLead role, in particular, bridged patient data, monitors, and team dynamics, reflecting a broad situational overview consistent with effective leadership [17,24].

Qualitative inspection of role-specific transition networks (Fig. 2) revealed recurring dyadic and triadic gaze motifs, such as CPR clinicians cycling attention between *Equipment - CPR*, *Patient*, and *Other Team Members*, and TeamLeads linking *Patient Vitals Monitor*, *Patient*, and *Other Team Members* in closed loops. These interpretive patterns mirror the micro-coordination strategies described in gaze-based situational awareness (SA) studies, where clinicians

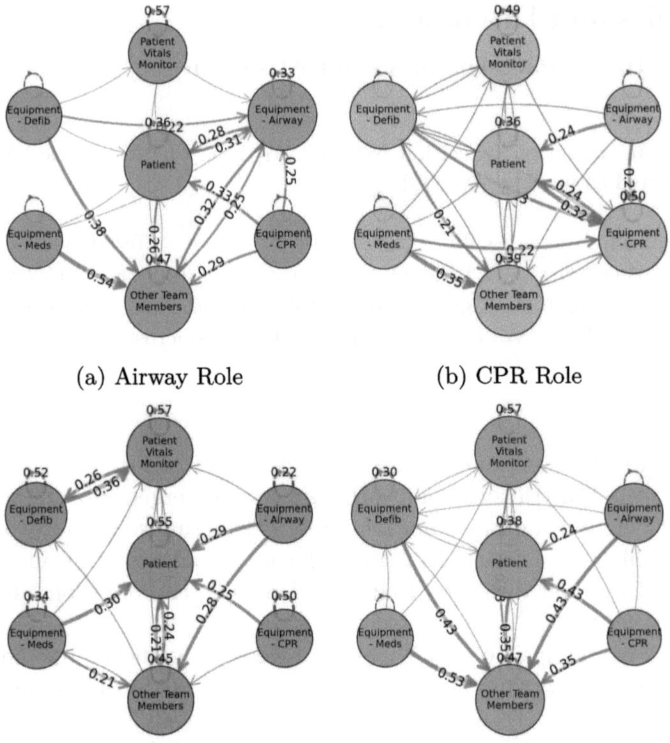

(a) Airway Role (b) CPR Role

(c) Defib Role (d) TeamLead Role

Fig. 2. Role-specific AOI transition networks for four resuscitation roles across seven AOIs, aggregated over all sessions. Node size reflects total fixations; edge thickness indicates transition probability; red edges denote self-loops. (Color figure online)

integrate perceptual cues with team interactions to maintain continuity of action [1,29]. Through the lens of Endsley's multi-level SA model [5], these motifs illustrate how roles support both Level 1 SA (cue perception) and Level 2 SA (meaning integration). In this framework, CPR clinicians couple patient status and feedback to take immediate action, and TeamLeads integrate information from multiple sources to provide a bird's-eye view and global oversight.

Altogether, these role-based analyses demonstrate that SA in acute cardiac resuscitation is encoded in the structure and dynamics of visual attention networks—distinctly shaped by role responsibilities, and emergent through both focused and distributed gaze behaviors that reflect task demands and teamwork situational imperatives.

3.2 Stage-Based Shifts in Attentional Structure

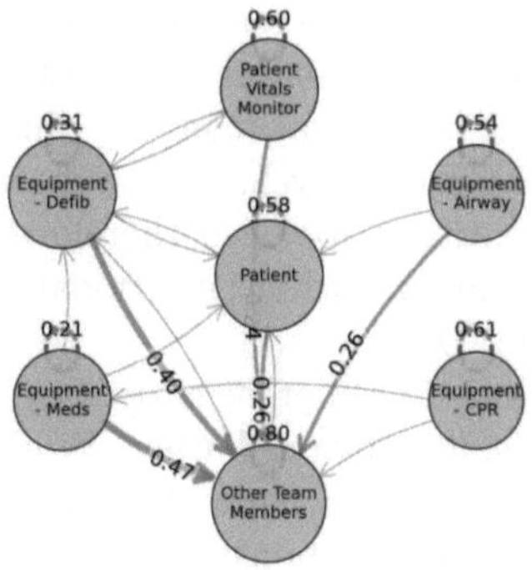

(a) CPR Role - Initial Simulation Stage

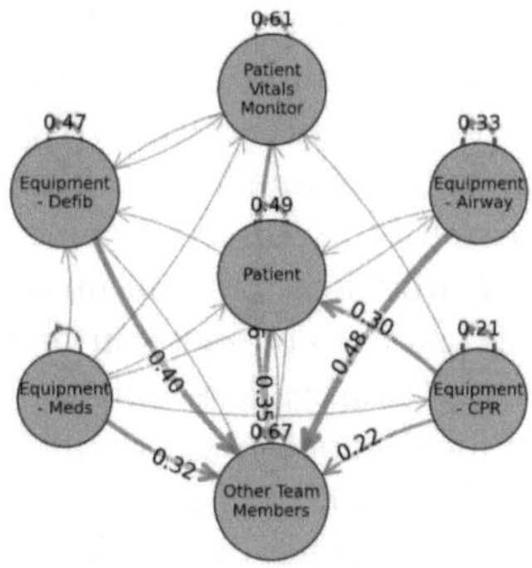

(b) TeamLead Role - Initial Simulation Stage

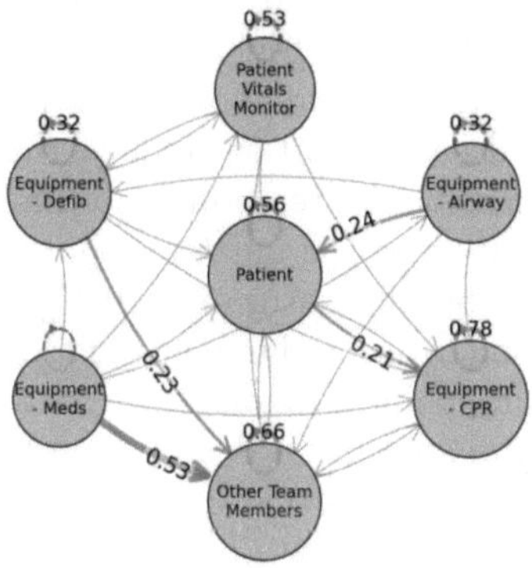

(c) CPR Role - Later-Intervention Stage

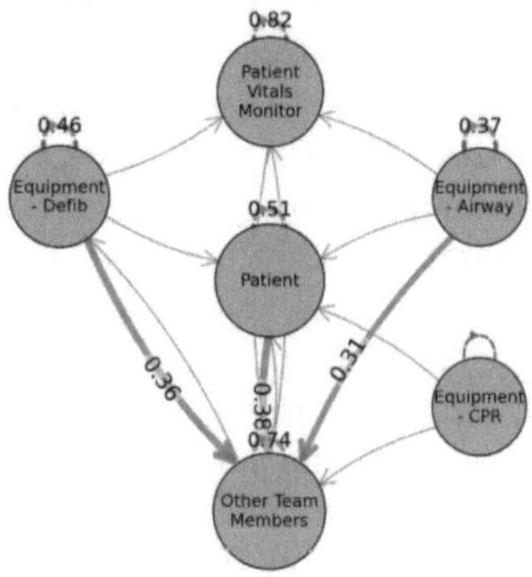

(d) TeamLead Role - Later-Intervention Stage

Fig. 3. Transition network diagrams for CPR and TeamLead roles across two stages of the cardiac arrest simulation. The top row depicts Stage 1 (early simulation), and the bottom row depicts Stage 5 (later intervention).

We focus on the CPR and TeamLead roles as they exemplify contrasting attentional strategies, with the CPR role expected to deliver hands-on chest compressions and track immediate patient response, while the TeamLead oversees team coordination, diagnoses, and decides on intervention steps. At the start of the simulation (Stage 1), clinicians in the CPR role showed broad exploratory scanning, distributing attention across multiple AOIs, including *Equipment - Defib*, *Patient*, and *Other Team Members*, with substantial self-loops on *Other Team Members* (.80), *Equipment - CPR* (.61), and *Patient Vitals Monitor* (.60). This pattern reflects the early diagnostic demands of rhythm confirmation, coordination with teammates, and integration of diverse perceptual cues before chest compression. As the scenario progressed to later intervention phases (Stage 5), the CPR gaze network became markedly more centralized around *Patient* and *Equipment - CPR*; self-looping on *Equipment - CPR* rose, while self-loops on *Other Team Members* and *Patient Vitals Monitor* decreased. This shift is consistent with increased motor workload during compressions, as attention is adaptively drawn to execution-critical AOIs and peripheral scanning diminishes—a phenomenon well documented in both perceptual psychology and acute resuscitation research [4,7,30]. Narrowing attentional focus is therefore adaptive, enabling CPR providers to maintain output quality while situational monitoring responsibilities shift to other team members [9,17].

In contrast, TeamLead participants followed a different trajectory. Their initial scanning focused on broad triadic motifs, integrating *Patient Vitals Monitor*, *Equipment - Defib*, and *Other Team Members*, with moderate self-loops at key anchors. This pattern highlights the leader's early responsibility for synthesizing information and stabilizing team workflow. By the intervention phase, TeamLead attention shifted toward monitoring-centric oversight: self-loops increased sharply on the *Patient Vitals Monitor* (.61 → .82) and *Other Team Members* (.67 → .74), while cross-node transitions declined. Figure 3 illustrates these stage-wise changes in attentional network structure for both CPR and TeamLead roles. Rather than indicating reduced situational awareness, this reflects an optimized supervisory strategy—leaders prioritize temporal coordination and team collaboration under high task intensity, assuming greater responsibility for global monitoring as execution-focused roles become saturated [10,17,24]. These stage-dependent shifts underscore how team cognition dynamically redistributes situational awareness in response to evolving clinical demands.

Taken together, the stage-wise shifts observed in CPR and TeamLead roles reveal a coordinated, functional reorganization of situational awareness (SA) across the resuscitation team. The divergent patterns observed illustrate the functional differentiation of SA, in which cognitive responsibilities are flexibly partitioned across roles in response to changing task demands. As CPR providers' attentional bandwidth contracts around execution, TeamLeads expand and stabilize their monitoring to maintain global team awareness—a compensatory strategy consistent with distributed cognition theories in acute care [10]. Importantly, TNA-derived motifs provide structural evidence for this redistribution: CPR networks converge into execution dyads, while TeamLead networks organize into high-stability self-loops. Overall, these findings demonstrate that SA in cardiac arrest resuscitation is not uniformly shared, but instead is dynamically rebalanced across roles and scenario stages to support coordinated performance under stress.

3.3 Limitations

Several considerations bound these findings. First, network metrics characterize gaze routing and persistence over clinically defined AOIs and should be interpreted as behavioral proxies of attention structure rather than direct measurements of higher-level situational comprehension or projection (Endsley Levels 2–

3; [5]). Second, with $n = 10$ per role this is an exploratory analysis; reported p-values are uncorrected for multiplicity, and the small sample limits detection of subtler role- or stage-level differences. Third, although VR provides a controlled and ecologically rich training environment, depth cues, peripheral vision, and field of view differ from in-person resuscitation and may shape AOI transition behavior in ways that do not generalize directly to bedside care.

4 Conclusion and Future Work

This study demonstrates how Transition Network Analysis (TNA) reveals the dynamic and compensatory nature of situational awareness in multiperson cardiac arrest VR simulations, including coordinated, adaptive redistribution of attention among team roles as scenarios unfold. CPR focus narrows during execution, while TeamLeads expand monitoring to support collective performance. Our findings highlight that situational awareness is neither static nor equally shared, but is dynamically reorganized across team roles, scenario phases, and clinical events. Recurring gaze patterns illustrate functional differentiation: as execution demands rise, monitoring responsibilities redistribute, supporting global performance, and preventing breakdowns in coordination. This network-analytic approach advances our understanding of team cognition in acute care. It showcases the utility of VR-based analytics for pinpointing phase-linked vulnerabilities and informing context-sensitive training.

For future work, we plan to extend our analyses beyond gaze data by integrating modalities such as team communication and physiological signals. We will also focus on event-centered analysis to capture how attention patterns reorganize around pivotal moments. Ultimately, these efforts aim to support richer modeling of individual and team situational awareness, guide training interventions, and enable real-time feedback for high-stakes collaborative environments.

References

1. Caloca-Amber, S., Mauriz, E., Vazquez-Casares, A.M.: Exploring eye-tracking data as an indicator of situational awareness in nursing students during a cardiorespiratory arrest simulation. Nurse Educ. Pract. **76**, 103911 (2024)
2. Cognitive3D: Cognitive3D: Objectives and Spatial Analytics. https://cognitive3d.com/product/objectives/ (2025)
3. Cui, Z., Sato, T., Jackson, A., Jayarathna, S., Itoh, M., Yamani, Y.: Gaze transition entropy as a measure of attention allocation in a dynamic workspace involving automation. Sci. Rep. **14**(1), 23405 (2024)
4. Duncan, J.: Information and uncertainty in a cumulative science of behavior: 25 years after broadbent's decision and stress. Am. J. Psychol. **109**(4), 617 (1996)
5. Endsley, M.R.: Toward a theory of situation awareness in dynamic systems. Hum. Factors **37**(1), 32–64 (1995)
6. Feller, S., Feller, L., Bhayat, A., Feller, G., Khammissa, R.A.G., Vally, Z.I.: Situational awareness in the context of clinical practice. In: Healthcare, vol. 11, p. 3098. MDPI (2023)

7. Hockey, G.R.J.: Effect of loud noise on attentional selectivity. Q. J. Exper. Psychol. **22**(1), 28–36 (1970)
8. Holmberg, M.J., et al.: Trends in survival after pediatric in-hospital cardiac arrest in the United States. Circulation **140**(17), 1398–1408 (2019)
9. Hunziker, S., et al.: Teamwork and leadership in cardiopulmonary resuscitation. J. Am. Coll. Cardiol. **57**(24), 2381–2388 (2011)
10. Keller, S., et al.: Behavioral sciences applied to acute care teams: a research agenda for the years ahead by a European research network. BMC Health Serv. Res. **24**(1), 71 (2024)
11. Kentros, M., Kamarianakis, M., Cole, M., Popov, V., Protopsaltis, A., Papagiannakis, G.: Non-linear, team-based VR training for cardiac arrest care with enhanced CRM toolkit. Eurographics technical report series (2025)
12. Kolbe, M., Boos, M.: Laborious but elaborate: the benefits of really studying team dynamics. Front. Psychol. **10**, 1478 (2019)
13. Kolbe, M., Burtscher, M.J., Manser, T.: Co-act–a framework for observing coordination behaviour in acute care teams. BMJ Qual. Saf. **22**(7), 596–605 (2013)
14. Krejtz, K., et al.: Gaze transition entropy. ACM Trans. Appl. Perception (TAP) **13**(1), 1–20 (2015)
15. Lavoie, P., et al.: A comparison of nurses' situation awareness and eye-tracking data in precardiac arrest simulations. Clin. Simul. Nurs. **81**, 101429 (2023)
16. Li, S., Duffy, M.C., Lajoie, S.P., Zheng, J., Lachapelle, K.: Using eye tracking to examine expert-novice differences during simulated surgical training: a case study. Comput. Hum. Behav. **144**, 107720 (2023)
17. Nallamothu, B.K., et al.: How do resuscitation teams at top-performing hospitals for in-hospital cardiac arrest succeed? A qualitative study. Circulation **138**(2), 154–163 (2018)
18. Perman, S.M., et al.: 2023 American heart association focused update on adult advanced cardiovascular life support: an update to the American heart association guidelines for cardiopulmonary resuscitation and emergency cardiovascular care. Circulation **149**(5), e254–e273 (2024)
19. Popov, V., et al.: Elucidating cognitive processes in cardiac arrest team leaders: a virtual reality-based cued-recall study of experts and novices. Ann. Med. **57**(1), 2470976 (2025)
20. Popov, V., Rochlen, L.R.: From communication to action: using ordered network analysis to model team performance in clinical simulation. BMC Med. Educ. **25**(1), 479 (2025)
21. Rasmussen, J., Lind, M.: A model of human decision making in complex systems and its use for design of system control strategies. In: American Control Conference, pp. 270–276. IEEE (1982)
22. Rasmussen, J., Rouse, W.B.: Human Detection and Diagnosis of System Failures, vol. 15. Springer Science & Business Media (2013)
23. Rosen, M.A., Dietz, A.S., Yang, T., Priebe, C.E., Pronovost, P.J.: An integrative framework for sensor-based measurement of teamwork in healthcare. J. Am. Med. Inform. Assoc. **22**(1), 11–18 (2015)
24. Rosenman, E.D., Branzetti, J.B., Fernandez, R.: Assessing team leadership in emergency medicine: the milestones and beyond. J. Grad. Med. Educ. **8**(3), 332–340 (2016)
25. Saqr, M., López-Pernas, S., Törmänen, T., Kaliisa, R., Misiejuk, K., Tikka, S.: Transition network analysis: a novel framework for modeling, visualizing, and identifying the temporal patterns of learners and learning processes. In: Proceedings of

the 15th International Learning Analytics and Knowledge Conference, pp. 351–361 (2025)
26. Sebok-Syer, S.S., Tawfik, D.: We cannot measure what we have not yet attempted to measure: steps towards reconceptualising team-based assessments in the health professions. Med. Educ. **59**(9), 895–897 (2025)
27. Thygesen, K., Alpert, J.S., Jaffe, A.S., Chaitman, B.R., Bax, J.J., Morrow, D.A., White, H.D., on behalf of the Joint European Society of Cardiology (ESC)/American College of Cardiology (ACC)/American Heart Association (AHA)/World Heart Federation (WHF) Task Force for the Universal Definition of Myocardial Infarction, E.G.: Fourth universal definition of myocardial infarction (2018). J. Am. College Cardiol. **72**(18), 2231–2264 (2018)
28. Trevi, R., Chiappinotto, S., Palese, A., Galazzi, A.: Virtual reality for cardiopulmonary resuscitation healthcare professionals training: a systematic review. J. Med. Syst. **48**(1), 50 (2024)
29. Weinberg, D.D., et al.: Visual attention patterns of team leaders during delivery room resuscitation. Resuscitation **147**, 21–25 (2020)
30. White, M.R., et al.: Getting inside the expert's head: an analysis of physician cognitive processes during trauma resuscitations. Ann. Emerg. Med. **72**(3), 289–298 (2018)

The Longitudinal Dynamics of GenAI Roles: An Idiographic Approach

Hesham Ahmed(✉), Aleya Siddika, Sonsoles López-Pernas, Markku Tukiainen, and Mohammed Saqr

University of Eastern Finland, Yliopistokatu 2, 80100 Joensuu, Finland
Hesham.ahmed@uef.fi

Abstract. This study explores the longitudinal dynamics of how eight PhD students perceive the role of GenAI in the effort they put in doing research tasks. We employed Experience Sampling Methods (ESM) to collect their perceptions on GenAI in relation to their effort whenever they utilized it for tasks requiring critical thinking over a month. We captured six dimensions of cognitive effort (knowledge, analysis, application, evaluation, understanding, and regulation). We applied a parsimonious Gaussian Mixture of Experts model to cluster students' effort-related variables, resulting in four perceived GenAI roles or states: Effortful, Cognitively Demanding, Facilitator, and Moderate. We then employed Transition Network Analysis with an Idiographic approach to understand how these states change longitudinally for every student. Our results reveal an inter-individual variability. Students exhibited different themes: some experienced unstable networks with no prominent patterns, others found GenAI interactions predominantly Effortful, while others viewed GenAI interactions solely as Moderate and Facilitator. These idiographic transitions outline the variable individual perceptions of GenAI roles and showcase the TNA's ability to provide a granular view of how such a temporal process unfolds over time.

Keywords: Transition Network Analysis · Idiographic · Learning Analytics · PhD Students · Self-regulation · Effort · Generative AI

1 Introduction

Improving students' performance and reaching educational outcomes has been a longstanding goal of educators and educational researchers [1–3]. The growing adoption of educational technology has allowed us to collect increasing amounts of information on students' learning processes and dynamics and what affects them [4, 5]. Using such data, students' self-regulation has been studied through various measures to capture how learners plan, monitor, and reflect on their learning [6, 7]. One of the significantly important variables found that impact students' performance is the effort exerted to study and learn. According to Carbonaro, (2005), effort in educational contexts is "the amount of time and energy that students expend in meeting the formal academic requirements established by their teacher and/or school" (p. 28) [8]. Students' effort can be directed

M. Saqr et al. (Eds.): TNA 2026, CCIS 3079, pp. 138–150, 2026.
https://doi.org/10.1007/978-3-032-34157-0_11

towards understanding, analyzing, recalling, or applying knowledge, and focusing on a specific task. With the recent rise of Generative Artificial Intelligence (GenAI), PhD students have integrated it in research tasks such as idea generation, data analysis, and writing [9], which might change how they direct and utilize their efforts.

Despite the abundance of research on self-regulation and effort, research addressing its relationship with GenAI tools is scarce. Further, research has mostly been one step or cross sectional with little research exploring the changing nature, perception, and role. Our study aims to showcase how PhD students' perceptions of GenAI roles in their research tasks. PhDs offer a distinct observation domain: students possess enough critical thinking skills and domain knowledge to maintain agency over GenAI. Furthermore, research is fundamentally composed of natural language tasks–the area where GenAI excels. This study's benefit is viewing the interaction with GenAI as a temporal journey, rather than a static event. In doing so, we utilize Transition Network Analysis (TNA) to allow us to represent how students' perceptions of GenAI roles change through time. Moreover, it will allow us to understand the process on an individual or idiographic level ($N = 1$) to show the different themes each student has followed. To this end, we aim to answer the following questions:

RQ1a: How do PhD students perceive the role of GenAI in research tasks that rely heavily on critical thinking?

RQ1b: How do the perceived GenAI roles change longitudinally for each student?

2 Background

The widespread use of Generative Artificial Intelligence (GenAI) prompted a similar investigation to understand its impact on cognitive effort and critical thinking [10]. For instance, Lee et al. (2025) surveyed 319 knowledge workers about their usage of GenAI. They concluded that GenAI changed the nature of tasks they engage in, for example, instead of cognitively engaging with the inquiry themselves, they review the GenAI's outputs [11]. Additionally, they found that GenAI might hinder critical engagement with work and lead to overreliance and diminished skills development. This outlines the double-edged sword nature of the GenAI-users interaction–although it might allow for optimization in efficiency, its users might risk failing to develop their skills due to the excessive cognitive offloading.

2.1 Group-Level and Idiographic Analysis

Previous studies in the learning analytics domain have predominantly focused on aggregate results and single time-points to analyze students' data. However, this approach can be limiting and potentially inaccurate. Group-level analysis relies on collecting data from a group, intending to generate statistics that represent the individuals within that group [12]; this method has been applied in the study of self-regulation processes, for example by [13]. The analysis of self-regulation processes using such an approach rest upon a false assumption that such processes are stable over time and lack inter-individual variations [14, 15]. Group-level analysis might then generate insights that, although useful in deriving broad patterns, are not applicable to all students, therefore limiting their usefulness [16]. Consequently, idiographic learning analytics emerged as a paradigm that rests upon the premise that students' learning process differs and group-level analysis might fail to reveal the individual differences of each student [17]. Specifically, the idiographic approach aims to discover the distinct process by studying the learning process on the individual level (N = 1) [18, 19]. The idiographic approach in education has been employed to study different aspects of educational psychology [20], such as stress [21] and self-regulation [22].

2.2 Methods Used in this Study

TNA is a novel framework that leverages stochastic process mining and probabilistic networks to model and identify the transition patterns in the learning process [23]. Nodes, for example, would represent the constructs under study (engagement, motivation, effort, etc.) and the transitions represented as weighted probabilistic directed edges between the nodes. Related work to our study includes research that targets understanding how the cognitive effort of PhD students' (N = 8) changes in relation to GenAI performance. They then used TNA to understand the overall transitions of all the students (Anonymized, 2026). Another study harnessed an idiographic approach to explore how a master's student's (N = 1) learning-related features such as anxiety, commitment, and regulation change over the course of thesis writing. Further, the study utilized TNA to understand how the learning states change intra-day, inter-day, and in relation to different activities (Anonymized, 2026). Sequence analysis is a method used to represent ordered events to discover patterns in them. It allows us to gain a bird's eye view of how a process evolved longitudinally by visualizing and summarizing large amounts of data [24]. Sequence analysis has been used in learning analytics to represent the changing nature of the learning process. Sequences can differ in the subject-under-study (states, events, or categories), actor (event-generator) time-granularity, and clustering method used to generate it. In education, it was used to represent students' roles in groups, learning management systems events, and interaction types on forums [25]. For example, actors could be a student, a teacher, a group of students, or pairs such as student-course. Clustering includes algorithms such as Hidden Markov Models, Differential sequence mining, and First Order Markov Models. Examples of related studies include An and Zhang, (2024) which utilized sequence analysis to understand the difference between heterogeneous and homogenous ability grouping on collaborative problem solving [26]. Another example is a study that investigated the differences in students' engagement trajectories through time at the course level and across a whole program [27].

3 Methodology

3.1 Data Collection and Preprocessing

In our study, eight PhD students participated in a month-long observational study to see how their cognitive processes changed when they used GenAI tools for tasks that required higher effort. We followed Lee et al.'s (2025) approach and used Experience Sampling Methods (ESM) [11]. The survey was administered as an external questionnaire. Each participant filled out a daily form whenever they used GenAI for a task that required critical thinking and understanding. The participants submitted multiple responses per day. The survey had a range of activities e.g., research support, writing and editing, data analysis and visualization. Regardless of task type, the same set of survey questions was used for all. We have measured six dimensions of cognitive effort, which is related to critical thinking. The collected dimensions are: effort in applying prior knowledge (application_effort), the effort needed to do the analysis (analysis_effort), effort that is needed to do the knowledge-based task (knowledge_effort), cognitive effort that is required to evaluate the critical thinking (evaluation_effort), understanding effort, and task-related effort (task_effort). The value of the effort variables was recorded on a 5-point Likert scale (1 = significantly less effort, 2 = slightly less effort, 3 = no change, 4 = slightly more effort, and 5 = significantly more effort). The entries of the dataset were first sorted by the participant's ID (user_code) and then by the date of the response.

3.2 Analysis Procedures

To highlight the individual variability in each of the effort variables, each was centered around its mean. To find patterns in the students' responses to each variable (RQ1a), clustering via parsimonious Gaussian Mixture of Experts [28] was implemented, through the MoEClust in R, in order to find a model that best provides an interpretable clustering of the different trends in the data. This process included testing different models (EII, VII, EEI, etc.) with different numbers of clusters (2–5). The criteria used to compare the suitability of the models and number of clusters were Akaike information criterion (AIC), Bayesian information criterion (BIC) [29], and interpretability. Additionally, the authors also verified that the selected cluster solution had high entropy (~0.85) —entropy close to 1 indicates delineation of classes [30]. As a result, Model EEV with 4 clusters was selected. EEV represents a model with equal volume & shape, variable orientation [28]. The following step included assigning descriptive labels to each cluster based on the different means of all the effort variables. Afterward, each cluster was mapped to a distinguishable color. Next, each of the students' responses was assigned a cluster and then created chronologically ordered sequences out of it using the From Variables to States to Trajectories method [31]. Finally, to answer RQ1b, we estimated a transition network for each PhD student and plotted it using the tna package in R [32].

4 Results and Discussion

To give an overview of PhD students' perceptions of the impact of GenAI on different categories of effort, descriptive statistics were calculated and shown in Table 1. The results show that the mean for all effort categories (excluding regulation) falls between 2 and 3. This indicates that GenAI has either decreased the effort slightly or created no change at all. The effort for regulation is relatively high with a mean of 3.83, indicating that the students are highly invested in their tasks.

The clustering of PhD students' daily responses resulted in four clusters (i.e., states) representing the roles students perceive GenAI to play during their daily research interactions in relation to their effort (RQ1a). Each student was assigned to one of these four

Table 1. Descriptive statistics of the features included in the analysis. M = Mean. SD = Standard Deviation. MED = Median.

Feature name	Question	M	SD	MED
Effort knowledge	How would you describe the effort required for knowledge-based tasks (e.g., recalling facts) when using a GenAI tool compared to not using one (e.g., Google or reading online)?	2.22	1.00	2.00
Effort analysis	How would you describe the effort required for analysis, synthesis, or critical thinking when using a GenAI tool compared to not using one?	2.45	1.09	2.00
Effort application	How would you describe the effort required for the application of your knowledge learned in your research in creating the task when using a GenAI tool compared to not using one?	2.38	1.06	2.00
Effort evaluation	How would you describe the effort required for evaluation, testing, or examining your ideas as you interact or build the assignment when using a GenAI tool compared to not using one?	2.36	1.05	2.00
Effort understands	How would you describe the effort required to understand ideas, new concepts, or techniques when using a GenAI tool compared to not using one?	2.22	1.12	2.00
Effort regulation	Effort (effort and effort regulation): "I have put enough effort into my learning/ tasks to accomplish them" "I am focused on performing my learning tasks and resisting distractions"	3.83	0.72	4.00

states based on their responses. **Effortful**(State 1) is characterized by above-average scores over all the effort variables. **CogDemand**(State 2) is characterized by above-average scores in cognitively demanding activities (analysis, evaluation, and understanding), below-average scores for (knowledge, application), and significantly low scores for regulation. **Facilitator**(State 3) is characterized by below-average scores for all features except effort for regulation. **Moderate**(State 4) is characterized by average scores for all variables. Subsequently, we studied how students' sequences of states evolved over time (RQ1b). Figure 1 showcases how the states changed for each PhD student over the days, grouped by similarity. There is a large variation in the way individuals perceive GenAI over the study period. Some students showed relatively stable patterns, whereas others alternated frequently between states.

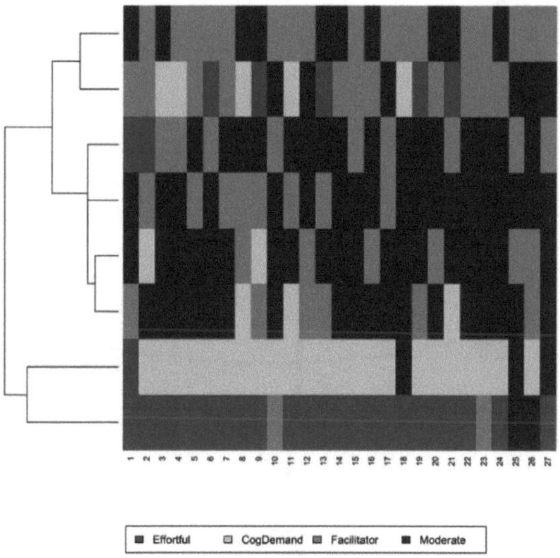

Fig. 1. Sequence index plot of the effort states for each PhD student ordered chronologically. The sequences are ordered by similarity (Color figure online).

We then zoomed in on each individual and their dynamics, whereby we used transition network analysis to represent the state transitions of each PhD student, grouped by similarity of patterns and connections. The nodes represent the effort states, and the directed connections represent the sequence of events. The bigger the node, the higher the frequency at which the student experienced the state. The thicker the lines, the more statistically reliable the transitions are.

Student 3 shows the most unstable effort states, as each state has 3 or more outward connections (Fig. 2). This might be indicative of undertaking tasks with different natures, changing GenAI output quality, or a mixture of both. The frequent change between states might represent a burnout cycle. The network shows that, contrary to other states, when this student perceived the GenAI as Effortful, there was 0% chance of remaining in such a state; changing to either **Facilitator**(0.8) or **Moderate**(0.2). When the student perceived the GenAI as a **Facilitator**, there was a 0.45 chance they remained unchanged.

Student 1 and Student 4 share a similarity, which is that they never viewed GenAI as **Cognitively demanding**. Student 1's was dominantly in an **Effortful** state, with a 0.86 chance of remaining in such a state (see Fig. 3). If they viewed the GenAI as **Facilitator**or **Moderate**, there was a 100% and 50% chance of transitioning to an **Effortful** view, respectively. This might indicate that GenAI for this student was mainly a liability. Meanwhile, Student 4's transitions mainly involved GenAI as **Moderate**and **Facilitator**. From state **Facilitator**, there was a 0.88 chance to move to state **Moderate**, and from **Moderate**, there was a 0.56 chance of remaining unchanged and 0.44 chance of returning to **Facilitator**.

Students 2 and 5 have never viewed GenAI as Effortful. Instead, they mostly exerted **Moderate**levels of effort in their interactions and tended to remain in such a state when reached (see Fig. 4). For Student 2, there was a notable change in perceptions

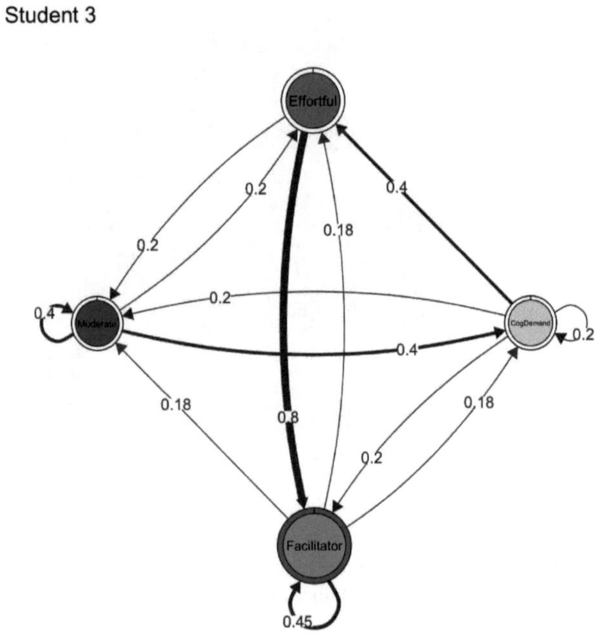

Fig. 2. A visualization of the transition network of the effort states of Student 3

that created a chain starting from **Cognitively demanding**, moving to **Facilitator**, and ending with **Moderate**. Meanwhile, for Student 5, whenever they were in state **Cognitively demanding**they always changed to **Moderate**levels of effort. Whenever they perceived GenAI as **Moderate**, there was a high chance of 0.71 (Student 2) and 0.67 (Student 5) of remaining unchanged.

Student 7 and Student 8's transitions involved only a loop between views **Moderate**and **Facilitator**(see Fig. 5). When Student 7 was in a **Moderate**effort state, there were 0.67 of them remaining in such a state. When they viewed GenAI **Facilitator**, there was a 0.75 chance of them transitioning to State **Moderate**. Contrarily, when Student 8 viewed GenAI as a **Facilitator**, there was a 0.62 chance of them remaining in such a state. When they were in the **Moderate**state, there was a 0.7 chance of transitioning to the **Facilitator**state.

Student 6 is unique as they never perceived GenAI as a **Facilitator**(see Fig. 6). The other unique characteristic is that whenever they were in either State **Effortful**or **Moderate**, they always changed their views of GenAI to State **Cognitively demanding**. Meanwhile, if they were in state **Cognitively demanding**, there was a 0.87 chance of remaining unchanged.

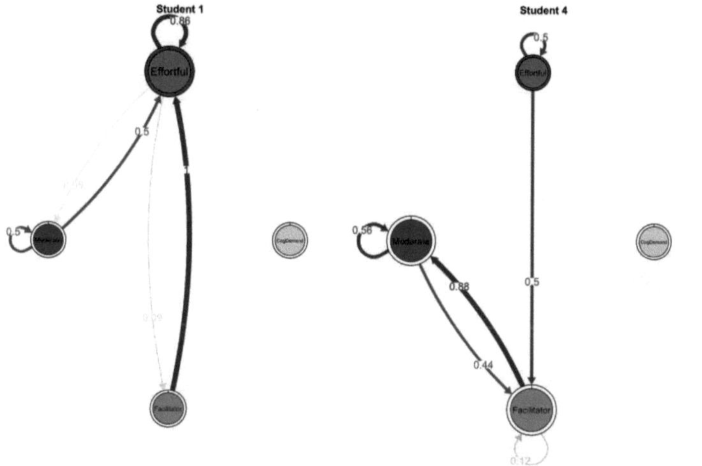

Fig. 3. A visualization of the transition network of the effort states of Student 1 (left) and Student 4 (right)

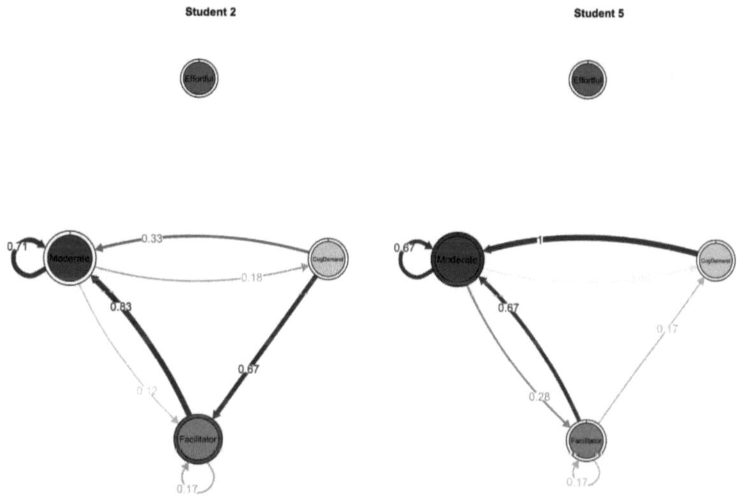

Fig. 4. A visualization of the transition network of the effort states of Student 2 (left) and Student 5 (right)

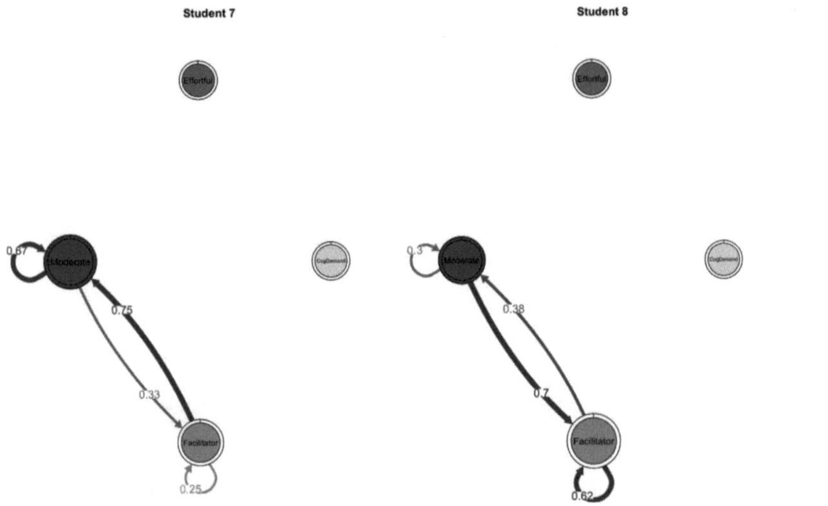

Fig. 5. A visualization of the transition network of the effort states of Student 7 (left) and Student 8 (right)

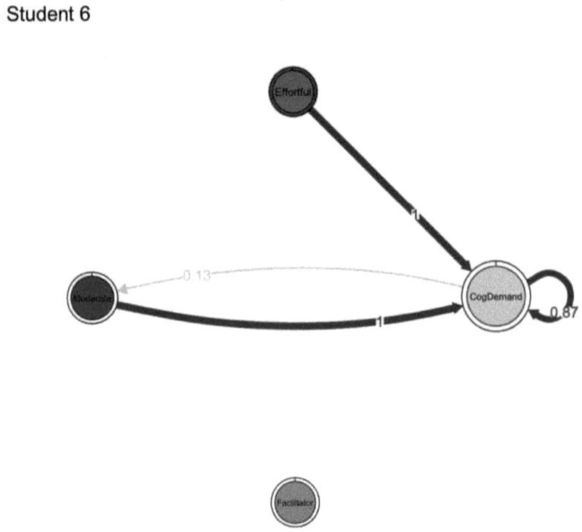

Fig. 6. A visualization of the transition network of the effort states of Student 6

5 Reflection and Future Directions

The relation between student effort and academic achievement has been studied over the years [8, 33–35]. For example, in a macroeconomics course, undergraduates responded to a survey on how much time (as a proxy for effort) they spent on various tasks, and such answers were used to model the relationship using Least Squares Estimates [36]. Similarly, to examine the relationship between learning environment and student effort, answers to a survey from primary and secondary students were analyzed through linear regression [37].

In this exploratory paper, we aimed to understand the longitudinal patterns of effort allocation during real-world GenAI use. Consequently, we collected data from eight PhD students on their ratings of how their effort changed while using GenAI for regular research tasks over a period of a month. The effort dimensions include applying prior knowledge, performing analysis, executing knowledge-based tasks, assessing critical thinking, comprehending information, and general task execution. We then used Gaussian Mixture of Experts Clusters to group the observations based on different data trends. The clustering resulted in four states: **Effortful**, **CogDemand**, **Facilitator**, and **Moderate**. We then created a TNA for each student.

Our results show that students' transitions vary greatly. For instance, Student 3 experienced all effort states and had transitions between all of them. This could be indicative of undertaking tasks with different natures, changing GenAI output quality, or a mixture of both. Students 1 and 4 did not find the GenAI interactions to be **Cognitively demanding**. Conversely, Student 1 mainly found GenAI interactions to be Effortful, while Student 4 found it to be **moderately**helpful. Students 2 and 5 never experienced State **Effortful** and they mainly viewed their interaction with GenAI as requiring moderate effort. Students 7 and 8 have found GenAI neither **Effortful** nor cognitively demanding compared to when not using it. Student 6 has found GenAI to be cognitively demanding for most of the time.

Reflecting on the recent work by Lee et al. (2025) [11], the **Effortful** state is a representative of cases where GenAI increased cognitive demands possibly due to task complexity, perceived high stakes, or high confidence in self of the researcher to question the GenAI output, which leads to more interactions. The **CogDemand**state might indicate a shift of effort toward the verification and integration of GenAI outputs instead of performing information gathering and application. The **Facilitator**state might correspond to low-stake tasks which the researcher trusts GenAI to perform well, which leads to decreased effort except for minimal oversight. Finally, the Moderate state may represent a neutral mode of interactions, in which perceived effort remains relatively unchanged. For future research, we aim to extend the observation window to collect more extensive data points per person to construct richer transition networks. Furthermore, we intend to map different GenAI roles to the specific tasks being performed to be able to investigate the dyadic and triadic patterns that were observed. Our study showcases how TNA can be used for idiographic analysis of ESM data as a variation of other established frameworks such as VaSSTra.

Acknowledgments. This work has been supported by FAST, the Finnish Software Engineering Doctoral Research Network, funded by the Ministry of Education and Culture, Finland. Additionally, this paper is co-funded by the Academy of Finland (Suomen Akatemia) Research Council for theproject "Towards precision education: Idiographic learning analytics (TOPEILA)", Decision Number350560 which was received by the last author, and the project "Optimizing Clinical Reasoning inTime-Critical Scenarios: A data-driven multimodal approach (CRETIC)", Decision Number 360746,which was received by the third author.

References

1. Missildine, K., Fountain, R., Summers, L., Gosselin, K.: Flipping the classroom to improve student performance and satisfaction. J. Nurs. Educ. **52**(10), 597–599 (2013). https://doi.org/10.3928/01484834-20130919-03
2. Papamitsiou, Z., Economides, A.A.: Learning analytics and educational data mining in practice: a systematic literature review of empirical evidence. J. Educ. Technol. Soc. **17**(4), 49–64 (2014)
3. G. Wiggins: Educative Assessment. Designing Assessments To Inform and Improve Student Performance. ERIC, (1998). Accessed 08 Dec 2025. https://eric.ed.gov/?id=ed418997
4. Chatti, M.A., Dyckhoff, A.L., Schroeder, U., Thüs, H.: A reference model for learning analytics. Int. J. Technol. Enhanc. Learn. **4**(5/6), 318 (2012). https://doi.org/10.1504/IJTEL.2012.051815
5. Clow, D.: An overview of learning analytics. Teach. High. Educ. **18**(6), 683–695 (2013). https://doi.org/10.1080/13562517.2013.827653
6. Schunk, D.H., Zimmerman, B.J.: Self-regulation in education: retrospect and Prospect. In: Self-Regulation of Learning and Performance. Routledge (1994)
7. Zimmerman, B.J., Kitsantas, A.: Comparing students' self-discipline and self-regulation measures and their prediction of academic achievement. Contemp. Educ. Psychol. **39**(2), 145–155 (2014). https://doi.org/10.1016/j.cedpsych.2014.03.004
8. Carbonaro, W.: Tracking, students' effort, and academic achievement. Sociol. Educ. **78**(1), 27–49 (2005). https://doi.org/10.1177/003804070507800102
9. Andersen, J.P., et al.: Generative artificial intelligence (GenAI) in the research process–a survey of researchers' practices and perceptions. Technol. Soc. **81**, 102813 (2025)
10. Yan, L., Pammer-Schindler, V., Mills, C., Nguyen, A., Gašević, D.: Beyond efficiency: empirical insights on generative AI's impact on cognition, metacognition and epistemic agency in learning. Br. J. Educ. Technol. **56**(5), 1675–1685 (2025). https://doi.org/10.1111/bjet.70000
11. Ler, H.-P., et al.: The impact of generative AI on critical thinking: self-reported reductions in cognitive effort and confidence effects from a survey of knowledge workers. Presented at the Proceedings of the ACM CHI Conference on Human Factors in Computing Systems, (2025). Accessed 07 Mar 2025
12. Hernández-García, Á., Conde, M.Á.: Beyond the average: person-specific analytics for precision education. Learn. Individ. Differ. **121**, 102730 (2025). https://doi.org/10.1016/j.lindif.2025.102730
13. Artino, A.R., Stephens, J.M.: Academic motivation and self-regulation: a comparative analysis of undergraduate and graduate students learning online. Internet High. Educ. **12**(3–4), 146–151 (2009). https://doi.org/10.1016/j.iheduc.2009.02.001
14. Molenaar, P.C.M., Campbell, C.G.: The new person-specific paradigm in psychology. Curr. Dir. Psychol. Sci. **18**(2), 112–117 (2009). https://doi.org/10.1111/j.1467-8721.2009.01619.x
15. Piccirillo, M.L., Rodebaugh, T.L.: Foundations of idiographic methods in psychology and applications for psychotherapy. Clin. Psychol. Rev. **71**, 90–100 (2019). https://doi.org/10.1016/j.cpr.2019.01.002
16. Saqr, M.: Group-level analysis of engagement poorly reflects individual students' processes: why we need idiographic learning analytics. Comput. Hum. Behav. **150**, 107991 (2024)
17. Saqr, M.: Modelling within-person idiographic variance could help explain and individualize learning. Br. J. Educ. Technol. **54**(5), 1077–1094 (2023). https://doi.org/10.1111/bjet.13309
18. Saqr, M., Ito, H., López-Pernas, S.: Individualized analytics: within-person and idiographic analysis. In: Saqr, M., López-Pernas, S. (eds.) Advanced Learning Analytics Methods: AI, Precision and Complexity, pp. 471–491. Springer Nature Switzerland, Cham (2026). https://doi.org/10.1007/978-3-031-95365-1_18

19. Saqr, M., López-Pernas, S.: Idiographic learning analytics: a definition and a case study. In: 2021 International Conference on Advanced Learning Technologies (ICALT), pp. 163–165 (2021). https://doi.org/10.1109/ICALT52272.2021.00056
20. Ito, H., López-Pernas, S., Saqr, M.: A scoping review of idiographic research in education: too little, but not too late. In: 2024 IEEE International Conference on Advanced Learning Technologies (ICALT), Nicosia, North Cyprus, Cyprus, pp. 10–12. IEEE (2024). https://doi.org/10.1109/ICALT61570.2024.00010
21. Aalbers, G., Hendrickson, A.T., Vanden Abeele, M.M., Keijsers, L.: Smartphone-tracked digital markers of momentary subjective stress in college students: idiographic machine learning analysis. JMIR Mhealth Uhealth. **11**, e37469 (2023). https://doi.org/10.2196/37469
22. Saqr, M., Cheng, R., López-Pernas, S., Beck, E.D.: Idiographic artificial intelligence to explain students' self-regulation: toward precision education. Learn. Individ. Differ. **114**, 102499 (2024). https://doi.org/10.1016/j.lindif.2024.102499
23. Saqr, M., López-Pernas, S., Törmänen, T., Kaliisa, R., Misiejuk, K., Tikka, S.: Transition network analysis: a novel framework for modeling, visualizing, and identifying the temporal patterns of learners and learning processes. In: Proceedings of the 15th International Learning Analytics and Knowledge Conference, pp. 351–361. ACM, Dublin Ireland (2025). https://doi.org/10.1145/3706468.3706513
24. Valle Torre, M., Oertel, C., Specht, M.: The sequence matters in learning - a systematic literature review. In: Proceedings of the 14th Learning Analytics and Knowledge Conference, in LAK '24, pp. 263–272. Association for Computing Machinery, New York, NY, USA (2024). https://doi.org/10.1145/3636555.3636880
25. M. Saqr et al.: Sequence Analysis in Education: Principles, Technique, and Tutorial with R. In: Learning Analytics Methods and Tutorials: A Practical Guide Using R, M. Saqr and S. López-Pernas, Eds., Cham: Springer Nature Switzerland, 2024, pp. 321–354. https://doi.org/10.1007/978-3-031-54464-4_10.
26. An, S., Zhang, S.: Effects of ability grouping on students' collaborative problem solving patterns: evidence from lag sequence analysis and epistemic network analysis. Think. Ski. Creat. **51**, 101453 (2024). https://doi.org/10.1016/j.tsc.2023.101453
27. Saqr, M., López-Pernas, S.: The longitudinal trajectories of online engagement over a full program. Comput. Educ. **175**, 104325 (2021). https://doi.org/10.1016/j.compedu.2021.104325
28. Murphy, K., Murphy, T.B.: Gaussian parsimonious clustering models with covariates and a noise component. ADAC **14**(2), 293–325 (2020). https://doi.org/10.1007/s11634-019-00373-8
29. Burnham, K.P., Anderson, D.R.: Multimodel inference: understanding AIC and BIC in model selection. Sociol. Methods Res. **33**(2), 261–304 (2004). https://doi.org/10.1177/0049124104268644
30. Celeux, G., Soromenho, G.: An entropy criterion for assessing the number of clusters in a mixture model. J. Classif. **13**(2), 195–212 (1996). https://doi.org/10.1007/BF01246098
31. López-Pernas, S., Saqr, M.: From variables to states to trajectories (VaSSTra): a method for modelling the longitudinal dynamics of learning and behaviour. In: García-Peñalvo, F.J., García-Holgado, A. (eds.) Proceedings TEEM 2022: Tenth International Conference on Technological Ecosystems for Enhancing Multiculturality, pp. 1169–1178. Springer Nature, Singapore (2023). https://doi.org/10.1007/978-981-99-0942-1_123
32. S. Tikka, tsn: Time-Series Network Analysis. (2025). R. Accessed 24 Nov 2025. https://github.com/santikka/tsn
33. Anaya, L.M., Zamarro, G.: The role of student effort on performance in PISA: revisiting the gender gap in achievement. Oxf. Econ. Pap. **76**(2), 533–560 (2024). https://doi.org/10.1093/oep/gpad018

34. Dunlosky, J., Badali, S., Rivers, M.L., Rawson, K.A.: The role of effort in understanding educational achievement: objective effort as an explanatory construct versus effort as a student perception. Educ. Psychol. Rev. **32**(4), 1163–1175 (2020). https://doi.org/10.1007/s10648-020-09577-3
35. Natriello, G., McDill, E.L.: Performance standards, student effort on homework, and academic achievement. Sociol. Educ. **59**(1), 18–31 (1986). https://doi.org/10.2307/2112483
36. Krohn, G.A., O'Connor, C.M.: Student effort and performance over the semester. J. Econ. Educ. **36**(1), 3–28 (2005). https://doi.org/10.3200/JECE.36.1.3-28
37. Hopland, A.O., Nyhus, O.H.: Learning environment and student effort. Int. J. Educ. Manag. **30**(2), 271–286 (2016). https://doi.org/10.1108/IJEM-05-2014-0070

Modeling Collaboration

Student-AI Dialogue Through Multiple Lenses: Interaction Profiles, Linguistic Patterns, and Content Trajectories

Kamila Misiejuk(✉), Stella Kolarik, Florence Lehnert, Daiana Rinja, Volkan Yücepur, and Marcus Specht

CATALPA, FernUniversität in Hagen, Germany, Germany
{kamila.misiejuk,stella.kolarik,florence.lehnert,daiana.rinja, volkan.yucepur,marcus.specht}@fernuni-hagen.de

Abstract. Generative AI has become an indispensable digital sparring partner for students in higher education and now plays a central role across a wide range of learning activities. This study aims to provide a nuanced view of student-AI interaction patterns and their relationships to both linguistic characteristics and the functional content of students' prompts in authentic contexts. First, k-means cluster analysis was applied based on student-AI interaction patterns to identify distinct student profiles. Second, methods from Natural Language Processing were applied to analyze linguistic features across profiles and assignment's based on indicators of writing accuracy, effort, writing style and emotional content. Third, Transition Network Analysis was used to compare students interaction patterns and prompt content across the identified profiles to reveal differences. As a result, we identified four student–AI interaction profiles—low, moderate, intensive, and multi-chat—that differed not only in the frequency and length of their chatbot interactions, but also in prompting style, sentiment, and prompt content. These patterns signal a need for pedagogical strategies that guide students toward reflective and learning-oriented uses of AI tools.

Keywords: Student-AI Interactions · Transition Network Analysis · Natural Language Processing · Student Profiles · Clustering

1 Introduction

Generative AI tools have rapidly entered higher education, offering students support with a personalized learning experience or direct help with completing assignments [2,7]. Compared to other learning support, AI can reduce perceived pressure and effort [7]. However, there are also anxieties and concerns surrounding the use of AI in higher education [33]. These concerns focus, for example, on misuse by students or risks for academic integrity [14,33]. To make informed decisions about the role of AI in courses and curricula, instructors need a clearer

M. Saqr et al. (Eds.): TNA 2026, CCIS 3079, pp. 153–171, 2026.
https://doi.org/10.1007/978-3-032-34157-0_12

understanding not only of students' attitudes toward AI, but of how students actually interact with these tools during learning activities.

Despite the growing interest concerning the use of AI for higher education, surprisingly little research focuses on the students' actual use through analyzing interaction traces. Past studies analyze students' knowledge and perceptions of AI and their intentions to use AI tools [5,12] or focus on prompting behaviors showing that interventions can improve the use of prompting strategies [29]. However, much less is known about students' authentic use of AI tools in real course contexts and how they formulate prompts while working through assignments. This creates a gap in understanding the underlying interaction processes, linguistic characteristics, and functional content of student prompts. These factors may influence learning behavior and the quality of AI responses. Prior work has examined prompting strategies or engagement patterns separately [27,34], but has rarely connected these dimensions or analyzed them at scale using actual student–AI interaction traces. A more integrated view is needed to understand how students position AI within their programming workflows and whether distinct usage styles emerge.

Identifying empirically grounded profiles can reveal whether students exhibit distinct ways of engaging with AI. This information is currently missing but crucial for developing individualized or adaptive support mechanisms (RQ1). Building on the identified profiles analyzing linguistic features allows us to uncover differences or similarities in how students express themselves through prompts, enriching our understanding of each interaction profile (RQ2). Adding further detail prompt content and temporal structure provide insight into the strategies students use when interacting with AI, whether they ask conceptual questions, request writing support, or engage in off-topic dialogue and how they transition between prompt types. By linking prompt content and transitions to the identified profiles, we explore whether students who interact differently with AI also systematically differ in the kinds of prompts they produce and transition patterns they create (RQ3).

To address the gap of research focusing on students' actual use of AI tools and prompting behaviors, we will examine prompt logs from students using a large language model (LLM) powered chatbot. The analysis will focus on interaction patterns, linguistic characteristics and prompt content. The aim is to characterize distinct profiles of student-AI prompting and answer the following research questions:

- RQ1: What types of profiles emerge from student-AI interaction patterns?
- RQ2: How do linguistic features differ across student profiles and assignments?
- RQ3: How do student-AI interaction profiles relate to the content of the prompts?

These three research questions enable a comprehensive understanding of how learners engage with AI tools during learning assignments. By examining interaction patterns, linguistic characteristics, and prompt content jointly, we can determine whether clear, distinguishable student profiles exist—or whether students tend to interact with AI in similar ways. The resulting insights can later support the development of analytics-based detection of these profiles and enable personalized guidance, scaffolding, or interventions tailored to distinct ways of working with AI.

2 Background

2.1 Student-AI Interactions

Within higher education, AI tools are increasingly being used not only as information retrieval systems but as collaborative learning partners that participate in joint meaning-making and regulation of learning processes [8,20]. With LLMs, these systems can be trained on broad domain knowledge and can engage through the use of natural language, enabling students to interact with them in ways that resemble peer collaboration. In educational settings, student-AI interaction can thus be understood as an iterative process in which learners use AI to explore ideas, complete academic tasks, solve problems, and seek formative feedback across different stages of the learning cycle [20]. In the present study, such interactions are captured through behavioral engagement metrics derived from chat logs, including the frequency and volume of prompts, chats, and assignment-level activity, which serve as the basis for identifying distinct interaction patterns.

To better understand how students actually learn with AI in this emerging landscape, a growing body of research has begun to examine student–AI interactions by identifying patterns or profiles of engagement. These profiles capture meaningful variation in how learners position AI within their study practices: from instrumental, surface-level reliance for task completion to more reflective, self-regulatory collaboration styles [1,30,34]. To characterize such interaction patterns, studies have applied a range of methods, such as latent profile analysis of self-report data [30], clustering based on engagement metrics from log data [34], and fine-grained coding of student–AI exchanges to distinguish different prompting strategies and information needs [1] - each offering a different lens on how students interact with AI systems.

For example, Stojanov et al. [30] identified five student–AI profiles based on university students' self-reported reliance on ChatGPT across a range of academic tasks, including groups such as *proactive learners*, who used AI for planning, feedback, and other self-regulatory purposes, and *assignment delegators*, who depended on AI primarily to generate or complete assignment products. These profiles, however, are derived solely from survey responses and do not incorporate actual interaction traces or the content of students' prompts.

Complementing these survey-based profiles, log-based work such as Wang et al. [34] has clustered learners by engagement metrics and performance when working with an AI coach (e.g., frequency of AI-supported activities and AI-generated learning scores), showing that engagement volume differentiates groups such as *most effective*, *passive*, and *inefficient* learners. In these studies, engagement is quantified through counts of activities and scores, not through the actual student-AI exchanges.

Finally, process-oriented research such as Amoozadeh et al. [1] has analyzed chat logs from CS1 students solving programming problems with ChatGPT, coding prompts by their information need (e.g., requests for full solutions vs. debugging help) and level of task decomposition (e.g., full-description, step-by-step, or hybrid prompting), and relating these strategies to how students navigate the problem-solving process. This work offers a detailed view into prompt content, but it is based on a small sample, remains largely descriptive, and does not develop broader, person-centred profiles or systematically link prompt types to aggregate engagement metrics.

Previous work has conceptualized interaction profiles predominantly through self-reported reliance patterns or aggregate engagement metrics (e.g., frequency of AI-supported activities), often without examining the linguistic or functional content of student prompts [30,34]. As a result, relatively little is known about how distinct engagement profiles map onto different prompting strategies, especially at scale. Even when prompt content is analysed in depth, as in Amoozadeh et al. [1], this is typically done in small case studies without integrating large-scale engagement metrics or deriving robust, content-informed profiles. In this study, we address this gap by deriving student–AI interaction profiles directly from large-scale chat logs and characterizing them using both engagement features and the linguistic and functional properties of students' prompts.

2.2 Student Prompting Strategies

Whereas interaction profiles describe how learners engage with AI across tasks and time, prompting captures the micro-level communicative actions through which this engagement is enacted. The prompt is the actionable unit through which students operationalize intentions, articulate goals, and seek support. As such, it provides a critical lens for understanding how students reason with and direct LLMs in authentic learning contexts. Although *prompting* in educational psychology, traditionally refers to instructional cues provided to learners to scaffold planning, self-regulation, or metacognitive processes [4,10,21], the present work examines prompts produced by learners when interacting with an AI system. While these traditions differ in agency and purpose, both conceptualize prompts as externalizations of cognitive processes. Accordingly, established linguistic indicators used in educational text analytics (e.g., readability, spelling accuracy, sentiment, and verbosity) can serve as proxies for engagement, cognitive effort, uncertainty, and affective state in student–AI interactions.

Empirical studies find substantial variation in students' prompting behaviors and their effects on outcomes. Sawalha et al. [27] show that simple copy-and-paste prompting produces substantially weaker model responses than reformulated or multi-question prompts, indicating that students' effort to structure their requests improves downstream performance. Carrasco-Sáez et al. [6] identify grammar quality, contextualization, and task specificity as predictors of output accuracy, further suggesting that prompts encode meaningful information about students' intentions, domain understanding, and strategy use. Given

LLMs' sensitivity to natural language, even subtle differences in wording, sentence structure, or contextual cues can alter system behavior [6,28]. These findings highlight prompting as a measurable interaction trace through which learners communicate uncertainty, decompose tasks, or delegate work to AI.

Functional analyses of student prompts provide greater insight into how students position AI within their learning activities. The dialogue act (DA) labeling schema of McNichols et al. [18], derived from authentic student–LLM interactions, distinguishes writing requests, editing requests, contextual questions tied to assignment requirements, conceptual questions addressing domain knowledge, verification prompts, context-providing inputs (e.g., instructions or code snippets), off-topic conversational turns, and miscellaneous utterances. These categories capture not only the informational target of a prompt, but also the learner's role expectations: whether the AI is treated as an explainer, editor, validator, or collaborator. Such functional distinctions position prompting as more than a surface linguistic artifact, instead reflecting students' task framing and problem-solving orientation.

Theoretical work in prompt engineering offers complementary mechanisms explaining why particular prompting strategies succeed. In the LLM interaction context, a prompt is the user input that guides or triggers the system's output [6,11]. For instance, Carrasco-Sáez et al. [6] distinguish the Guide Contextualization Strategy, in which students provide explicit contextual information to steer the model, from the Specific Purpose Strategy, in which the objective of the request is narrowly defined. These strategies align with functional prompt patterns described in White et al.'s Prompt Pattern Catalog [36], including context control, input semantics, output customization, error identification, prompt improvement, and interaction management. Many empirical student prompt types map naturally to these mechanisms: context-providing prompts reflect context control, verification prompts correspond to error identification, and writing or editing requests instantiate output customization. This correspondence suggests that students routinely deploy strategies that resemble prompt engineering principles, even without formal training.

Despite the growing research on prompting strategies, little work integrates interaction metrics, linguistic characteristics, and theoretically grounded prompt-content categories to examine heterogeneous prompting behaviors. Few studies have used clustering approaches to identify prompting profiles at scale, and existing efforts are typically context-specific or based on small cohorts [1]. As a result, little is known about how prompting behaviors vary across learners, how they relate to interaction trajectories, or how linguistic and functional prompting features co-occur within distinct engagement patterns.

To address these gaps, the present study extends the StudyChat coding scheme [18] by introducing additional conversational categories, such as agreement, disagreement, and polite language (i.e., sentiment analysis), to better capture the social and dialogic nature of student–AI interactions. This multidimensional approach enables a systematic investigation of emergent interaction patterns through three perspectives: (RQ1) identifying what types of student–AI interaction profiles emerge, (RQ2) examining how linguistic features differ across these profiles and across assignments, and (RQ3) analyzing how interaction profiles relate to the content of students' prompts. By integrating behavioral, linguistic, and content-level dimensions, the study contributes a novel perspective on how students engage with LLMs in higher education.

3 Methods

3.1 Dataset

In this research, we utilized the StudyChat dataset [18], publicly available on HuggingFace (huggingface.co/datasets/wmcnicho/StudyChat). The dataset was collected over two offerings of an AI course. Student interactions were captured through a web-based LLM chatbot powered by GPT-4o-mini, which students were encouraged to use freely across all seven course assignments. In total, the dataset comprises 16,849 prompts from 2,213 chats by 203 students. The prompts in the StudyChat dataset were annotated using dialogue acts, following the work of Wood et al. [37] (see Table 1). A sample of 150 utterances was annotated by four human annotators through an iterative process, while the remaining data was coded by an LLM using a prompt-based approach. The LLM annotations were then validated by the same four annotators, who independently re-annotated a new sample of 154 utterances. More details about the annotation procedure and its validation are provided in McNichols et al. [18].

Table 1. Prompt coding scheme (from [18])

Prompt type	Description
Writing	The student asks the LLM to generate text, such as code, explanations, or summaries.
Editing	The student asks for modifications or improvements to existing code or text.
Contextual Questions	The student asks a question based on something from the assignment or prior conversation.
Conceptual Questions	The student asks a general question about programming, libraries, tools, or CS concepts unrelated to the conversation.
Verification	The student requests validation of their code, writing, or output to ensure correctness.
Context	The student supplies relevant information to the LLM, such as assignment instructions, code snippets, or error messages.
Off Topic	Conversations unrelated to the assignment, such as casual discussions, greetings, or expressions of gratitude.
Misc	A catch-all category for dialogue acts that do not fit elsewhere.

3.2 Analysis

To identify profiles based on student-AI interaction patterns (RQ1), we applied k-means clustering, which is well-suited for larger datasets and continuous variables [24]. Student profiles were clustered using the following metrics: the total number of assignments in which a student interacted with the LLM chatbot, the total number of chats, the total number of student prompts, the number of prompts per chat, and the total number of chats per assignment. The number of clusters was determined using the elbow method, which indicated k = 4 as the optimal solution (see Fig. 1). The four-cluster solution explained 67.7% of the total variance (between- to total sum of squares ratio, BSS/TSS = 0.677), while silhouette analysis indicated weak-to-moderate cluster separation (mean silhouette width = 0.301). Findings should be interpreted as tendencies rather than discrete categories.

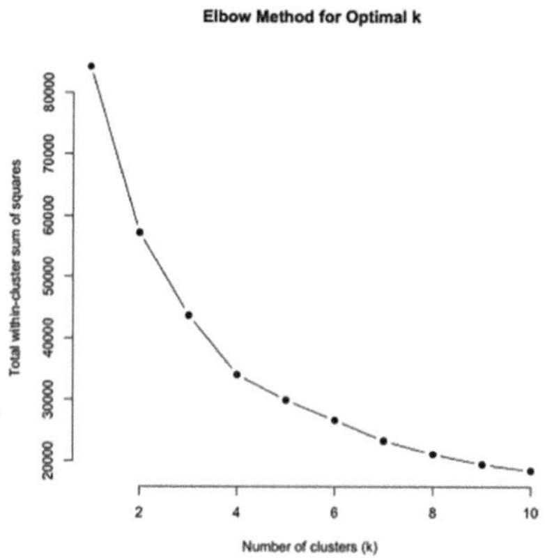

Fig. 1. Optimal k determination by elbow method for student-AI interaction patterns

To address the research question on the linguistic characteristics of different student-AI interaction profiles (RQ2), we first extracted linguistic features from the student prompts. Specifically, we used the compound sentiment score metric (`VADER` R package [23]), Flesch-Kincaid Readability Score (`quanteda` R package [3]), spelling error rate (`hunspell` R package [19]), punctuation density, and the number of words per prompt. These linguistic indicators were selected to capture different aspects of student writing: spelling error rate and punctuation density as proxies for writing accuracy, words per prompt as a measure of effort or dedication, Flesch-Kincaid Readability Score to reflect writing style, and sentiment to capture emotional content. We first used descriptive statistics (mean and standard deviation) to summarize these features across student-AI interaction profiles. To test whether linguistic features differed across profiles, we conducted Kruskal–Wallis tests (`stats` R package [22]). In addition, we plotted the means for each linguistic feature per assignment and student-AI interaction profile.

To investigate how student-AI interaction profiles relate to the content of the prompts (RQ3), we first examined the standardized residuals of prompt types by student-AI interaction types to identify over- and underrepresented prompt types within each interaction category. Next, we applied Transition Network

Analysis (TNA) [26] (TNA R package [31]) to explore the patterns of prompt type transitions across different student–AI interaction profiles. TNA is based on stochastic process mining and probabilistic network models, and it operationalizes first-order Markov models to capture transition patterns in learning processes. Previously, it has been applied to study transition probabilities between stimulus events, emotional reactions, and emotion regulation strategies during collaborative learning [32], as well as to model transition trajectories in student engagement across academic programs [17]. We also explored communities within the TNA networks, defined as groups of states that frequently transition between one another [25], and examined the out-strength, betweenness and diffusion centralities across all interaction profiles for different prompt types. All TNA comparison plots for RQ3 can be found here figshare.com/s/85fb7c268176b1b6e071.

4 Results

4.1 RQ1: What Types of Profiles Emerge from Student-AI Interaction Patterns?

The k-means cluster analysis revealed four main interaction types in our dataset (see Table 2), with each student classified based on their interaction patterns. The majority of students ($n = 99$) exhibited a *low interaction* pattern. These students showed very low engagement across all metrics, with minimal participation and few prompts per chat. The second-largest group ($n = 76$) demonstrated *moderate interactions*. Here, students interacted with the LLM chatbot selectively across multiple assignments, contributing a few prompts per chat and engaging in a moderate number of chats overall. A smaller group ($n = 16$) showed *intensive interactions*. These students sent many prompts per chat and had higher total prompts per student than average, while their activity was concentrated in fewer chats. Finally, a group of students ($n = 12$) exhibited *multi-chat interactions*. They broke their work into many chats, resulting in above-average chats per student and chats per assignment, as well as higher total prompts per student. However, prompts per chat were slightly below average.

Table 2. K-means cluster summary of student–AI interactions

	Low (n = 99)	Moderate (n = 76)	Intensive (n = 16)	Multi-Chat (n = 12)
Prompts per chat	−0.3716	−0.3926	1.4379	−0.3581
Total prompts per student	−0.9052	−0.3741	0.7212	1.2327
Chats per student	−0.7678	−0.2424	−0.1173	1.8038
Chats per assignment	−0.3434	−0.2522	−0.4419	1.7009
Total assignments	−1.5418	0.4186	0.3165	0.4894

4.2 RQ2: How Do Linguistic Features Differ Across Student Profiles and Assignments?

Students with the *intensive* interaction profile produced the highest number of words ($M = 8743$, $SD = 8295$), followed by *multi-chat* ($M = 4842$), *moderate* ($M = 4152$), and *low* ($M = 3308$) (see Table 3). The Kruskal–Wallis test indicated a significant difference in word counts across interaction profiles ($\chi^2(3) = 1279$, $p < 0.001$). Sentiment scores were similar across *intensive* ($M = 0.153$), *low* ($M = 0.153$), and *moderate* ($M = 0.156$), but lower in *multi-chat* ($M = 0.120$); the Kruskal–Wallis test confirmed a significant difference across profiles ($\chi^2(3) = 24$, $p < 0.001$). Flesch-Kincaid readability scores were slightly higher in *multi-chat* ($M = 34.58$) than in the other profiles (*intensive* $M = 21.89$, *low* $M = 21.98$, *moderate* $M = 21.45$), but differences were not statistically significant ($\chi^2(3) = 4.9$, $p = 0.177$). Spelling error rates were lowest in *intensive* ($M = 0.005$) and highest in *low* and *multi-chat* ($M = 0.007$), with significant differences across profiles ($\chi^2(3) = 17$, $p < 0.001$). Punctuation density was highest in *multi-chat* ($M = 38.70$) and lower in the other profiles (*intensive* $M = 31.21$, *low* $M = 28.52$, *moderate* $M = 28.96$), but the Kruskal–Wallis test indicated no significant difference ($\chi^2(3) = 3.7$, $p = 0.29$).

Table 3. Descriptive and inferential statistics of linguistic features across student-AI interaction profiles.

		Intensive	Low	Moderate	Multi-Chat	Kruskal–Wallis Test	
						χ^2 (df = 3)	*p*-value
Number of Words	M	8743	3308	4152	4842	1279	< 0.001***
	SD	8295	3770	5248	5854		
Sentiment Score	M	0.153	0.153	0.156	0.120	24	< 0.001***
	SD	0.377	0.374	0.368	0.368		
Flesch-Kincaid Score	M	21.89	21.98	21.45	34.58	4.9	0.177
	SD	104.08	103.21	85.35	219.59		
Spelling Error Rate	M	0.005	0.007	0.006	0.007	17	< 0.001***
	SD	0.039	0.058	0.049	0.053		
Punctuation Density	M	31.21	28.52	28.96	38.70	3.7	0.29
	SD	166.01	26.11	34.12	564.39		

Significance levels: *** p < 0.001; ** p < 0.01; * p < 0.05.
Sample sizes: Intensive = 3395; Low = 3370; Moderate = 7238; Multi-Chat = 2846

Across assignments, students with *intensive* interaction profile consistently produced the most words (7656–10865), showing a stable trend (see Fig. 2). Students with *low* profile wrote fewer words (2636–4070) with a slight increasing trend, *moderate* students were stable (3499–5274), and students with *multi-chat* profile were variable, increasing overall (3278–7210). Sentiment scores were stable for students with *intensive* profile (0.082–0.232) and *low* profile (0.121–0.219), mildly increasing for students with *multi-chat* profile (0.072–0.175), and variable for students with *moderate* profile (0.104–0.232). Flesch-Kincaid readability was mostly stable for students with *intensive*, *low*, and *moderate* profiles (13–48), but highly variable for students with *multi-chat* profile (16–94). Spelling error rate remained stable and low for students with *intensive* (0.002–0.007) and *multi-chat* (0.004–0.010), with slight fluctuations for students with *low* and *moderate* profiles (0.002–0.017). Punctuation density was stable for students with *intensive*, *low*, and *moderate* profiles, but variable for students with *multi-chat* profile, peaking at assignment 3 (95.10).

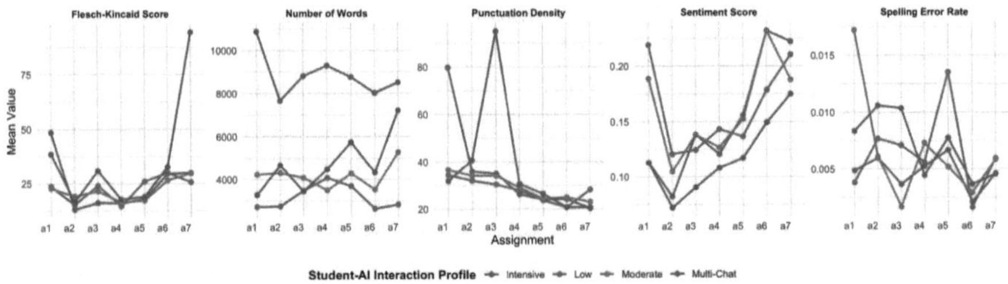

Fig. 2. Mean values of linguistic features across assignments, grouped by student-AI interaction profile. Each panel shows trends for a specific feature.

4.3 RQ3: How Do Student-AI Interaction Types Relate to the Content of the Prompts?

The most common prompt type in our dataset was *conceptual questions* (n = 5,199), followed by *writing requests* (n = 4,336), *provide context* (n = 3,028), and *contextual questions* (n = 2,933). Less frequent prompt types included *verification* (n = 647), *editing requests* (n = 418), *off-topic* prompts (n = 250), and *miscellaneous* prompts (n = 33).

The Mosaic plot revealed distinct distributions of prompt types across student interaction patterns (see Fig. 3). Within the *Intensive* interaction group, *writing request* and *conceptual questions* prompts were underrepresented, while *provide context*, *off-topic* and *contextual questions* prompts were overrepresented. A similar profile was observed for the *Multi-Chat* group, although in this case, *conceptual questions* were overrepresented and *provide context* prompts were underrepresented. Students in the *Low* and *Moderate* interaction groups both showed an overrepresentation of *writing request* prompts and an underrepresentation of *provide context.* Additionally, the *Low Interaction* group had fewer *verification* prompts but more *off-topic* and *miscellaneous* prompts, while the *Moderate Interaction* group had fewer *conceptual questions* and *off-topic* prompts. All reported differences were statistically significant.

For the *Intensive Interaction* group (see Fig. 4a, students frequently moved from *verification* prompts, where they checked their code or output for correctness, to *writing request* prompts. Many transitions also targeted *writing request*, highlighting a strong focus on text or code generation. *Writing request* prompts exhibit the highest in-strength centrality, followed by *contextual questions* and

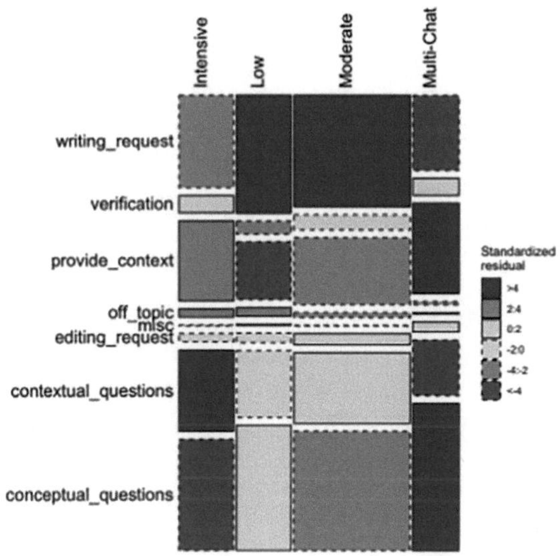

Fig. 3. Mosaic plot of association between student interaction types and prompt types. Standardized residuals indicate where specific prompt types are overrepresented (blue) or underrepresented (red) within each interaction group. Grey indicates no statistical significance. (Color figure online)

conceptual questions, indicating that these prompts are frequent destinations within workflows (see Fig. 5). Out-strength and diffusion centralities are highest for *miscellaneous* prompts, while *off-topic* and *conceptual questions* show the highest betweenness centrality. Additionally, transitions from *miscellaneous* to *contextual questions*, *conceptual questions*, and *writing request* suggest that students often supplied information or sought clarification before requesting new content, while transitions from *editing request* to *contextual questions* indicate iterative refinement as students modified existing content while clarifying assignment requirements.

In the *Moderate Interaction* group (see Fig. 4b), transitions commonly occurred from *provide context* prompts, where students provided assignment instructions, code snippets, or error messages, to *writing request* prompts, and from *editing request* to *writing request*, reflecting attempts to produce or improve text based on supplied context. *Conceptual questions* exhibit the highest in-strength centrality. Out-strength and diffusion centrality are highest for *miscellaneous* prompts. *Off-topic* prompts show the highest betweenness centrality. Occasional transitions from *off-topic* to *provide context* prompts suggest brief digressions before students returned to task-relevant information.

For the *Multi-Chat* group (see Fig. 4c), students demonstrated complex transition patterns. *Conceptual questions*, where they asked about programming languages, libraries, or computer science concepts, received input from *miscellaneous*, *verification*, and *contextual questions*, highlighting a blend of general

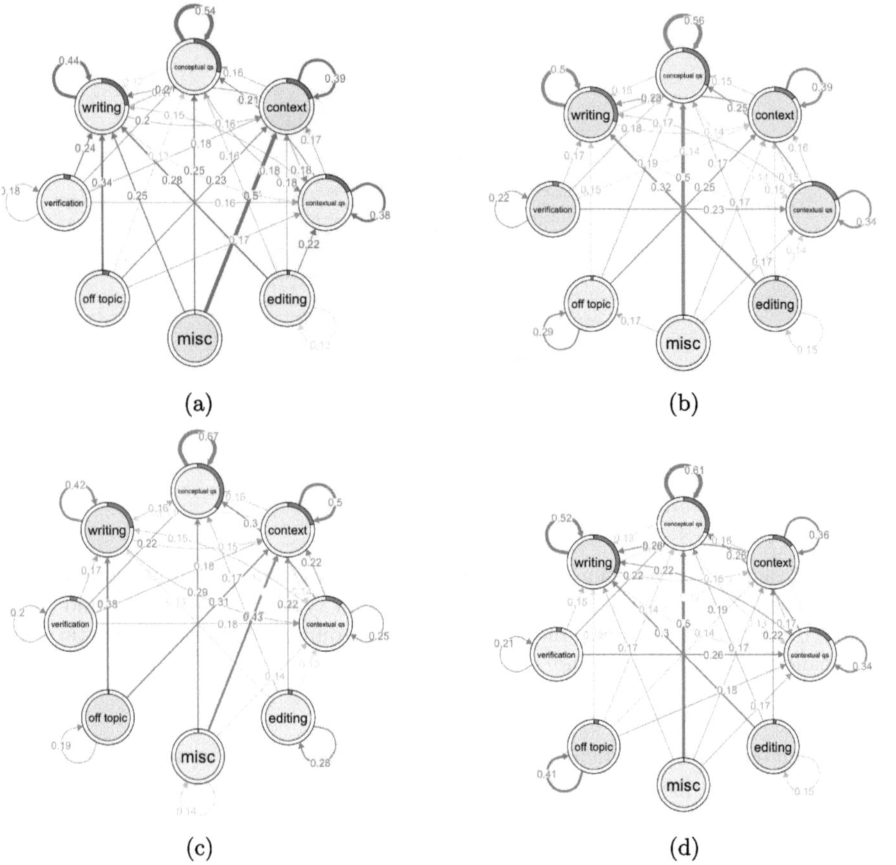

Fig. 4. TNA plots of prompt type transitions for (a) *Intensive* (green) (b) *Moderate* (yellow), (c) *Multi-Chat* (purple) (d) *Low* (red) interaction types. Only probabilities of at least 0.1 are shown. Node colors indicate different communities. (Color figure online)

inquiry, validation, and contextual reasoning. *Contextual* prompts received transitions from *contextual questions*, *miscellaneous*, *off-topic*, and *editing request*, reflecting iterative information provision and refinement. *Verification* prompts also transitioned to *conceptual questions*, showing cycles of checking outputs and seeking conceptual understanding.

Finally, the *Low Interaction* group (see Fig. 4d) displayed the strongest self-loop in *off-topic* prompts, indicating occasional disengagement or casual conversation, which is also reflected in the highest betweenness centrality for *off-topic*. *Conceptual questions* had the highest in-strength centrality, followed by *writing request* prompts. Out-strength and diffusion centralities are highest for *miscellaneous* prompts. Transitions from *verification*, *miscellaneous*, and *contextual questions* to *conceptual questions*, as well as from *context*, *contextual questions*, and *editing* to *writing*, suggest that students alternated between providing information, asking questions, and generating content.

The differences among the various prompt types across student-AI interaction profiles are also reflected in the community structures. The *Intensive Interaction* group features one community that combines *miscellaneous* and *context* prompts, and another community encompassing all other prompt types, highlighting a distinction between information-providing and task-focused prompts. In the *Moderate Interaction* group, one community includes *miscellaneous*, *off-topic*, and *conceptual questions*, while the remaining prompt types form a separate community, suggesting occasional digressions or clarifications before returning to core tasks. The *Multi-Chat* group exhibits a community comprising *writing* and *off-topic* prompts, and another containing all other types, emphasizing the interplay between content generation and casual interaction. Finally, the *Low Interaction* group shows two communities with four prompt types each: one including *writing*, *editing*, *context*, and *off-topic*, and the other consisting of *conceptual questions*, *contextual questions*, *verification*, and *miscellaneous*, reflecting a clear separation between task execution and information-seeking or clarification prompts.

5 Discussions

Our analysis highlighted four student-AI interaction patterns that differed substantially not only in how they interacted with the AI but also in the linguistic features and content of their prompts and prompting patterns.

The low interaction group engaged with the AI only minimally, producing very few prompts and showing little sustained use across assignments. Their language use reflected this limited engagement: they wrote the fewest words and made the most spelling errors. Despite this minimal and less accurate language production, their sentiment remained relatively positive. This pattern suggests that their limited use of the LLM-chatbot was unlikely to stem from frustration with the tool and may instead be driven by other factors. Their prompts were dominated by writing requests, off-topic questions, and miscellaneous inputs, with strong off-topic loops suggesting unfocused or exploratory use rather than task-driven engagement. Conceptual questions functioned as the central point around which many other prompt types converged, whereas off-topic prompts frequently bridged otherwise separate prompt types, further reinforcing the group's diffuse and inconsistent interaction style.

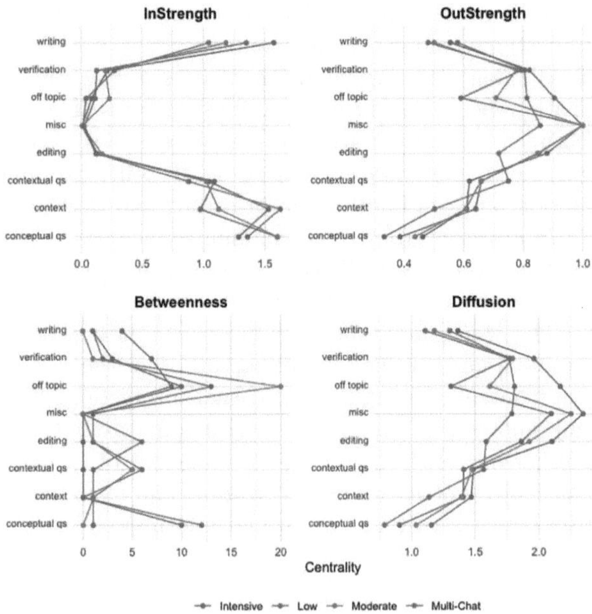

Fig. 5. In-strength, out-strength, betweenness, and diffusion centralities of each prompt types for each student-AI interaction types.

In contrast, the moderate interaction group participated selectively but consistently across assignments, producing moderate word counts, stable sentiment, and mid-level spelling accuracy. Their prompt patterns centered on writing requests, which commonly followed contextual or editing prompts, indicating a process-oriented approach to writing support. Conceptual questions remained the most influential prompt type in their network structure, while off-topic prompts again held the highest betweenness centrality, although they were far less disruptive than in the low interaction group. This pattern may be partly explained by the community analysis, which showed that off-topic, miscellaneous, and conceptual questions clustered within a single community. This suggests that students in this group may have used the chatbot in two distinct modes: a more exploratory mode, where they shifted between off-topic and conceptual inquiries to better understand the topic, and a more task-focused mode that was directed toward completing the assignment.

The intensive student–AI interaction pattern differed from both low and moderate users. Students in this group produced many prompts within fewer chats, which may reflect a completion-focused prompting style rather than frustration, as suggested by their maintained moderate sentiment. Linguistically, they generated the longest responses, which could result from longer individual prompts as well as extensive copy-pasting behavior. This interpretation is further supported by their low rate of spelling errors. Their prompt content patterns highlighted an emphasis on providing context and off-topic prompts, while writing requests and conceptual questions were relatively rare but played a structurally central role, bridging interactions with the AI when they occurred. The high out-strength and diffusion centralities of multiple prompt types suggest that intensive users explored diverse conversational paths.

Finally, students in the multi-chat student–AI interaction group exhibited a breadth-oriented rather than depth-oriented pattern, initiating many chats across assignments while using slightly fewer prompts per chat. Their linguistic profile contrasted with that of the intensive group: their prompts grew longer over successive assignments, their sentiment was the lowest among all students, although it increased over time, and they had relatively high spelling error rates. Conceptual questions and prompts providing context were the most prominent in this group. Context prompts also had the highest in-strength centrality, while verification prompts showed the highest betweenness centrality across all interaction groups, reflecting frequent requests for validation of code, writing, or outputs to ensure correctness. Writing requests and off-topic prompts formed a distinct community within their interactions, suggesting that writing requests were treated separately from other academic inquiries, with students primarily focused on generating text or engaging in off-topic discussion. Together, these patterns indicate more effortful or uncertain engagement with the LLM-chatbot and may also reflect dissatisfaction with its performance.

These four interaction patterns highlight emerging differences in how students integrate AI into their assignment-solving practices. Although our data do not allow us to make strong causal claims, the substantial differences in prompting styles suggest that students may be engaging with AI in ways that mirror their existing study habits, which could potentially reinforce both productive and less productive learning behavior. This insight reflects emerging findings that students may turn to AI for quick solutions, which can limit opportunities for deeper learning [13,16,35]. These patterns highlight a key challenge: AI can support understanding and provide rapid feedback [15], but it may also exacerbate disparities in self-regulation, encourage overreliance on automated reasoning, and obscure students' actual learning needs [1,9,38]. Without pedagogical guidance, these divergent patterns could become normalized in ways that reinforce existing inequities or undermine student learning.

This study presents a rich picture of student–AI interactions while solving computer science assignments; however, it is not without limitations. The primary limitation concerns the labeling of prompts, which was conducted mostly by an LLM with only partial human validation. This approach was necessary due to the large volume of data (over 16,000 prompts), which made careful, fully manual coding infeasible. Future research could therefore explore alternative, potentially more reliable methods for coding datasets of this scale. In addition, we did not triangulate our findings with student grades to examine whether specific patterns of AI use were associated with higher assignment or course performance. This limitation arose because complete grade data were not available for all students, and our aim was to fully utilize the entire dataset rather than restrict the analysis to a smaller subsample. Future studies could also examine the assignment tasks in more detail. For example, the observed drop in sentiment scores in Assignment 2 may be related to characteristics of that particular assignment, which warrants further investigation. Finally, while the large number of data points provides strong quantitative power, it constrains the depth of qualitative interpretation. For instance, the higher word counts observed in the intensive-use group could reflect more elaborate and thoughtful prompts, but they could also be the result of copy-pasted content. Distinguishing between such interpretations would require more fine-grained qualitative analysis.

6 Conclusions

This study identified four distinct patterns of student–AI interaction during computer science assignments, reflecting differences in engagement intensity, prompting style, and language use. These patterns suggest that students integrate AI into their assignment-solving practices in ways that may mirror their broader study habits, with some students using AI as a focused tool for task completion and others engaging more diffusely or with greater uncertainty. As AI becomes increasingly present in educational settings, understanding how students interact with it and what those interactions reveal about their learning becomes essential. The findings point to the need for pedagogical guidance that helps students engage with AI in ways that support rather than shortcut their learning.

Acknowledgments. K.M. was partially funded by the *Development of the Ecosystem for Novel Learning Resources and Network Data Techniques* project (Postdoktorandinnenförderung: Eigenes Sachkostenbudget funding, FernUniversität in Hagen) and conducted this research in cooperation with the LEAD:FUH project funded by the Stiftung Innovation in der Hochschullehre (1001-3223).

Declaration on Generative AI. During the preparation of this work, the authors used ChatGPT to improve on the readability and check language mistakes. After using this tool, the authors reviewed and edited the content as needed and took full responsibility for the content of the publication.

References

1. Amoozadeh, M., et al.: Student-AI interaction: a case study of cs1 students. In: Proceedings of the 24th Koli Calling International Conference on Computing Education Research, pp. 1–13 (2024)
2. Bahroun, Z., Anane, C., Ahmed, V., Zacca, A.: Transforming education: a comprehensive review of generative artificial intelligence in educational settings through bibliometric and content analysis. Sustainability **15**(17) (2023). https://doi.org/10.3390/su151712983, https://www.mdpi.com/2071-1050/15/17/12983
3. Benoit, K., et al.: quanteda: An R package for the quantitative analysis of textual data. J. Open Source Softw. **3**(30), 774 (2018). https://doi.org/10.21105/joss.00774, https://quanteda.io

4. Bouchet, F., Harley, J.M., Azevedo, R.: Can adaptive pedagogical agents' prompting strategies improve students' learning and self-regulation? In: International Conference on Intelligent Tutoring Systems, pp. 368–374 (2016). https://doi.org/10.1007/978-3-319-39583-8_43
5. Cano, J.R., Nunez, N.A.: Unlocking innovation: how enjoyment drives genai use in higher education. Front. Educ. **9** (2024)
6. Carrasco-Sáez, J.L., Contreras-Saavedra, C., San-Martín-Quiroga, S., Contreras-Saavedra, C.E., Viveros-Muñoz, R.: Analyzing higher education students' prompting techniques and their impact on ChatGPT's performance: an exploratory study in Spanish. Appl. Sci. **15**(14) (2025). https://doi.org/10.3390/app15147651
7. Cubillos, C., Mellado, R., Cabrera-Paniagua, D., Urra, E.: Generative artificial intelligence in computer programming: does it enhance learning, motivation, and the learning environment? IEEE Access **1**, 40438–40455 (2025)
8. D'Mello, S.K., et al.: From learning optimization to learner flourishing: reimagining AI in education at the institute for student-AI teaming (iSAT). AI Mag. **45**(1), 61–68 (2024)
9. Fan, Y., et al.: Beware of metacognitive laziness: effects of generative artificial intelligence on learning motivation, processes, and performance. Br. J. Edu. Technol. **56**(2), 489–530 (2025)
10. Gentner, N.M., Respondek, L., Seufert, T.: Effects of short- and long-term prompting in learning journals on strategy use, self-efficacy, and learning outcomes. Instr. Sci. **52**(6), 919–950 (2024). https://doi.org/10.1007/s11251-024-09671-x
11. Giray, F.: Prompt engineering with ChatGPT: a guide for academic writers. Ann. Biomed. Eng. **51**(12), 2629–2633 (2023). https://doi.org/10.1007/s10439-023-03272-4
12. Guillén-Yparrea, N., Hernández-Rodríguez, F.: Unveiling generative AI in higher education: insights from engineering students and professors. In: IEEE Global Engineering Education Conference (EDUCON), pp, 1–5 (2024)
13. Güner, H., Er, E.: AI in the classroom: exploring students' interaction with ChatGPT in programming learning. Educ. Inf. Technol. 1–27 (2025)
14. Kasneci, E., et al.: ChatGPT for good? On opportunities and challenges of large language models for education. Learn. Individ. Differ. **103**, 102274 (2023)
15. Kim, J., Lee, S.S.: Are two heads better than one?: The effect of student-AI collaboration on students' learning task performance. TechTrends **67**(2), 365–375 (2023)
16. López-Pernas, S., Misiejuk, K., Oliveira, E., Saqr, M.: The dynamics of the self-regulation process in student-AI interactions: the case of problem-solving in programming education. In: Proceedings of the 25th Koli Calling International Conference on Computing Education Research, pp. 1–12 (2025)
17. López-Pernas, S., Saqr, M.: How the dynamics of engagement explain the momentum of achievement and the inertia of disengagement: a complex systems theory approach. Comput. Hum. Behav. **153**, 108126 (2024)
18. McNichols, H., Ikram, F., Lan, A.: The studychat dataset: analyzing student dialogues with ChatGPT in an artificial intelligence course. In: Proceedings of the LAK26: 16th International Learning Analytics and Knowledge Conference, pp. 53–63 (2026). https://doi.org/10.1145/3785022.3785029
19. Ooms, J.: hunspell: High-Performance Stemmer, Tokenizer, and Spell Checker (2025). https://docs.ropensci.org/hunspell/, R package version 3.0.7
20. Oppenheimer, D.M., Cash, T.N., Connell Pensky, A.E.: You've got AI friend in me: LLMs as collaborative learning partners. Int. J. Artif. Intell. Educ. 1–26 (2025)

21. Papadopoulos, P.M., Demetriadis, S.N., Stamelos, I.G., Tsoukalas, I.A.: The effect of prompting to students with different learning styles. Multicultural Educ. Technol. J. **4**(3), 198–213 (2010). https://doi.org/10.1108/17504971011075192
22. R Core Team: R: A Language and Environment for Statistical Computing. R Foundation for Statistical Computing, Vienna, Austria (2013). http://www.R-project.org/
23. Roehrick, K.: vader: Valence Aware Dictionary and sEntiment Reasoner (VADER) (2020). https://CRAN.R-project.org/package=vader, R package version 0.2.1
24. Rokach, L., Maimon, O.: Clustering methods. In: Data Mining and Knowledge Discovery Handbook, pp. 321–352. Springer, Boston, MA (2005)
25. Saqr, M., López-Pernas, S., Tikka, S.: Mapping relational dynamics with transition network analysis: a primer and tutorial. Advanced learning analytics methods: AI, Precision and Complexity (2025)
26. Saqr, M., López-Pernas, S., Törmänen, T., Kaliisa, R., Misiejuk, K., Tikka, S.: Transition network analysis: a novel framework for modeling, visualizing, and identifying the temporal patterns of learners and learning processes. In: Proceedings of the 15th International Learning Analytics and Knowledge Conference, pp. 351–361 (2025)
27. Sawalha, G., Taj, I., Shoufan, A.: Analyzing student prompts and their effect on ChatGPT's performance. Cogent Educ. **11**(1), 2397200 (2024). https://doi.org/10.1080/2331186X.2024.2397200
28. Sclar, M., Choi, Y., Tsvetkov, Y., Suhr, A.: Quantifying language models' sensitivity to spurious features in prompt design or: how i learned to start worrying about prompt formatting. arXiv:2310.11324 (2024). https://doi.org/10.48550/arXiv.2310.11324
29. Sigot, M., Tassoti, S.: An investigation of change in prompting strategies in a semester-long course on the use of genai. J. Chem. Educ. **102**(6), 2507–2513 (2025)
30. Stojanov, A., Liu, Q., Koh, J.H.L.: University students' self-reported reliance on ChatGPT for learning: a latent profile analysis. Comput. Educ. Artif. Intell. **6**(4), 100243 (2024)
31. Tikka, S., López-Pernas, S., Saqr, M.: TNA: an R package for transition network analysis. Appl. Psychol. Meas. (2025)
32. Törmänen, T., et al.: Emotional dynamics and regulation in collaborative learning. Learn. Instr. **100**, 102188 (2025)
33. Wang, H., Dang, A., Wu, Z., Mac, S.: Emotional dynamics and regulation in collaborative learning. Comput. Educ.: Artif. Intell. **7**, 100326 (2024)
34. Wang, X., et al.: What matters in AI-supported learning: a study of human-AI interactions in language learning using cluster analysis and epistemic network analysis. Comput. Educ. **194**, 104703 (2023)
35. Weng, X., Xia, Q., Ahmad, Z., Chiu, T.K.: Personality traits for self-regulated learning with generative artificial intelligence: the case of ChatGPT. Comput. Educ. Artif. Intell. **7**, 100315 (2024)
36. White, J., et al.: A prompt pattern catalog to enhance prompt engineering with ChatGPT. arXiv preprint arXiv:2302.11382 (2023)

37. Wood, A., Rodeghero, P., Armaly, A., McMillan, C.: Detecting speech act types in developer question/answer conversations during bug repair. In: Proceedings of the 2018 26th ACM Joint Meeting on European Software Engineering Conference and Symposium on the Foundations of Software Engineering, pp. 491–502 (2018)
38. Zheng, J., et al.: Do students rely on AI? Analysis of student-ChatGPT conversations from a field study. In: Proceedings of the AAAI/ACM Conference on AI, Ethics, and Society, pp. 2796–2807 (2025)

Penny: Transition Network Analysis of Learner-Chatbot Interactions in Scaffolded EFL Writing

Steve Woollaston[1(✉)], Brendan Flanagan[2], Yuko Toyokawa[1], and Hiroaki Ogata[1]

[1] Academic Center for Computing and Media Studies, Kyoto University, Kyoto, Japan
s.m.woollaston@gmail.com,
{toyokawa.yuko.2j,ogata.hiroaki.3e}@kyoto-u.ac.jp

[2] College of Information Science and Engineering, Ritsumeikan University, Kyoto, Japan
flanagan@fc.ritsumei.ac.jp

Abstract. Generative AI chatbots promise to transform English as a Foreign Language (EFL) writing by providing immediate, personalised feedback. However, their pedagogical value depends on how learners engage with them - a process often treated as a "black box." This study uses Transition Network Analysis to model the temporal dynamics of Japanese EFL learners using "Penny," an LLM-powered writing chatbot. Analysis of over 4,500 writing sessions and 21,000 chatbot interactions reveals two dominant behavioural loops: a"Revision Loop," where feedback leads directly to successful error correction, and a "Chat Loop," where learners engage in sustained dialogue with the chatbot following feedback. Crucially, EFL proficiency significantly shapes interaction: high-proficiency learners engage more in open dialogue and negotiation with the chatbot, while low-proficiency learners rely more heavily on repetitive corrective feedback cycles. The findings demonstrate that AI-scaffolded writing is a non-linear, dialogic process and highlight the need for differentiated chatbot design to move beyond simple error correction and foster deeper cognitive engagement for all learners.

Keywords: chatbot · log data · LLM · generative AI · EFL writing · transition network analysis (TNA) · written corrective feedback

1 Introduction

Writing in English as a Foreign Language (EFL) is a complex cognitive activity, often fraught with challenges for learners. To address these difficulties, instructors have traditionally relied on Written Corrective Feedback (WCF) to provide feedback and scaffold learning. However, providing timely and personalised feedback in large classes remains a significant burden for busy teachers. The emergence of Large Language Models (LLMs) offers a promising solution [25], with

M. Saqr et al. (Eds.): TNA 2026, CCIS 3079, pp. 172–186, 2026.
https://doi.org/10.1007/978-3-032-34157-0_13

generative AI (genAI) chatbots acting as "tireless assistants" capable of providing immediate feedback on various aspects of the writing, from surface features such as spelling and punctuation, to higher level feedback such as word choice, style, and organisation.

While recent research has begun to demonstrate the efficacy of these tools in improving writing quality [1,7], the pedagogical value of AI chatbots depends on how learners actually engage with them. Current literature often treats the learner-chatbot interaction as a "black box," focusing primarily on output metrics such as final essay scores or error rates. However, understanding how learners navigate the cycle of writing, feedback, and revision is critical to designing effective scaffolding and learning support [3]. For instance, do learners simply accept corrections at face value, or do they engage in a dialogue to negotiate meaning? Do English proficiency levels dictate different interactional strategies? To answer these, we must examine the sequential dynamics of the learning process.

In this study, we examine the chat and interaction logs of Japanese junior high school learners using *Penny*, an LLM-powered writing support chatbot. By mapping the specific pathways learners take between writing, receiving feedback, and chat, we aim to uncover the behavioural mechanisms that underlie AI-scaffolded writing at different proficiency levels. This investigation is guided by the following research questions:

Research Questions:

1. What are the common transition patterns and behavioural loops learners exhibit when using a generative AI chatbot for EFL writing practice?
2. How do the temporal interaction patterns and feedback uptake behaviours differ between high-proficiency and low-proficiency learners?

2 Related Work

2.1 From Simple Correction to Dialogic Interaction

Corrective feedback is well established as an important pedagogical intervention for improving second language (L2) accuracy [2], yet its provision by teachers is constrained by workload, time pressures, and at times inconsistency in feedback [13]. To help mitigate these, Automated Writing Evaluation (AWE) systems, such as *Criterion* and *Grammarly*, have been integrated into language learning classrooms to provide immediate, form-focused feedback [5,11,20]. However, traditional AWE have faced criticism for being formulaic and prioritising surface-level mechanics over higher level issues like content and organisation [13]. Further, while AWE tools identify errors, they often lack the interactive capability to guide learners through the cognitive process of understanding the *why* of the correction or allowing follow up discussion to deepen understanding.

The integration of genAI and chatbots represents an opportunity for pedagogical shift from static error correction to "negotiated meaning". Unlike traditional AWE, chatbots can facilitate a "didactic function of negotiation," where feedback pushes learners to refine their output through dialogue rather than passive reception [13,19]. Recent studies indicate that AI-generated feedback can be more comprehensive than human feedback, addressing content and organisation with greater balance, thereby potentially fostering higher learner engagement through dialogue [4].

2.2 Process vs. Product

Despite the recent proliferation of AI writing tools, a significant gap remains in Second Language Acquisition (SLA) research regarding the *process* of learner engagement versus the *product* of writing quality. Existing literature focuses on outcome-oriented measures, such as pre- and post-test accuracy scores or final draft quality [22,23]. This product-based focus treats the learner's interaction with the feedback as a "black box," failing to reveal how learners process and act upon feedback during revision [10,28].

Furthermore, much research often relies on self-reported data, such as surveys [8,11]. Self-reports may not accurately reflect behavioural engagement, as discrepancies often exist between learners' stated preferences and their actual revision practices. For instance, while learners may claim to value global feedback, their actual revisions often prioritise surface-level corrections [14]. Storch [24] and others [6,15,29] have called for research that moves beyond static measures to investigate the temporal nature of the "feedback-uptake sequence".

2.3 Mapping Behavioural Sequences

While research shows that L2 writing proficiency levels influence strategy use during planning, translating, and reviewing [9,27], the sequential relationship between stochastic genAI chatbot feedback and subsequent learner behaviours remains underexplored. To move beyond static measures of feedback uptake, we must analyse how learners navigate the dynamic, non-linear dialogue of AI-mediated knowledge construction. To address this, Transition Network Analysis (TNA) offers a robust framework for modeling temporal patterns, allowing researchers to visualise learning as a network of states and directed transitions [21]. Unlike traditional methods that focus on feedback frequency, TNA maps the temporal trajectory of learner actions, such as moving from writing feedback to a clarification request and then to a revision. By visualising the probability of these shifts, TNA operationalises the "error treatment sequence" [19] in interactionist SLA, providing a roadmap for explicitly teaching low-proficiency learners the specific strategies needed to negotiate meaning, improve their writing process, and ultimately improve their writing.

Much EFL learning feedback research focuses on higher education [12,18], leaving a significant data gap in secondary school settings. This is a critical oversight: younger learners often lack the metacognitive maturity to handle automated feedback without explicit scaffolding. As feedback effectiveness is highly dependent on cultural and instructional variables, temporal analysis is essential to determine if the dialogic benefits of AI writing feedback extend to this younger demographic.

3 Methodology

3.1 Participants

The study was conducted at a high performing public school in Japan with three EFL classes ($n = 119$) over four months. Learners were between 14 and 16 years of age. Based on a median split of average scores from three school-based English examinations and one comprehensive external English proficiency assessment (GTEC), learners were classified into high and low English proficiency groups. Written informed consent was obtained from all legal guardians of the students. Participants retained the right to withdraw their data at any time while continuing to use the chatbot for learning.

3.2 System and Procedure

The learners utilised *Penny* (Fig. 1), a generative AI chatbot powered by `GPT-4o` `(gpt-4o-2024--08--06)` designed to scaffold English writing practice three to four times per week with different writing prompts (see Appendix for the system prompt). *Penny* was provided with the learner's up-to-date writing and full chat history each time they interacted.

Each day a new writing prompt was displayed. The classroom routine began with a five-minute "Think-Pair-Share" activity where learners brainstormed ideas for the day's writing prompt. The prompts were simple: e.g. *What is your favorite hobby? Describe a place you would like to visit. What do you like to do when it rains?* These were designed to encourage variety of output and engagement.

Learners were required to write a minimum of 100 characters before a **Check my writing** button became active, enabling interaction with the chatbot. The writing textbox only accepted English characters, but the Penny interface and feedback was provided in English or Japanese (set in the *Penny* options), defaulting to the browser's language. Learners could use the system freely outside the classroom, but could not engage with future writing prompts past the present day.

3.3 Data Processing

Log data, including chat logs and revision history, were collected for analysis and where necessary classified by LLM. LLM-based classification for large datasets has proven effective in similar chatbot research [26]. To construct the transition networks, events were coded into discrete states:

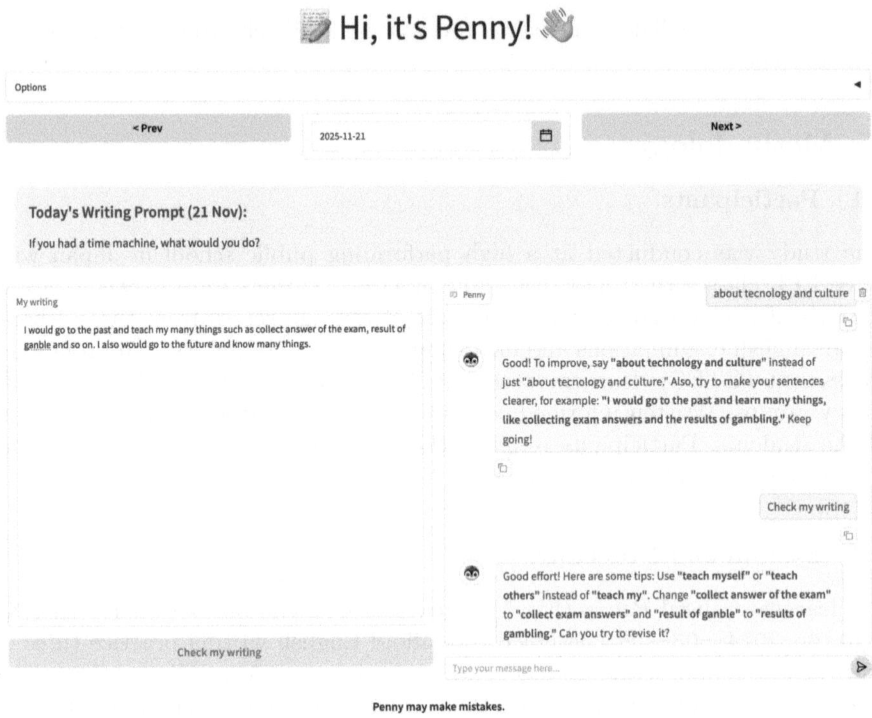

Fig. 1. Penny interface used by learners

- **Chatbot Interaction:** Penny's responses were classified as either `penny_feedback` (containing explicit corrective feedback or advice) or `penny_chat` (general conversation, encouragement, or clarification). Classifications were performed using `gpt-4o-mini-2024-07-18`. Validation against a random sample of 100 interactions coded by two independent researchers (experienced in EFL teaching) yielded a Fleiss' κ of 0.70 (substantial agreement between all three raters).
- **Learner Uptake:** Learner revisions following feedback were classified into three outcomes: `successful_uptake` (one or more errors repaired), `unsuccessful_uptake` (attempted but failed repair), or `no_uptake` (feedback ignored). Within this sample, 50 interactions involved subsequent revisions. To validate the LLM classification process, these were also independently coded by researchers, achieving a Fleiss' κ of 0.71; again indicating substantial agreement.
- **Other Nodes:** Remaining actions were coded as `start_session`, `end_session`, `check_button` (requesting feedback), `revise_writing` (writing has changed since last interaction), and `user_chat` (learner sending a message to Penny).

3.4 Transition Network Analysis

We employed TNA to model the temporal dynamics of the interaction process using the web-based TNA Shiny app [17]. The calculated network-level metrics (density, reciprocity) and performed statistical comparisons to identify significant differences in transition probabilities between the two proficiency groups.

4 Results

4.1 Penny Interaction Metrics

There were a total of 4,651 writing sessions and 21,061 messages exchanged with the Penny chatbot. As shown in Table 1, the engagement levels varied significantly among learners. On average, each learner completed approximately 39 sessions ($SD = 12.57$) and exchanged nearly 177 messages ($SD = 156.53$) over the course of the semester. The high standard deviation in message count highlights the presence of distinct usage patterns, ranging from minimal interaction to highly active engagement ($max = 917$ messages sent). Learners overwhelmingly chose to interact with Penny in their native language of Japanese (98.16%) instead of English (1.84%).

Table 1. Interaction Summary ($n = 119$)

Metric	Mean	SD	Median	Min	Max
Writing sessions per learner	39.06	12.57	40	4	101
Total messages per learner	176.92	156.53	137	7	917
Messages per session	5.58	6.96	4	1	116
Messages per session (excl. `check_button`)	5.43	7.84	3	0	114
Characters (before chatbot interaction)	210.05	151.54	177	100	3000
Characters (final text at session end)	183.66	166.54	167	0	3000

On average, learners produced an average initial draft of 210 characters ($SD = 151.54$) or approximately 40 words; double the minimum requirement of 100 characters. Interestingly, the final submitted texts averaged 183.66 characters ($SD = 166.54$), slightly shorter than the initial drafts, suggesting that revisions often involved condensation or correction rather than purely additive expansion. Session duration showed a notable skew; while the mean duration was approximately 32 min, the median was roughly seven minutes, indicating that while many interactions were quick check-ins, a subset of sessions involved prolonged engagement.

4.2 Coded Behaviours

Table 2 presents the frequency and distribution of the 63,328 events. The most frequent state was penny_feedback (23.13%), occurring on average 123.11 times per learner, followed by user_chat (18.38%), indicating that the sessions were driven by a high volume of chatbot-learner interaction. Explicit requests for feedback (check_button) accounted for 15.14% of events.

Table 2. Frequency and Distribution of Coded Behaviours by Proficiency Group

Code	Freq.	%	Mean per Learner	Mean per Session	High ($n = 60$)		Low ($n = 59$)	
					Freq.	%	Freq.	%
start_session	3808	6.01	32.00	1.00	2230	5.91	1578	6.16
check_button	9587	15.14	80.56	2.52	5566	14.76	4021	15.70
texttttpenny_feedback	14650	23.13	123.11	3.85	8739	23.17	5911	23.08
revise_writing	6627	10.46	55.69	1.74	3968	10.52	2659	10.38
successful_uptake	4592	7.25	38.59	1.21	2733	7.25	1859	7.26
unsuccessful_uptake	1053	1.66	8.85	0.28	622	1.65	431	1.68
no_uptake	982	1.55	8.25	0.26	613	1.63	369	1.44
user_chat	11642	18.38	97.83	3.06	7097	18.81	4545	17.75
penny_chat	6579	10.39	55.29	1.73	3924	10.40	2655	10.37
end_session	3808	6.01	32.00	1.00	2230	5.91	1578	6.16
Total	**63328**	**100.00**	**532.17**	**16.63**	**37722**	**100.00**	**25606**	**100.00**

Regarding revision behaviours, revise_writing constituted 10.46% of the total events. Notably, successful_uptake (7.25%) was observed significantly more often than unsuccessful_uptake (1.66%) or no_uptake (1.55%), suggesting that learners frequently and effectively incorporated the feedback provided.

When comparing proficiency groups, interactions remained proportionally similar across most categories. High-proficiency learners engaged slightly more frequently in open dialogue (user_chat: 18.81% vs. 17.75%; penny_chat: 10.40% vs. 10.37%). Conversely, low-proficiency learners relied more on the automated feedback tools, showing higher relative tendencies to click the check_button (15.70% vs. 14.76%). The percentage of penny_feedback received was nearly identical between groups (High: 23.17%; Low: 23.08%).

4.3 Transition Network Analysis

The network (Fig. 2) consists of 10 nodes and 26 directed edges. It exhibits a network density of 0.29 (the proportion of observed transitions relative to all possible connections) indicating that learners favoured specific behavioural sequences rather than transitioning randomly between states. Furthermore, the reciprocity of 0.31, which quantifies the degree to which connections are bidirectional, reflects a moderate level of back-and-forth exchange between the learner and the chatbot's feedback mechanisms. Complementing these, the network shows an in-degree centralisation of 0.42 and mean in- and out-strength of 0.90, indicating that while interaction is distributed, the network features specific 'gravitational' nodes (such as `penny_feedback`) that serve as the primary hubs for learner activity. Transitions with a probability below 0.05 were omitted from the visualisation to enhance clarity; aforementioned network metrics were calculated from the full dataset.

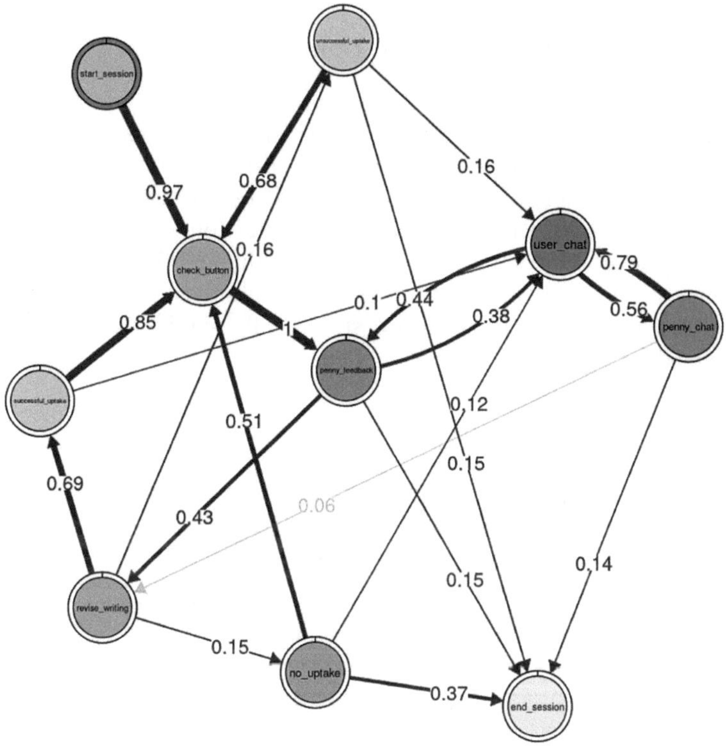

Fig. 2. Pruned Transition Network (min value = 0.05)

The transition probabilities reveal a distinct "Revision Loop" and "Chat Loop" within the learning process. By design, sessions began with a linear sequence where `start_session` transitions almost exclusively to `check_button` (0.97), which in turn triggers `penny_feedback` (1.00). In rare cases learners may have returned to previous sessions, leading to other states.

Following `penny_feedback`, learner behaviour diverges into two primary paths:

- **Revision (42.6%):** The most frequent response to Penny's feedback is to `revise_writing`, where learners edit their text.
- **Dialogue (38.3%):** Alternatively, learners transition to `user_chat`, where the learner replies to the chatbot rather than immediately revising their writing.

When learners chose to revise (`revise_writing`), the subsequent state was predominantly `successful_uptake` (0.69), indicating a high rate of effective error correction. Conversely, when learners engage in dialogue (`user_chat`), the interaction frequently loops back to `penny_feedback` (0.44), creating a sustained cycle of feedback and response, or transitions to `penny_chat` (0.56) for non-corrective interaction.

4.4 Proficiency-Based Difference Comparison

To visualise the variation in behavioural states across proficiency groups, we generated a mosaic plot displaying the standardised residuals of interaction frequencies (Fig. 3). To determine whether this distribution was independent of learner proficiency, we conducted a chi-squared test of independence. The null hypothesis (H_0) posited that the frequency of behavioural states does not differ by proficiency level. Our analysis yielded a χ^2 value of 25.4 ($p < .003$). Rejecting H_0 suggests that the observed differences in interaction frequencies between high- and low-proficiency learners are statistically significant and unlikely to have occurred by chance.

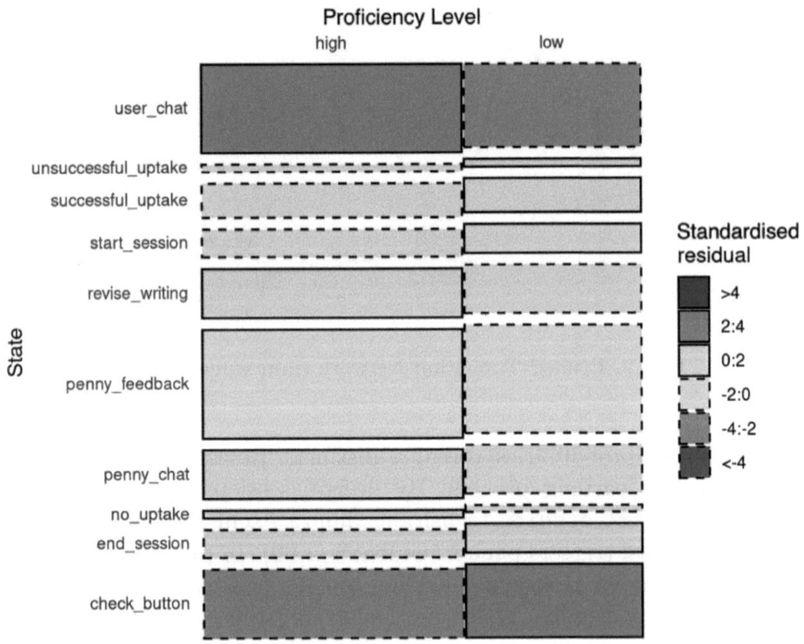

Fig. 3. Mosaic plot of behavioural state frequencies by proficiency group

The width of the columns corresponds to the relative sample size of events for each proficiency group (High-proficiency: $n = 37,722$; Low-proficiency: $n =$

25, 606). The height of each tile represents the proportion of that state within the proficiency group, while the colour indicates the magnitude of the standardised residual; i.e., the difference between the observed and expected frequency if the variables were independent.

High-proficiency learners displayed a distinct over-representation in conversational states. Specifically, `user_chat` showed a positive association (residual between 2 and 4), indicating these learners engaged in significantly more dialogue than expected. Conversely, this group showed a significant under-representation (residual between −2 and −4) in the `check_button` state, suggesting less reliance on general feedback requests.

The pattern was largely inverted for low-proficiency learners. This group showed a statistically significant over-representation for `check_button` (residual between 2 and 4), indicating a higher dependency on general feedback. In contrast, they were significantly under-represented in conversational engagement, with `user_chat` showing a negative association (residual between −2 and −4).

Other states, including `penny_feedback`, `penny_chat`, `revise_writing`, and both `successful_uptake` and `unsuccessful_uptake`, showed residuals between −2 and 2. This indicates that while the raw frequencies may differ, the distribution of these specific actions did not deviate significantly from expected values based on the proficiency group size alone.

5 Discussion

5.1 RQ1: Common Transition Patterns

This study utilised TNA to open the "black box" of learner-chatbot interaction, revealing that chatbot-scaffolded writing is not a linear process of submission and correction. The network topology highlights a divergence following chatbot feedback: learners almost equally choose to engage in dialogue (`user_chat`: 37.3%) or immediately apply revisions (`revise_writing`: 43.8%).

The strong transition probability from `revise_writing` to `successful_uptake` (69%) confirms that when learners choose to revise their writing, the Penny chatbot effectively facilitates error repair. However, the substantial proportion of learners entering the "Chat Loop" (transitioning from feedback to chat and often back to feedback) suggests that for many, the chatbot may serve as a partner for the "negotiation of meaning" rather than just a corrective tool. This aligns with internationalist SLA theories where "pushed output" and dialogue facilitate hypothesis testing [19]. Unlike traditional AWE systems that provide static error identification, the TNA model shows that learners actively utilise the chatbot's conversational capabilities to mediate and support their writing process.

5.2 RQ2: Proficiency Interaction and Uptake Differences

Navigational strategies within the network differ slightly but significantly by proficiency. High-proficiency learners are significantly more likely to transition into penny_chat states, perhaps suggesting they are capable of sustaining metalinguistic conversations, using the chatbot to discuss ideas or seek clarification without direct feedback on their writing. Conversely, low-proficiency learners appear to rely on corrective loops more heavily. They are more likely to use the check_button, and their dialogue with the chatbot (user_chat) is significantly more likely to trigger further corrective feedback (penny_feedback). This finding supports previous research suggesting that lower-level learners may struggle to process long and/or complex chatbot feedback [8]. For these learners, the chatbot functions less as a partner and more as a persistent corrector, which may explain their tendency to use the check_button rather than clarify or negotiate the feedback.

5.3 Limitations

This study is limited by the coarse granularity of the user_chat node. While we know learners are chatting, we did not distinguish between off-task behaviour, clarification requests, frustration, or social pleasantries. Further analysis of the chatlogs is required to better understand the intent behind the "Chat Loop." Furthermore, while the automated classification of chatbot interactions (penny_feedback vs. penny_chat) yielded substantial inter-rater agreement (Fleiss' $\kappa = 0.70$), there were disagreements. This suggests that the distinction between explicit pedagogical feedback and general conversational scaffolding can be somewhat ambiguous, particularly in short-form chatbot responses. This introduces a degree of uncertainty into the transition probabilities. Consequently, the observed frequencies of these states should be interpreted as approximations of general trends rather than absolute measures. The study was conducted within a specific cultural and educational context with a specific chatbot and LLM model, limiting generalisability. Finally, while successful_uptake measures immediate repair, this does not necessarily equate to long-term language acquisition or retention.

5.4 Future Work

Future work should qualitatively analyse the content of the user_chat nodes to distinguish between productive negotiation and off-task behaviour. Additionally, longitudinal studies are required to determine if the high immediate uptake rates translate to long-term writing improvements. Further research could also investigate why low-proficiency learners tended to rely more on the check_button for feedback, so as to design a better system that encourages them to move beyond the corrective loop. Our statistical analysis employed a chi-squared test to identify differences in the distribution of behavioural states between proficiency groups. While this identifies overall behavioural differences, it does not isolate specific edge-level differences. Future work should employ permutation testing to identify statistically significant differences in specific transition pathways between groups. As a cross-sectional analysis, this research identifies behavioural difference, but cannot establish causality. Future experimental designs are necessary to investigate any causal impact of AI scaffolding on writing development.

5.5 Conclusion

This study contributes to the field of chatbot feedback in EFL education by visualising the temporal dynamics of learner-chatbot interaction. The TNA model demonstrates that while generative AI successfully scaffolds immediate revision, it also reveals that learners of different proficiencies interact with the chatbot and their writing differently. High English proficiency learners engage in more dialogue and negotiation of meaning, while low-proficiency learners tend to enter a cycle of correction. This dichotomy highlights a critical design challenge: to maximise effectiveness, chatbots must engage with varying EFL proficiencies in a way that transcends simple error correction and stimulates the deep cognitive processing necessary for language acquisition.

Acknowledgments. Special thanks to Mayumi Yamanaka for facilitating the use of Penny within her classes, and to her students for their invaluable contributions and enthusiasm. This research is supported by Council for Science, 3rd SIP JPJ012347, and JSPS Grant-in-Aid for Scientific Research (B) JP20H01722 and JP23H01001, (Exploratory) JP21K19824, JP22KJ1914, (A) JP23H00505, and NEDO JPNP20006.

Disclosure of Interests. The authors have no competing interests to declare.

Availability of Dataset. Data analysed in this paper contains confidential information and will not be made publicly available.

A System Prompt

The system prompt for the Penny chatbot, including the insertion of student variables and the guidelines for the persona.

```
**Role:** You are Penny, an intelligent English writing
    tutor dedicated to helping {student_name}, a Japanese
    EFL student improve their English writing skills. Your
    role is to provide clear explanations, constructive
    feedback, and helpful guidance tailored to each student'
    s proficiency level.

**Guidelines:**
- Adapt to the student's level: Tailor your feedback and
    explanations to the student's current language
    proficiency.
- Grammar and Syntax Review: Identify and correct
    grammatical errors, awkward phrasing, and incorrect
    syntax.
- Vocabulary Enhancement: Suggest alternative words or
    phrases to improve clarity, tone, and variety.
```

```
- Structure and Coherence: Provide guidance on how to
   structure sentences, paragraphs, and essays effectively.
- Encourage and Support: Foster a positive learning
   environment by providing constructive criticism balanced
    with positive reinforcement.
- Engagement: Keep interactions engaging by asking
   questions to clarify the student's intent and offering
   examples.
- Cultural Sensitivity: Be mindful of cultural differences
   that might affect the student's writing style or choice
   of words.
- Choose just one area to focus on at a time
- Be concise and clear in your explanations, providing
   examples when necessary.
- Show any revised English text in **bold** to highlight
   changes made.
- Give short responses to ensure the student can absorb the
    feedback effectively.
- Adjust the writing as necessary without adding extra
   material.
- Encourage the student to put any changes or corrections
   into the writing textbox (i.e. apply the feedback).

**Tone:** Be friendly, patient, and supportive, focusing on
    helping the student build confidence in their writing
   abilities while making the learning process enjoyable
   and informative.

### Limit your response to 50 words. Keep the student on
   topic. If the student is off-topic, guide them back to
   the writing prompt.

** For explanations, respond to the user in {chat_language
   }. Always give writing revisions in English. **

**Today's writing prompt:** {writing_prompt}
```

References

1. Apriani, E., et al.: Impact of AI-powered ChatBots on EFL students' writing skills, self-efficacy, and self-regulation: a mixed-methods study. Glob. Educ. Res. Rev. **1**(2), 57–72 (2024)
2. Bitchener, J., Storch, N.: Written corrective feedback for L2 development. Multilingual Matters **96** (2016)
3. Crosthwaite, P., Sun, S.: Generative AI and L2 written feedback studies: a scoping review. RELC J. (2025). https://doi.org/10.1177/00336882251386530
4. Dai, W., et al.: Assessing the proficiency of large language models in automatic feedback generation: an evaluation study. Comput. Educ. Artif. Intell. **7**, 100299 (2024). https://doi.org/10.1016/j.caeai.2024.100299

5. Dikli, S., Bleyle, S.: Automated essay scoring feedback for second language writers: how does it compare to instructor feedback? Assess. Writ. **22**, 1–17 (2014). https://doi.org/10.1016/j.asw.2014.03.006
6. Ellis, R.: EPILOGUE: a framework for investigating oral and written corrective feedback. Stud. Second. Lang. Acquis. **32**(2), 335–349 (2010). https://doi.org/10.1017/s0272263109990544
7. Ghafouri, M., Hassaskhah, J., Mahdavi-Zafarghandi, A.: From virtual assistant to writing mentor: exploring the impact of a ChatGPT-based writing instruction protocol on EFL teachers' self-efficacy and learners' writing skill. Lang. Teach. Res. (2024). https://doi.org/10.1177/13621688241239764
8. Guo, K., Wang, D.: To resist it or to embrace it? Examining ChatGPT's potential to support teacher feedback in EFL writing. Educ. Inf. Technol. **29**(7), 8435–8463 (2024). https://doi.org/10.1007/s10639-023-12146-0
9. Habók, A., Magyar, A., Molnár, G.: Investigating the relationship among English language learning strategies, language achievement, and attitude. Front. Psychol. **13**, 867714 (2022). https://doi.org/10.3389/fpsyg.2022.867714
10. Kim, J.H.: Learner understanding of written corrective feedback and its relationship with immediate uptake and retention in EFL classrooms. English Teach. **68**, 109–130 (2013). https://doi.org/10.15858/ENGTEA.68.3.201309.109
11. Koltovskaia, S.: Student engagement with automated written corrective feedback (AWCF) provided by Grammarly: a multiple case study. Assess. Writ. **44**, 100450 (2020). https://doi.org/10.1016/j.asw.2020.100450
12. Li, S.: The effectiveness of corrective feedback in SLA: a meta-analysis: Meta-analysis of corrective feedback. Lang. Learn. **60**(2), 309–365 (2010). https://doi.org/10.1111/j.1467-9922.2010.00561.x
13. Lin, S., Crosthwaite, P.: The grass is not always greener: teacher vs GPT-assisted written corrective feedback. System **127**, 103529 (2024). https://doi.org/10.1016/j.system.2024.103529
14. Link, S., Mehrzad, M., Rahimi, M.: Impact of automated writing evaluation on teacher feedback, student revision, and writing improvement. Comput. Assist. Lang. Learn. **35**(4), 605–634 (2022). https://doi.org/10.1080/09588221.2020.1743323
15. Liu, K.: How language proficiency and peer familiarity shape engagement with feedback in English as a Foreign language writing. Lang. Teach. Res. (2025). https://doi.org/10.1177/13621688251369331
16. López-Pernas, S., Saqr, M., Tikka, S.: TNA: An R Package for Transition Network Analysis. R package version 0.4.0 (2024)
17. López-Pernas, S., Tikka, S., Misiejuk, K., Saqr, M.: TNA-web: advanced analytics just a few clicks away. In: Proceedings of Technological Ecosystems for Enhancing Multiculturality (TEEM 2025), Salamanca, Spain (2025)
18. Lv, X., Ren, W., Xie, Y.: The effects of online feedback on ESL/EFL writing: a meta-analysis. Asia Pac. Educ. Res. **30**(6), 643–653 (2021). https://doi.org/10.1007/s40299-021-00594-6
19. Lyster, R., Ranta, L.: Corrective feedback and learner uptake: negotiation of form in communicative classrooms. Stud. Second. Lang. Acquis. **19**(1), 37–66 (1997). https://doi.org/10.1017/S0272263197001034
20. Saeli, H., Rahmati, P., Koltovskaia, S.: Learner engagement with written corrective feedback: the case of automated writing evaluation. J. Response Writ. **9**(2) (2023)

21. Saqr, M., López-Pernas, S., Törmänen, T., Kaliisa, R., Misiejuk, K., Tikka, S.: Transition network analysis: a novel framework for modeling, visualizing, and identifying the temporal patterns of learners and learning processes. In: Proceedings of the 15th International Learning Analytics and Knowledge Conference, pp. 351–361. ACM, New York, NY, USA (2025). https://doi.org/10.1145/3706468.3706513
22. Shi, H., Aryadoust, V.: A systematic review of AI-based automated written feedback research. ReCALL **36**(2), 187–209 (2024). https://doi.org/10.1017/s0958344023000265
23. Stevenson, M., Phakiti, A.: Automated feedback and second language writing. In: Feedback in Second Language Writing, pp. 125–142. Cambridge University Press (2019). https://doi.org/10.1017/9781108635547.009
24. Storch, N.: Collaborative writing in L2 contexts: processes, outcomes, and future directions. Annu. Rev. Appl. Linguist. **31**, 275–288 (2011). https://doi.org/10.1017/s0267190511000079
25. Woollaston, S., Flanagan, B., Ogata, H.: Chatbots and EFL learning: a systematic review. In: Joint Proceedings of the 14th International Conference on Learning Analytics and Knowledge (LAK 2024) Workshops, pp. 89–98. Kyoto University, Kyoto, Japan (2024)
26. Woollaston, S., Flanagan, B., Ocheja, P., Ogata, H.: ARCHIE: EFL learning processes in chatbot-supported active reading using transition network analysis. In: International Conference on Learning Evidence and Analytics. APSCE, Fukuoka, Japan (2025)
27. Wu, Y.: Language learning strategies used by students at different proficiency levels. Asian EFL J. **10**, 75–95 (2008)
28. Zhang, Z.: Student engagement with computer-generated feedback: a case study. ELT J. **71**(3), 317–328 (2016). https://doi.org/10.1093/elt/ccw089
29. Zhang, X., Zhang, R.: Feedback, response, and learner development: a sociocultural approach to corrective feedback in second language writing. SAGE Open **13**(1) (2023). https://doi.org/10.1177/21582440231157680

Capturing the Dynamics of Collaborative Project Discourse on Discord Using Transition Network Analysis

Fitsum Gizachew Deriba[1,2](✉), Ramy Elmoazen[2], and Wajdi Aljedaani[3]

[1] Computer Science Department, Wachemo University, Hossana, Ethiopia
fgizache@uef.fi

[2] University of Eastern Finland, Joensuu, Yliopistokatu 2, fi-80100 Joensuu, Finland
ramy.elmoazen@uef.fi

[3] Saudi Data & Artificial Intelligence Authority, Riyadh, Saudi Arabia
waljedaani@sdaia.gov.sa

Abstract. Understanding the learning process, motivation shifts, and social interaction in the education domain is relevant for enhancing educational practices and informing policy. However, there was limited empirical evidence that analyzed the student transition in their learning process and used TNA to analyze learning processes in collaborative project work, even though there is a recent novel development of a framework, specifically Transition Network Analysis (TNA). This study uses the TNA approach to identify and examine the sequential transitions and interactions in Master's Computer Science students in Big Data analytics courses. Based on the Community of Inquiry (CoI) framework, this work examined 543 chat log data from students' collaborative project work. The findings reveal that students' online discourse is dominated by non-cognitive activities, with Social and Teaching Presence collectively accounting for 76.2% of all actions, indicating that learners prioritize building relationships and task organization. The findings of the transition analysis indicate that students frequently transitioned from social bonding to administrative organization ($P = 0.41$), bypassing cognitive engagement. Furthermore, the results identify a cognitive bottleneck, although there were productive transitions between exploration and integration ($P = 0.27$), students facing cognitive triggers (new problems) returned to social interaction ($p = 0.36$) while supposed to advance to exploration, indicating a tendency to seek peer validation over deep inquiry when challenged. Consequently, the findings suggest that educators should implement targeted interventions to break administrative patterns and help learners transition from organizational tasks to higher-order cognitive processing, or to bridge the gap between social coordination and practical cognitive resolution.

Keywords: Transition Network Analysis · Learning Analytics · Big Data analytics Education · Project-Based Learning · Collaborative Learning · Community of Inquiry

M. Saqr et al. (Eds.): TNA 2026, CCIS 3079, pp. 187–198, 2026.
https://doi.org/10.1007/978-3-032-34157-0_14

1 Introduction

The education domain is characterized by complex and dynamic systems, including student enrollment or admission, learning, progress monitoring, and the need for intervention [1, 2], where learners accumulate knowledge through a dynamic process of movement through various learning states via transitions. Understanding how this complex system moves between different learning states—for instance, in online learning, whether students move from reading materials to watching videos, taking quizzes, or doing their assignments—is relevant to uncovering hidden patterns in the complex process of education [3]. Thus, it reveals students' learning patterns, identifies difficulties, and informs pedagogical strategies relevant to understanding their interactions and interaction transitions across different activities, such as assignments and project tasks [4]. For instance, it helps to identify the learner's challenging state or bottleneck that influences their achievement [5], understand students' next journey based on the observed transition state [6], and furthermore, it supports decision making to provide where intervention is more relevant in their learning process [7].

To investigate the nature of online interactions, many frameworks have been employed. However, the Community of Inquiry (CoI) framework has become widely used as an established theoretical model [8]. CoI defines online education as the interaction among three elements: Social Presence, Cognitive Presence, and Teaching Presence [9]. CoI categorizes the content of student discourse to be analyzed using traditional analytical methods, such as frequency counts or co-occurrence analysis, including Epistemic Network Analysis (ENA), which failed to properly model the temporal nature of the interactions [10, 11].

While learning analytics (LA) encompasses various methodological approaches, such as process and sequence mining, which are used to analyze data sequences to discover patterns, predict future behavior of learners, and model complex processes, TNA represents a contemporary advancement used to establish a novel analytic framework [6]. This method integrates Stochastic Process Mining with probabilistic graph representations to model, visualize, and scrutinize patterns in learning process data [12]. By capturing both relational and temporal aspects, TNA provides a rigorous and holistic perspective on learning behaviors [13].

Although the TNA was introduced more recently in 2024, there is growing interest among researchers to employ this methodological approach due to its integrated and statistically rigorous data sequence, such as the learning process. For example, Woolla ston et al. [14] employed TNA to investigate the interaction patterns and characteristics of English learners during chatbot-supported reading sections, model how students transitioned between actions, and demonstrate the role of chatbot engagement in the learning sequence. The use of TNA in modeling interaction sequences can provide insights for designing more effective AI-supported language learning tools [14].

This study aimed to model and analyze the temporal interaction patterns of students engaged in collaborative project work in a big data analytics course by applying TNA to Community of Inquiry–coded discourse data, to uncover the probabilistic transitions between social, cognitive, and teaching presence during the online collaborative process, guided by the following research question:

RQ: What sequential transition patterns between Social, Cognitive, and Teaching Presence are revealed by Transition Network Analysis of student collaborative project work discourse?

2 Methodolgy

2.1 Study Setting and Participants

The study was conducted at Wachemo University, Ethiopia, within the Computer Science master's program. Data were collected from the Big Data Analytics course (CoSc6222), a five-credit in-person course delivered during the second semester of 2024. Twelve students (2 female, 10 male; aged 25–34) participated, with project work organized into two groups of six members each.

2.2 Project Task and Description

Two case studies were used for this study, focusing on collaborative group project work in Big Data Analytics (BDA). Students were asked to select two project topics aligned with the course objectives (15% of the total grade). Following the project selection process, students chose to work on the design of a *Mental Health Evaluation Framework* and an *E-commerce Recommendation System.* The project's goal was to conceptualize BDA system awareness. Students were tasked with creating a conceptual design using the Figma tool, incorporating indicators of the blueprint functionality of their project system. They used asynchronous text-based communication (Discord) and synchronous virtual meetings (Zoom) to coordinate their design and final reporting. The groups were tasked with communicating their project ideas on Discord. The final deliverable was a five-page project report, incorporating the system mockup design, followed by an oral group presentation of their work.

2.3 Data Preparation and Coding

The student discourse data from the Discord platform [15] was extracted in CSV format using Discord ChatExporter. A total of 543 chat data entries underwent preprocessing by Coder 1. This involved exporting the chatlog and removing data irrelevant to transition network analysis, such as tags, empty entries, and redundant data, resulting in 382 relevant data entries. This data includes the date (timestamp), username, content, and mentions.

Based on the work of Elmoazen [16], we used the Community of Inquiry (CoI) framework. Coder 1 and Coder 2 met to discuss and define codes, agreeing to use three indicators (social, teaching, and cognitive presence) with specific codes for each dimension, totaling ten codes (see Table 1). Initially, both coders coded the same 15 student discourses (qualitative data) into the specified 10 codes. The codes were assigned sequentially (1, 2, 3) in each discourse. One sentence or post (utterance) may contain more than one category. For messages containing multiple cognitive or social dimensions, each distinct indicator was coded as a separate sequential step in the transition chain to ensure the temporal flow was preserved. The agreement between the two coders was 0.92; disagreements were discussed and resolved through consensus. Coder 1 continued the remaining coding.

Subsequently, both coders met to discuss how to convert the coded dataset into a format understandable by the transition network tool and identify transitions between users or states in the conversation. Secondly, the coder 2 converted the CoI-coded data (date, username, content mapped to 10 codes) into timestamp, username, interaction (how many times the user interacts with each code), and value (the sequence number).

Table 1. CoI coding scheme with indicators and examples

Dimension	Codes	Indicators	Example (from used data)
Social presence	**S Affective**	Emotion, humor, self-disclosure, gratitude, praise	Congratulations all...Thank you for the support. I tried to draw some sketches... ...😁
	S Interactive	Replying, acknowledging, (dis)agreeing, validating, complementing, asking	This is true. I think we should also choose who the stakeholders are. Yes, I thought about that, it seems to be the simplest way
	S Cohesion	Salutations, group addressing, group identity (we, us, our), greetings, closures	Hi all, if I am correct, in the last meeting we decided that..
Cognitive presence	**C Trigger**	Identify new problems/confusion, questions, or constraints	How would the system know this? Should we include a paragraph on ethics and anonymisation?
	C Explore	suggesting specific ideas, critique, exchange opinions/information	What do you think if we extract activities like Appointment Requests vs. Actual Appointments
	C Integrate	Connecting ideas, synthesis, justification (dis) agreement, creating a solution	I think it would be right to include a paragraph on ethics since the system would involve the use of patients... in a real-life scenario.
	C Reson	Resolution, applying/finalizing idea, artifact	Stakeholders are at least Admins and Counselors.

(continued)

Table 1. *(continued)*

Dimension	Codes	Indicators	Example (from used data)
Teacher presence	**T Organize**	Scheduling, task allocation, administrative management, timeline, rules, and roles	How about Friday morning? 9 AM to 11 AM... we can run a Zoom as well
	T Facilitate	Ensuring engagement, keeping focus, and checking in consensus	Just so that everyone's on board with what we're doing
	T Instruct	Direct instruction/task, defining constraints and rules, clarifying requirements,	Were we asked not to include specific medical records, right?

2.4 Sequence Modeling and Network Interpretation

These coded transition data datasets were then imported into Jamovi software and analyzed using the JTNA module [17]. This software was used to compute transition probabilities between codes and to generate directed network graphs that visualize the sequential flow and structural patterns of student interaction. We selected different centrality measures for our study. For instance, we chose OutStrength to identify which states frequently trigger subsequent actions, Betweenness to identify bridge activities like Integration that connect phases of inquiry, and Diffusion to measure how a specific behavior's influence spreads through the network. The findings, including the frequency of discourse, its transitions, and centrality, were then reported based on the students' discourse data.

3 Findings

3.1 Frequency of Observed Discourse Codes

The analysis of the coded student discourse revealed a total of 595 CoI actions (Fig. 1). **Social Presence** was the most dominant presence with 40.4% of the total actions. Specifically, Social Interactive was the most frequent code (19.5%), indicating the predominance of direct replies, acknowledgments, and validation among peers to reinforce their collective bond in addressing group work and to define their shared tasks clearly. Also, a high frequency was observed for Social Affective (12.3%), characterised by salutations and supportive closure, with participants viewing themselves as a unified team with shared responsibility for their project's success.

Teaching Presence was the second most common dimension with 35.8% of the discourse with the highest frequency for *Teaching Organization* (18.0%) which showed the self-management and task allocation in the collaborative project; for instance, directing of instructions on agreed task such as mental health framework mockup, following privacy and ethics in reporting and gathering health data, and structuring their report in these concepts.

Finally, **Cognitive Presence** was the least frequent dimension, accounting for 23.8% of the total interactions. The highest percentage was for *Cognitive Exploration* (11.4%) characterized by the group's brainstorming and debate over data sources (hospital data against privacy constraints), metrics and inputs for dashboard, and design choices (University Admin vs. Doctors) to determine the appropriate stakeholders, and infrequent occurrence of the higher-order cognitive codes: *Cognitive Reasoning* (1.7%) and *Cognitive Trigger* (2.5%) such as asking for clarification on what content belongs in the mockups, how specific indicators work, and what analytics should be displayed on the admin dashboard.

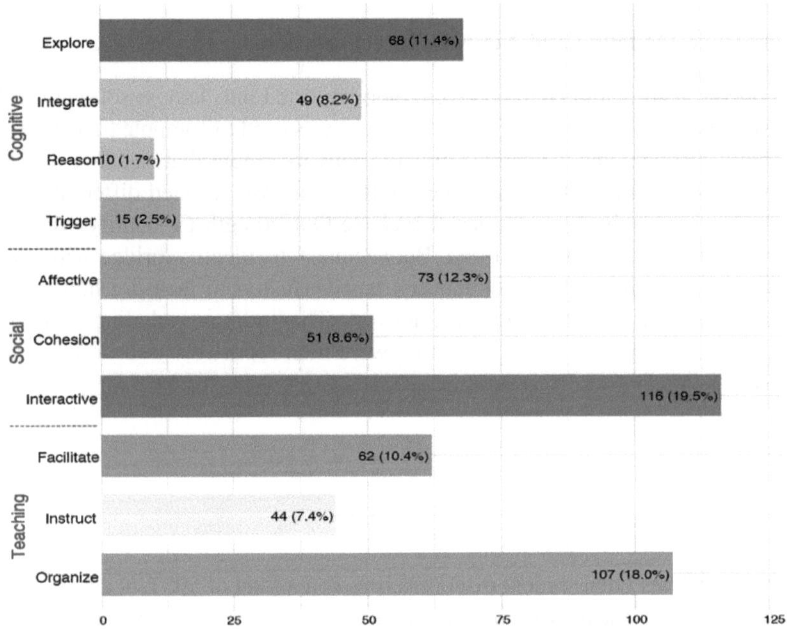

Fig. 1. Frequency and percentage distribution of discourse codes based on the CoI framework

3.2 Initial Probabilities of Discourse Codes

The initial probabilities for the coded student of each CoI represent the likelihood that a specific action will initiate a transition of interactions. The Social Presence was the most frequent starting point for student interaction, accounting for 59% of all initial coded actions, followed by Interactive (28%), Group Cohesion (19%), and Affective (12%). Teacher Presence codes were the second most common initial state, driven by organization at 22%, and the less frequent Facilitation and Instructions, both at 5% of the initial coded actions. Finally, Cognitive Presence codes were the least likely to appear in the initial conversation sequence, with Exploration the most probable at 5%, while Integration, Trigger, and Reasoning had low initial probabilities, ranging from 1% to 2% (Table 2).

Table 2. Initial probabilities of discourse codes

Presence	Code	Initial Probability
Cognitive	Explore	0.05
	Integrate	0.02
	Triger	0.01
Social	Affective	0.12
	Cohesion	0.19
	Interactive	0.28
Teaching	Facilitate	0.05
	Instruct	0.05
	Organize	0.22

3.3 Transition Network Analysis of Students' Discourse on Project Work

TNA computed the probability of transition from one CoI code to another (Fig. 2). The most significant transitions identified indicate a strong tendency for discourse to shift directly from Social Presence activities into **Teacher Presence** activities. For example, the highest probability transition was observed from *Social Cohesion* to *Teacher Organization* (0.41), indicating that students, after connecting, move toward administrative tasks, such as task allocation or scheduling. After *Teacher Organization*, students shift to *Teacher Facilitation* with a probability of 0.26.

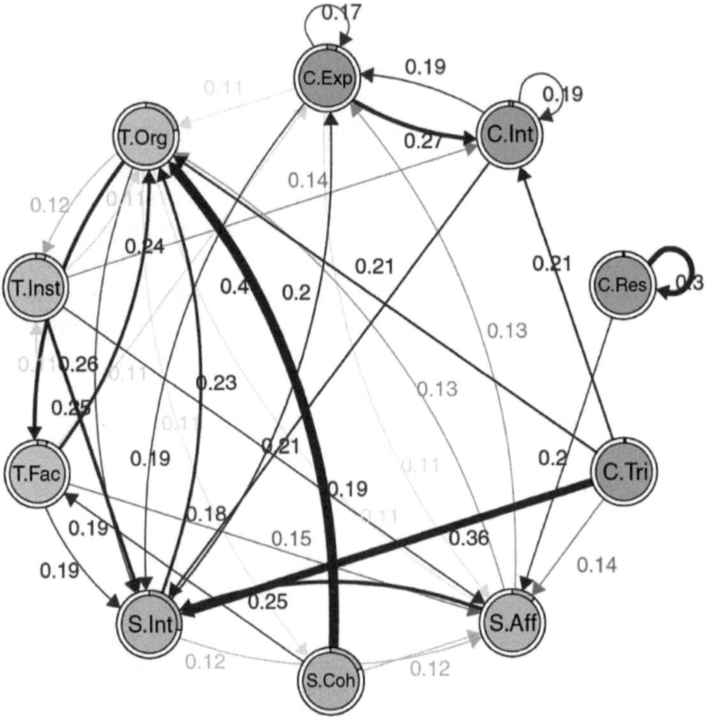

Fig. 2 TNA plot showing the sequential flow and transition probabilities of student discourse using the CoI framework**.** *Social Presence Codes* (**S. Aff:** Affective, **S. Int:** Interactive, **S. Coh**: Group Cohesion), *Cognitive Presence Codes* (**C. Tri:** Triger, C. Exp.: Explore, **C. Int.**: Integrate, **C. Res**: Reasoning), and *Teaching Presence Codes* (**T. Org**: Organize, **T. Fac**.: Facilitation, **T. Inst**: Instruction)

TNA also showed productive flow in **Cognitive Presence**, as in *Cognitive Exploration*, which led to justification in *Cognitive Integration* with a probability of 0.27. However, when students face the challenge of a new problem in *Cognitive Trigger*, they return to *Social Interactive* activities with a probability of 0.36, seeking replies or agreements from peers, rather than exploration. Similarly, posts including *Teacher Instruction* and *Social Affective* activities also continue the *Social Interaction.* Specifically, in direct instruction or clarification, students often responded with direct replies with a probability of 0.25, and expressions of gratitude or humor in Social Affective led to replies and acknowledgments in Social Interactive in 0.25 of the cases as well.

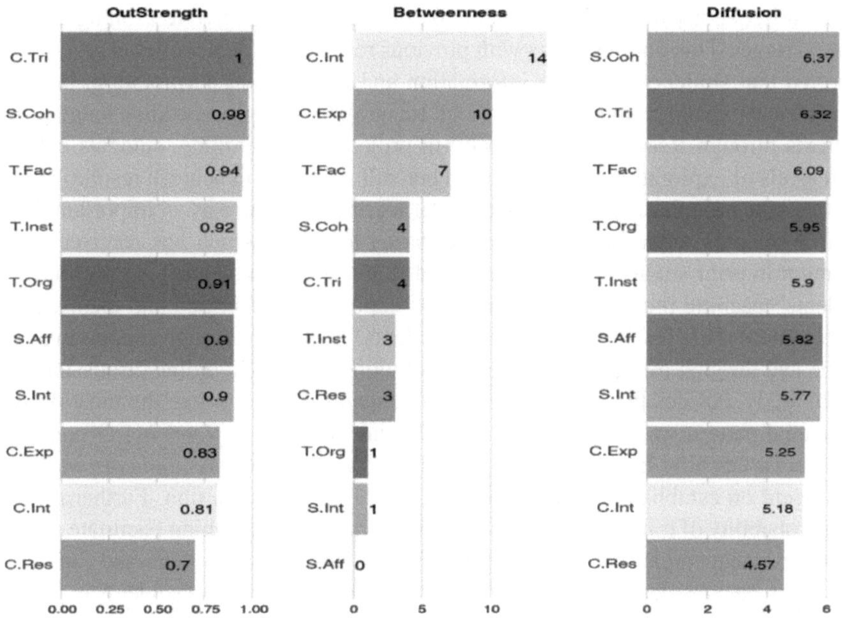

Fig. 3. Betweenness centrality, in-strength, and interaction diffusion

As indicated in Fig. 3 of the centrality measure analysis, communication of student interaction in their BDA group project was mostly driven by cognitive triggering and social cohesion with high OutStreanth (1.0 and 0.98) and diffusion (6.32 and 6.37). These show how they are influential in initiating or spreading the information in group interaction about their project tasks. Cognitive integration holds the highest betweenness (14), making it the bridge for communication of their information flow within groups, while lower OutStrength (0.81) and Diffusion (5.1) suggest most group members acted as mediators. The Cognitive Resolution and Social Affective shows the lowest level of engagement and influence, suggesting they were peripheral to the project discourse. Thus, the project communication relies on a few high-influence leaders of the group for idea generation about their project, while a specific intermediary (C.Int) ensures connectivity across the communication network.

4 Discussion and Conclusion

This study aimed to investigate the sequential interaction of master's students during collaborative project work, using TNA to analyze CoI–coded discourse. The frequency analysis demonstrated that Social Presence and Teaching Presence collectively accounted for over three-quarters of the entire discourse (76.2%), with the dominance of Social Interactive and Teaching Organization codes, which highlights that the students' primary focus was on establishing group connections and organizing task allocation and scheduling. The initial probability analysis also supported this finding, as students are most likely to begin by establishing a connection through Social Presence or by organizing tasks rather than engaging in cognitive activities. The Cognitive Presence was the least frequently observed dimension, particularly in Cognitive Reasoning and Cognitive Trigger. This finding aligns with previous research by deNoyelles et al. [18], who reported that students exchange information and ideas during Exploration, but rarely connect and expand on these ideas through Integration or apply new knowledge to other contexts through Resolution. Especially in project-based learning, students exhibited high levels of exploration and integration but still struggled to achieve resolution [18].

Our study emphasizes the importance of teaching presence as an important dimension of students' contributions in project-based learning, which has received limited attention in prior studies. Both teachers and students can show teaching presence, and students' teaching presence was found to be important for learning and metacognition development [19]. Teaching presence for students was shown through support in conversation and through offering guidance and solutions to peers in online discussions [20]. In our study, besides the high frequency of *Teaching Organization*, the most probable sequential pattern was the transition from Social Cohesion to *Teaching Organization.* This social-teaching link suggests that students' work on task assignments was highly contingent on establishing a sense of group presence and cohesion. Furthermore, the high probability of transitioning from Teaching Organize to Teaching Facilitate confirms that task management was followed by efforts to ensure engagement and facilitation, which can be considered a two-step organizational process among students in the BDA conceptualization.

A critical finding was the high probability of transition from *Cognitive Trigger* to *Social Interactive.* Accordingly, when students identified a problem, they were most likely to respond by starting a discussion with peers (Interactive) rather than immediately exploring and sharing knowledge. These findings indicate uncertainty or challenges in the complex BDA conceptualization task, which necessitate the need for social scaffolding to address any confusion. This pattern is consistent with the foundational hypothesis of the CoI, which emphasizes that Social Presence is important to facilitate cognitive objectives after a triggering event by instigating and supporting critical thinking among learners [9].

The TNA also confirmed a productive flow within cognitive presence, from Cognitive Exploration to Cognitive Integration, demonstrating that knowledge sharing transitioned into synthesis and justification. This finding is supported by the theoretical definitions of the CoI framework, such as those reported by Moore & Miller [21]. In their systematic review, which stated that the Integration phase occurs after information gathering, during which students integrate different components and filter out irrelevant information. Furthermore, they emphasize that the transition to Integration involves higher levels of cognitive presence than the knowledge-sharing characteristic of the Exploration phase.

4.1 Limitations and Future Direction

The study has several limitations that warrant discussion. First, the analysis was restricted to asynchronous text-based discourse on Discord. As noted by Bach and Thiel [22], students in collaborative learning often use multiple modalities; thus, high-level cognitive processing likely occurred during unrecorded synchronous Zoom sessions, leaving the text logs primarily as records of coordination. This limitation may reduce the visibility of cognitive depth and may not accurately reflect learners' actual capabilities. Second, the sample size ($N = 12$) and number of groups (two) were small. Although TNA offers rigorous probabilistic modeling [6], reliable estimation of transition probabilities may require a larger dataset. To capture the broader ecosystem of student interaction, future studies should explore multimodal learning analytics that integrate synchronous video and audio data with asynchronous text logs. Such triangulation could offer a more holistic view of cognitive workflows and help determine whether the observed cognitive bottleneck is a recurring pattern or an artifact of the communication channel. Additionally, incorporating covariate analysis may clarify how external factors (e.g., prior knowledge, group gender composition) influence the emergence of specific regulatory patterns. Finally, longitudinal TNA models could track how transition patterns evolve over a semester, revealing whether students adjust their collaborative strategies as project complexity increases.

Declaration on Generative AI. During the preparation of this work, the author(s) used Gemini 3 and Grammarly to fix grammar and spelling-related issues. After using these tool(s)/service (s), the author (s) reviewed and edited the content as needed and take (s) full responsibility for the publication's content.

References

1. Gibson, D., Kovanovic, V., Ifenthaler, D., Dexter, S., Feng, S.: Learning theories for artificial intelligence promoting learning processes. Br. J. Educ. Technol. **54**(5), 1125–1146 (2023)
2. Kitto, K., Gibson, A.: Places to intervene in complex learning systems. In: Proceedings of the 14th Learning Analytics and Knowledge Conference, pp. 929–935 (2024)
3. Tikka, S., López-Pernas, S., Saqr, M.: Tna: an R package for transition network analysis. Appl. Psychol. Meas., 01466216251348840 (2025)
4. Amri, M., Sert, O.: Establishing understanding during student-initiated between-desk instructions in project work. Cambridge J. Educ. **52**(6), 667–689 (2022)
5. Saqr, M., López-Pernas, S.: Why learning and teaching learning analytics is hard: an experience from a real-life LA course using LA methods. In: International Conference on Technological Ecosystems for Enhancing Multiculturality, pp. 781–789 (2023)
6. Saqr, M., López-Pernas, S., Törmänen, T., Kaliisa, R., Misiejuk, K., Tikka, S.: Transition network analysis: a novel framework for modeling, visualizing, and identifying the temporal patterns of learners and learning processes. In: Proceedings of the 15th International Learning Analytics and Knowledge Conference, pp. 351–361 (2025)
7. Baric, V., Munkholm, M., Wilder, J., Lidström, H.: Development of a practical guide to facilitate smooth transitions in and between schools for students with special educational needs–a co-creation study. Eur. J. Spec. Needs Educ., 1–18 (2025)
8. Castellanos-Reyes, D.: 20 years of the community of inquiry framework. TechTrends **64**(4), 557–560 (2020)
9. Garrison, D.R., Anderson, T., Archer, W.: Critical inquiry in a text-based environment: computer conferencing in higher education. Internet High. Educ. **2**(2–3), 87–105 (1999)
10. Elmoazen, R., Saqr, M., Tedre, M., Hirsto, L.: A systematic literature review of empirical research on epistemic network analysis in education. IEEE Access **10**, 17330–17348 (2022). https://doi.org/10.1109/ACCESS.2022.3149812
11. F. Deriba: Enhancing the Education of Accessibility with Artificial Intelligence. Itä-Suomen yliopisto, (2025). https://erepo.uef.fi/server/api/core/bitstreams/1426332a-3a5e-484e-9459-8606455733c8/content

12. Saqr, M., López-Pernas, S., Tikka, S.: Mapping relational dynamics with transition network analysis: a primer and tutorial. In: Advanced Learning Analytics Methods: AI, Precision and Complexity, pp. 371–411. Springer (2025)
13. Saqr, M., López-Pernas, S., Tikka, S.: Capturing the breadth and dynamics of the temporal processes with frequency. Adv. Learn. Anal. Methods AI, Precis. Complex., 413 (2025)
14. Woollaston, S., Flanagan, B., Ocheja, P., Ogata, H.: ARCHIE: EFL learning processes in Chatbot-supported active Reading using transition network analysis. In: International Conference on Learning Evidence and Analytics (2025)
15. Kruglyk, V.S., et al.: Using the discord platform in the educational process. In: Proceedings of the Symposium on Advances in Educational Technology, Aet (2020)
16. Elmoazen, R., Saqr, M., Hirsto, L., Tedre, M.: Capturing temporal pathways of collaborative roles: a multilayered analytical approach using community of inquiry. Int. J. Comput. Collab. Learn. **20**(1), 41–77 (2025)
17. López-Pernas, S., Girault, D., Tikka, S., Saqr, M.: JTNA: A Desktop Software for Transition Network Analysis
18. DeNoyelles, A., Mannheimer Zydney, J.: Strategies for creating a community of inquiry through online asynchronous discussions. J. Online Learn. Teach. **10**(1) (2014)
19. Garrison, D.R., Akyol, Z.: Toward the development of a metacognition construct for communities of inquiry. Internet High. Educ. **24**, 66–71 (2015)
20. Anderson, T., Liam, R., Garrison, D. R., Archer, W.: Assessing teaching presence in a computer conferencing context (2001)
21. Moore, R.L., Miller, C.N.: Fostering cognitive presence in online courses: a systematic review (2008–2020). Online Learn. **26**(1), 130–149 (2022)
22. Bach, A., Thiel, F.: Collaborative online learning in higher education—quality of digital interaction and associations with individual and group-related factors. In: Frontiers in Education, vol. 9, p. 1356271 (2024)

Author Index

M. Saqr et al. (Eds.): TNA 2026, CCIS 3079, p. 199, 2026.
https://doi.org/10.1007/978-3-032-34157-0

MIX
Papier aus verantwortungsvollen Quellen
Paper from responsible sources
FSC® C105338

If you have any concerns about our products,
you can contact us on
ProductSafety@springernature.com

In case Publisher is established outside the EU,
the EU authorized representative is:
Springer Nature Customer Service Center GmbH
Europaplatz 3, 69115 Heidelberg, Germany

Printed by Libri Plureos GmbH
in Hamburg, Germany